The Economics of Labor Migration

A BEHAVIORAL ANALYSIS

STUDIES IN URBAN ECONOMICS

Under the Editorship of

Edwin S. Mills
Princeton University

The Economics of Labor Migration

A BEHAVIORAL ANALYSIS

CHARLES F. MUELLER

The Planning Economics Group—Boston
Woburn, Massachusetts

ACADEMIC PRESS

A Subsidiary of Harcourt Brace Jovanovich, Publishers

New York   London
Paris   San Diego   San Francisco   São Paulo
Sydney   Tokyo   Toronto

COPYRIGHT © 1982, BY ACADEMIC PRESS, INC.
ALL RIGHTS RESERVED.
NO PART OF THIS PUBLICATION MAY BE REPRODUCED OR
TRANSMITTED IN ANY FORM OR BY ANY MEANS, ELECTRONIC
OR MECHANICAL, INCLUDING PHOTOCOPY, RECORDING, OR ANY
INFORMATION STORAGE AND RETRIEVAL SYSTEM, WITHOUT
PERMISSION IN WRITING FROM THE PUBLISHER.

ACADEMIC PRESS, INC.
111 Fifth Avenue, New York, New York 10003

United Kingdom Edition published by
ACADEMIC PRESS, INC. (LONDON) LTD.
24/28 Oval Road, London NW1 7DX

Library of Congress Cataloging in Publication Data

Mueller, Charles F. (Charles Francis)
    The economics of labor migration.

    (Studies in urban economics)
    Bibliography: p.
    Includes index.
    1. Labor mobility. 2. Emigration and immigration.
3. Migration, Internal. I. Title. II. Series.
HD5717.M83   331.12'79   81-19046
ISBN 0-12-509580-5   AACR2

PRINTED IN THE UNITED STATES OF AMERICA

82 83 84 85   9 8 7 6 5 4 3 2 1

To Mother and Father

Contents

3
An Economic Theory of Migration   71

4
Data Requirements and Migration Propensities   91

5
Empirical Specification and Results   125

6
A Diagnosis of Collinearity   147

7
Summary, Recommendations, and Conclusions   157

Appendix   165

References   185

Index   193

List of Tables

Preface

While the individual man is an insoluble puzzle, in the aggregate he becomes a mathematical certainty. You can, for example, never foretell what any one man will do, but you can say with precision what an average number will be up to. Individuals vary, but percentages remain constant [Sherlock Holmes in Sir Arthur Conan Doyle, *The Sign of Four*].

This book deals with one important aspect of the interrelationship between migration and regional economic growth: the worker's decision to migrate. With equally important goals of providing a logic of inquiry to the migration decision and exploring that logic empirically, the book has four objectives. The first is the development of a decision model of migration that has roles for economic gains, amenities, separation costs, and uncertainty and that considers the trade-offs between alternative destinations as well as between the origin and the actual destination. The second is the assessment of previous migration studies that furnish a perspective on our approach to the migration decision. Third, the migration behavior of workers is evaluated empirically in light of our decision model using recently developed estimation techniques suitable to analyzing disaggregate choice behavior. The fourth objective is to assess the ability of the data used in the empirical analysis to shed light on separate hypotheses. Together, these objectives represent a thorough application of theoretical and empirical procedures to the analysis and understanding of an important social phenomenon.

The book serves as a useful text and reference to scholars of migration in the disciplines of economics, sociology, demography, geography, and regional science as well as to practitioners in private industry and government whose difficult task it is to account for migration. And since this study applies empirical techniques associated with qualitative choice analysis and collinearity diagnostics, it has value as a collateral reference for courses in applied econometrics in addition to urban, regional, and labor economics.

The organization of the book parallels its objectives. The review of previous studies on the determinants of interregional migration and geographic mobility is the subject of Chapter 2. In Chapter 3, I develop the theoretical model of the migration decision and specialize it to an empirical multinomial logit model. The judgments used in developing a data base suitable for estimation purposes and the aggregate characteristics of the sample of workers is presented in Chapter 4. The estimation results are discussed in Chapter 5. In Chapter 6, the conditioning of the data is evaluated using collinearity diagnostics that identify sources of collinearity.

ACKNOWLEDGMENTS

This book is largely drawn from my Ph.D. dissertation at Boston College, a co-winner of the 1980 Irving Fisher Award. I am especially grateful to Marvin Kraus who, as my dissertation advisor, was a skillful and consistent sounding board and a careful reader of the earlier drafts of the manuscript. I am grateful as well to David Belsley, Robert Wallace, and Geoffrey Woglom for their valuable comments on early drafts. James Freund, James Kneafsey, and Steven Lerman have made helpful suggestions on certain aspects of this study.

The data analysis undertaken herein was considerable, and I acknowledge the computing support of the Boston College Computer Center. Special thanks are due to Laura Appleton, George Hetrick, and James Kidd for their programming assistance.

I would also like to acknowledge the support of the Advanced Study Program of the Brookings Institution, where I completed the manuscript. Finally, The Planning Economics Group, Boston, has supported the preparation of the manuscript, and Rick Lesaar has been especially helpful in monitoring the preparation of the various drafts.

C.F.M.
Brookline, Massachusetts

The Economics of Labor Migration

A BEHAVIORAL ANALYSIS

1

Introduction

Only recently have those interested in the growth and welfare of local areas begun to understand the interrelationship among population changes, economic conditions, and regional development policy. The process of migration is an essential key to the interrelationship. It both is affected by and causes changes in local populations and economic conditions. The purpose of this research is to investigate one important aspect of this interrelationship: the worker's decision to migrate.

The conventional wisdom concerning migration decisions is that they bring about movements that enhance public welfare. That is, migration is an equilibrating adjustment mechanism that shifts local labor market supplies from areas where labor is underemployed to areas in which it could be fully employed. Even if we grant, for the moment, that this is indeed the direction of movement, there are possible consequences of such movement that can conflict with the popular wisdom of enhancing public welfare.[1] Potential conflicts arise because migration can affect the growth prospects of both the sending and receiving areas.[2] For example, suppose that the sending areas are depressed whereas the receiving areas are prosperous. There is evidence indicating that such migrants possess attractive

[1] For a detailed discussion, see Morrison (1972b).

[2] The characterization can be appropriate to both interarea and intraarea migration. In the case of intraarea migration, consider the movement from central cities to suburban areas.

1

labor force characteristics relative to their origin counterparts but that the characteristics are not distinctive compared to those of destination residents.[3] If the receiving areas are few or the migrant flows concentrated, both sending and receiving areas may have their growth prospects impaired by migration in the "right direction." The sending areas would be characterized by labor forces with low-quality characteristics, which can impair any prospects the areas have for attracting industry. This might induce further migratory outflows and accelerate area decline. Receiving areas, on the other hand, experience increased demands on their public infrastructure and services. Since marginal cost pricing does not characterize the pricing of public services, this usually results in increased taxation to provide the additional capacity needed to meet the new demands. Additionally, if the new arrivals have low-quality characteristics relative to those of the present residents, the inmigrants are likely to be burdens on the welfare rolls creating additional pressure for increased taxation.[4] The drain on community resources that these burdens impose can lead to the decentralization of activity on the part of the more productive members of a community, which can further aggravate the burdens on receiving areas. The recent attempts of policymakers in Oregon and Hawaii to discourage inmigration illustrate the concern and possible impairment of public welfare that such burdens cause.

As we have just seen, the effects of movement in the right direction—from underemployment to full-employment areas—can provide challenging problems to those responsible for public welfare. Other problems arise, if movement is not in the right direction. The immobility of local populations in certain areas, the tendency for migration to follow well-beaten paths, and the occurrence of return migration indicate that migration is complex behaviorally. Potential economic gains are not the only inducements affecting migration. The availability of information and the nonpecuniary costs incurred by leaving one's social and work environs are certainly factors influencing migration decisions. They can outweigh economic inducements and cause either no movement or movement in apparently the wrong direction. Knowledge of how potential migrants evaluate these factors is essential in forming effective policy for influencing population redistribution and regional development.

There is currently debate over whether place-oriented regional policy has any effect on stemming the migratory losses of certain areas, and resolution of the debate has serious implications for how regional develop-

[3] See Hoover (1975, p. 185), Lansing and Mueller (1967, pp. 318, 319), and Michigan Survey Research Center (1966, p. 26).

[4] Migrants from depressed areas have, in the past, shared more than proportionately in urban poverty. See Kain and Persky (1967), and U.S. Congress (1972).

ment policy will be shaped in the future.[5] Indeed, President Carter's Commission for a National Agenda for the Eighties recently took the politically risky stand of urging government to emphasize people-oriented, spatially neutral programs over the traditional place-oriented policies.[6] Both sides to this debate rely in part upon the empirical results of migration studies to lend credibility to their arguments.[7] However, as will be seen in Chapter 2, previous migration studies are generally faulty on two grounds: They do not model the migration decision adequately, and they do not allow a sufficiently rich role for differences among potential migrants in the consideration of either personally relevant measures of economic opportunity or personal mobility characteristics. Thus, conclusions and inferences drawn from such work are subject to methodological and empirical shortcomings.

The scope of this study is not as grand as to include decisive comment on the future direction of regional policy. Instead, it is limited to three research objectives. First, the existing literature on migration research will be reviewed, with emphasis on its methodological shortcomings. Second, a behavioral model of the migration decision will be developed which meets the shortcomings of earlier work. Third, a disaggregate empirical model will be estimated to assess the influence of several mobility characteristics on the decision to move and the evaluation potential migrants have of information and economic and amenity attributes of alternatives. Since the study is disaggregate, personally relevant measures of economic opportunity are included in the empirical analysis. It is expected that this study will lead to further disaggregate empirical work and subsequently to constructive comment on the orientation of regional policy.

OVERVIEW

The previous empirical studies of interregional migration have largely analyzed aggregate movements. They have been typically based on spinoffs of a synthesized gravity-economic model, and their framework

[5] Place-oriented policy attempts to improve individuals' welfare by improving the economic well-being of an area. Such policy consists in efforts designed to create jobs by stimulating local growth in employment through infrastructure investment, area planning assistance, tax incentives, and so forth. This policy is in contrast to people-oriented policy, which promotes the welfare of individuals by providing them with education, retraining, job information, and mobility assistance. For a detailed discussion, see Winnick (1966). For representative discussion of the sides to the debate see Hansen (1972) and Hoover (1972).

[6] See U.S. President's Commission for a National Agenda for the Eighties (1980).

[7] An example is Alonso (1972a, pp. 143–151).

has been either an origin, a destination, or an origin–destination perspective. The aggregate approach of these works does not allow the examination of the influence of personal attributes, so-called mobility characteristics, and personally relevant measures of economic opportunity. And the gravity inertia in the field has not tended to lead the literature toward framing the migration decision within a choice-theoretic perspective. This research is partly a response to the importance of correcting the modeling shortcomings and the empirical gaps arising from reliance upon aggregate data and from the gravity inertia in understanding the migration process. Geographic mobility studies, on the other hand, are both disaggregate and typically more behavioral than other studies, and they consequently have emphasized the role of personal attributes on the decision to move. However, mobility studies generally stop short of assessing the decision to move in the simultaneous context of the destination choice.

This study is the first disaggregate study of interregional migration in the United States in that it simultaneously analyzes the decision to move and the destination choice.[8] The empirical model is in a choice-theoretic framework and uses micro locational choices as a base for assessing the influence of mobility characteristics on the decision to migrate and the implicit valuation the potential migrant has of economic factors, some of which are personally relevant, and amenity attributes. In the choice model, the potential migrant is viewed as a neoclassical consumer maximizing lifetime expected utility over space. The utility at each place is defined over the place's economic and amenity attributes and, for the origin, over personal attributes. The potential migrant scans the expected utilities obtainable at each alternative location open to him and selects to locate at the alternative for which the expected utility is greatest.

Experimentally, the choice behavior of a sample of potential migrants is considered as the trial outcomes of a multinomial experiment. The parameters of the experiment are, through multinomial logit probabilities, the parameters of the potential migrant's utility function. Data from the Social Security Administration's Longitudinal Employer–Employee Data (LEED) file are the base for locational choices and personal attributes of potential migrants. The LEED file is rich in work history information. Using a nonlinear estimation technique, maximum-likelihood estimates of the parameters of the potential migrant's utility are obtained.

In the empirical analysis, each potential migrant's choice set is restricted to a subset of counties. For our sample of 1996 potential migrants, 28 alternatives on average are available to each potential migrant. The variables used for each alternative are measures of mobility

---

[8] DaVanzo (1977) examined the destination choices of migrants in a disaggregate study but the analysis did not simultaneously consider the decision to move.

characteristics such as job tenure, of economic attributes such as expected lifetime income, of amenity attributes such as housing conditions, and of the variance associated with knowing an alternative's attributes.

The results of estimating the migratory choice model support our modeling efforts. Personal attributes have strong influences on migratory behavior. And the observed effects of personally relevant measures of economic opportunity provide some support for our model. Employment in the potential migrant's industry exerts a positive significant influence on the potential migrant's utility. Another personally relevant measure, the potential migrant's lifetime income, was not found to be as important. This is probably due to measurement problems of the income variable imposed by data restrictions—the income measure is specific to one's industry rather than one's occupation.

The migratory choice model was estimated for both the full sample and stratifications of the sample by race, income, and sex. The results for the stratified subgroups are indicative of heterogeneous behavior. In the case of certain attributes, estimates using the full sample were misleading due to opposite directional relationships for subgroups. The model developed here allows for extensive stratification since it easily and directly uses micro data. The stratification possibilities are extremely limited in any study using aggregate data.

Since the potential migrant's utility function is specified to be quadratic in place attributes, which allows for risk aversion under uncertainty, there are several pairs of linear and quadratic terms used in the empirical analysis. This tends to introduce collinearity among the explanatory variables. To assess this possibility, a technique recently developed to diagnose collinearity in regression analysis is adapted to maximum-likelihood, multinomial logit analysis and applied to our data. A few collinear relations between pairs of linear and quadratic terms are indeed found.

OUTLINE

The organization of the remaining chapters provides an outline of this study. Chapter 2 is an intensive review of many of the empirical studies of migration. The focus of the review is to assess how earlier works have characterized the migration decision. The behavioral model of the migration decision is developed in Chapter 3. Special attention is devoted to the theory of internal labor markets to aid in specifying the model, and the discussion is extended to the empirical model, which will be seen to be linked uniquely to the choice model. Chapter 4 describes the data sources and the working assumptions used to construct an integrated data base for use in estimation. The characteristics of the sample of potential migrants from the LEED file are also discussed, as are aggregate migration propensities. In Chapter 5, the assumptions and variables used in specifying the empirical model are detailed. Also, the results of estimation are discussed. Chapter 6 develops a diagnostic of collinearity suited to multinomial logit analysis and examines the collinearity in the data used to estimate our migration model. A summary of this study, recommendations for further research, and an assessment of current migration policy in the United States are provided in the final chapter.

2

A Review of Migration Research

Population migration is central to many disciplines and has received extensive attention from economists, sociologists, demographers, and geographers. The economic literature has been usefully grouped by Greenwood (1975a) into two general categories: studies concerning the determinants of migration and those assessing the consequences of migration. The present study investigates the factors influencing the decision to migrate, and this review is primarily concerned with studies assessing the determinants of interregional migration. Since many of the current themes in migration literature originate with the study by Lowry (1966), post-Lowry contributions to migration research are mainly discussed. The review is distinguished from others by its focus on how the studies view the migration decision and is essentially in five parts: the Lowry model, inmigration models, outmigration models, place-to-place models, and geographic mobility models.

THE LOWRY SYNTHESIS

Since Lowry's work is a synthesis of earlier work, studies prior to that of Lowry are briefly discussed for their perspective. Early migration studies were principally based on one of two alternative theories. The first explains social interactions in terms of physical laws. Like the Newtonian laws governing force and mass, migration between two regions is related to laws governing the intervening distance and the populations. The social–physical law governing social interaction has come to be known as the gravity law. While there are numerous specific forms by which it has been expressed, the gravity model is essentially a descriptive and predictive model for aggregate migration flows.[1] Even though the model does not provide much explanation for an individual move, population and distance have been considered as proxies for the behavioral variables of market size and transportation costs.

The other early theory is from neoclassical economics and is expressed by Hicks (1932, p. 76): "differences in net economic advantages, chiefly differences in wages, are the main causes of migration." Given competitive market assumptions and Marshallian period-analysis of markets, changes in the regional distribution of the demand for labor result in regional differences in wages.[2] Migration is then an equilibrating force that adjusts regional labor supplies so that wage disparities are eliminated. The same equilibrating role of migration is obtained by using Keynesian period-analysis.[3] Changes in the regional distribution of the demand for labor would then result in regional differentials in employment rates. In response to so-called job vacancies, migration takes place between regions until all employment rates are equalized. Thus in the neoclassical world, migration by responding to wage differentials or job vacancies is the important mechanism that eliminates regional disparities in per capita income. Most economic studies prior to Lowry were mainly concerned with verifying the role ascribed to migration by the neoclassical model.[4]

In the neoclassical vein, Lowry (1966) viewed migration as the key link between regional economic growth and regional population growth, that is, as a behavioral response to economic opportunity. To assess this, Lowry synthesized the gravity and neoclassical approaches and modeled migration as

$$M_{ij} = k\left(\frac{U_i}{U_j} \cdot \frac{W_j}{W_i} \cdot \frac{L_i L_j}{D_{ij}}\right), \tag{2.1}$$

[1] The reader is referred to a thorough review of gravity models by Isard (1969), Chapter 11). For economic contexts for the gravity model, see Niedercorn and Bechdolt (1969, pp. 273–282) and Anderson (1979).

[2] The competitive assumptions are: Income is the sole argument of the preference function, information is perfect, and mobility is costless. In Marshallian period-analysis of markets, price adjusts infinitely fast relative to quantity.

[3] Keynesian period-analysis reverses the relative speed of adjustment held by price and quantity in Marshallian analysis.

[4] A good example of such work is Raimon (1962, pp. 428–438).

where M_{ij} is migration from i to j, U_i and U_j are the unemployment rates at i and j, W_i and W_j are the wage rates, L_i and L_j are the labor forces, D_{ij} is the intervening distance, and k is a constant.

Migration between two areas was considered by Lowry to be the result of neoclassical and gravity effects. Once the equilibrating effects of migration eliminated any differences in economic opportunity, wages and unemployment, by appropriately shifting local labor supplies, migration would only be the random interchange of persons between two areas, which is related to population sizes and intervening distance. A noteworthy aspect of Eq. (2.1) is that relative economic conditions were considered to be the important behavioral variables. That is, economic conditions at origins and destinations would have symmetric effects on migration.

When the model was estimated using data on the 1955–1960 migratory streams between SMSAs, the results were less than satisfactory. Migration was found to be unrelated to relative economic conditions. The model was then altered so that economic conditions at origins and destinations might exhibit separate effects. The most successful specification was

$$M_{ij} = e^{a_0}\left(\frac{U_i^{a_1}}{U_j^{a_2}} \cdot \frac{W_j^{a_3}}{W_i^{a_4}} \cdot \frac{C_i^{a_5} C_j^{a_6} A_i^{a_7} A_j^{a_8}}{D_{ij}^{a_9}} \right),$$

where C_i and C_j are civilian labor forces, A_i and A_j represent the armed forces, e is the exponential constant, and $a_0, \ldots, a_9$ are constants. In the empirical analysis, the variables U_i and W_i, origin economic conditions, were surprisingly not significant. Thus, relative economic conditions were not important determinants of migration, since migrants reacted only to economic conditions in destinations.

These results apparently held a clear implication for migration theory. Analyses of internal migration need not consider economic conditions at origins and destinations simultaneously. Instead, the migratory behavior of places could be understood by separately studying the inmigration and outmigration components of migration.[5] Outmigration from a place is related only to the size and mobility characteristics of its population, while inmigration is responsive to labor market conditions and to the destination's population size. Pursuant to Lowry's work, many authors have sought to explain migration in either an origin or a destination framework.[6] The underlying presumption is that the migration decision is a two-

[5] See Lowry (1966, p. 35).

[6] It should also be noted that the studies of inmigration and outmigration, reviewed in the next two sections, which followed Lowry's work, were not solely the outgrowth of Lowry's findings. Another consideration leading to these analyses was the apparent success of net

stage process wherein the decision to migrate is independent of the destination decision.

INMIGRATION MODELS

An apparent corollary to Lowry's findings is that the attention of economists should be upon the choice of destination since this is the decision influenced by economic factors. This section reviews several such studies of inmigration. The inmigration studies are categorically grouped as job-vacancy models, structural models, simultaneous-equations models, and alternative-opportunities models.

Job-Vacancy Models

Studies by Mazek (1966) and Glantz (1973) constitute job-vacancy models in that the emphasis of each is employment opportunity. And each utilizes uniquely constructed measures of opportunity. As a part of his study of net migration, Mazek examined the 1955–1960 inmigration to metropolitan areas. Assuming sticky wages, Mazek assessed the responsiveness of the labor force to regional differences in employment opportunity—unemployment levels. Mazek recognized an interdependence between migration and unemployment and considered inmigration to be largely dependent on potential unemployment, a construct representing the rate of unemployment that would have prevailed at the end of the migration period if there had been no migration.[7] In the empirical analysis, median income was also included as an independent variable to examine its role relative to potential unemployment. Using data on the 1955–1960 inmigration rates of 47 SMSAs, the regression results supported the importance of potential unemployment. It was significantly negatively related to inmigration, while income was an insignificant factor.[8]

---

migration studies, another type of study popular in the mid-1960s. Inmigration and outmigration, the components of net migration, were understandably then the next to be studied. For example, Blanco's success (1964) in explaining the 1950–1957 net migration of the 48 states was a major influence in Mazek's study of inmigration and outmigration (1966).

[7] The concept of potential unemployment was first used by Blanco (1964), who termed it *prospective unemployment*.

[8] Mazek also examined outmigration rates using the same two variables. Neither variable was significantly related to outmigration, and none of the variation in outmigration rates was explained by the two variables. Apparently, there was economic pull but no push, and Mazek's results supported the asymmetry found by Lowry (1966).

Mazek also stratified the inmigrants into eight occupational groups and six age groups.[9] For each group, the regression model employed group-specific measures of potential unemployment and median income. Each model also included the regional unemployment rate as a measure of alternative employment opportunities. Inmigrants would presumably be inclined to migrate to a place where their chance of obtaining alternative employment was high, in the event they were unable to find a job in their particular occupation. The empirical results were generally similar to those for the total sample.[10] Potential unemployment was a significant factor, and median income was consistently insignificant. The measure of regional unemployment met with mixed results, though more often than not it was a significant variable.

Following the work of Lowry and Mazek, Glantz (1973) analyzed metropolitan inmigration for three inmigrant groups: the 1955–1960 and 1965–1970 inmigration of the poor, the 1955–1960 inmigration of nonwhites, and the 1965–1970 inmigration of low-income blacks. In assessing the responsiveness of inmigration to economic opportunities, Glantz essentially maintained two arguments. First, the appropriate measure of job vacancy for inmigrants is one reflecting the excess demand for labor. Second, income opportunities for the economically disadvantaged are not measured well by customary variables and measures of unearned income such as transfer payments are more relevant to low-income potential migrants.[11] To measure the excess demand for labor, Glantz constructed two variables—employment potential and industrial relocation. The first reflected the demand for labor resulting if employment in each of a region's industries grew at the national rate. The second captured

---

[9] Another major aspect of Mazek's work was the assessment of migration's impact upon the age and occupational compositions of depressed areas. The 10 SMSAs with the highest average unemployment of the original 47 were considered as depressed areas. Mazek found that unemployment in depressed areas was not due to disproportionate shares of population subgroups that have high national rates of unemployment. And he found that migration did not substantially alter this population. Nonetheless, the impact of migration upon these areas was disfavorable. The least mobile occupational groups were craftsmen, operatives, and laborers, all of whom had high national unemployment rates. In terms of age, the older groups demonstrated the least mobility. With persistent migratory loss, the composition of a depressed area's population could be significantly altered. It would lean heavily toward highly unemployable and immobile groups.

[10] Mazek's stratified evidence (1966, Tables 3, 4, 11, and 12) also supports the pull more than the push. Only a few subgroups of outmigrants demonstrated a responsiveness to economic conditions. The strongest relations were found for professionals and managers and for those aged 20–24 and 35–44.

[11] See Herrick (1973) for a more formal treatment of the role of nonwage income on migration.

whether employment in each of a region's industries was growing more quickly than that of the nation.

In the empirical work, inmigration was modeled as a function of welfare payments, employment potential, industrial relocation, amenities, and friends and relatives.[12] The welfare measure was total payments per recipient, and amenities were captured by population. The measure of friends and relatives was the proportion poor, and for nonwhites and low-income blacks the proportion nonwhite was also used. Using data on 102 SMSAs in 1955–1960 and 64 SMSAs in 1965–1970, three inmigration flows were analyzed: migration into SMSAs, migration into central cities, and migration into SMSAs outside central cities.

The empirical results varied for different groups of inmigrants. For the poor, the measures of excess demand for labor—employment potential and industrial relocation—and the proportion poor were generally significant. The welfare measure was a significant factor influencing the 1965–1970 inmigration, but it was insignificant in the period 1955–1960. For nonwhites and low-income blacks, the only consistently significant variable was the proportion nonwhite. Nonwhite movements in 1955–1960 were to large SMSAs. The nonwhite inmigration to central cities of SMSAs was influenced by the measures of excess demand for labor. The migration into areas outside the central city was influenced only by the presence of friends and relatives. For low-income blacks in 1965–1970, economic opportunities influenced inmigration to areas outside central cities, but they were not a factor in the movement to central cities.

Thus, Glantz's study indicates that poor migrants are pulled by economic opportunity, and that nonwage income can be an important aspect of economic opportunity.[13] Also, the results suggest that less is known about the determinants of nonwhite migration.[14] Apparently, nonwhites select destinations primarily due to factors associated with the presence of other nonwhites.

---

[12] The empirical model allows for the interaction of welfare and inmigration and is a simultaneous-equations model estimated using two-stage least squares.

[13] The relation between welfare payments and migration was also investigated by Cebula (1974). Like Glantz, Cebula (1974) considered a simultaneous-equations model in which migration and welfare payments were jointly determined. Welfare payments were most attractive to male and female black migrants aged 20 to 39 and were significant deterrents to the migration of white males and females.

[14] Other research on the migration of disadvantaged groups supports this. For example, both Bowles (1970, p. 360) and Rogers (1967) had substantially less success in explaining nonwhite than white migration.

Structural Models

The job-vacancy models stress the role of employment opportunities as influences on inmigration. As such, they pay less attention to other structural aspects of destinations—such as housing conditions and amenities. These factors have been given more thorough consideration in work by von Böventer (1969) and Pack (1973).

Von Böventer's analysis of inmigration to cities in West Germany is unique in its treatment of the role of city size and the relationship of the city to the region. A nonlinear relation between inmigration and city size was considered since neither the costs of providing public services and infrastructure nor the benefits that firms and households derive from agglomeration economies are linearly related to population.[15] The nonlinear relation between inmigration and city size was explored empirically by using five separate population variables pertaining to five classes of city size.

With respect to the city's position in the region's spatial structure, von Böventer examined hypotheses concerning a city's distance and accessibility from other cities. In particular, as the distance from a given city to other cities increases, two opposite effects on inmigration to the city were considered. With increasing distance, agglomeration economies and spillover effects derived from the proximity of the cities would decline. At the same time, however, a city's dominance over its hinterland would increase. The first effect, the agglomeration effect, would reduce the city's attractiveness, while the second, the hinterland effect, would reduce the intervening opportunities confronting migrants, which increases the city's attractiveness to migrants. If the agglomeration effect were to decline more rapidly than the hinterland effect increases, the net effect of increasing distance between cities on inmigration would be negative up to a point, the so-called pessimum distance. Thereafter, the hinterland effect would dominate the more slowly diminishing agglomeration effect, and beyond pessimum distance the net effect of increasing distance on inmigration would be positive. In the empirical work, a pessimum distance was calculated for each city, and its value depended uniquely on the city's size.

The second aspect of the city's position relative to the region's spatial structure investigated by von Böventer was the accessibility of the city to potential migrants in the other places. The greater the accessibility to the

---

[15] Agglomeration economies from spatial concentration refer to benefits resulting from scale economies in production, complementarities in labor supply and production, and personal interactions that generate innovative ideas. See Mills (1972, pp. 16, 17).

city, the greater should be the flow of inmigrants to it. Since the primary modes of intercity travel in West Germany are rail and auto, inmigration to the city might increase along with the number of rail and highway connections.

Additionally, von Böventer considered several variables as measures of the city's economic, fiscal, and amenity attributes. In particular, the change in per capita income, industrial composition, tax receipts, public infrastructure investments, the city's recreational and cultural opportunities, and the condition of its housing market were included in the empirical analysis.

In the empirical work, the sample was stratified by city size into two groups: cities above 75,000 in population and those with 10,000 to 75,000 persons. For each size group, regression equations were estimated for two time periods: 1956–1961 and 1961–1966. As expected, the determinants of inmigration differed substantially between the large and small cities. For large cities, the significant variables were industrial composition, housing conditions, cultural importance, city size, and distance from other centers. Inmigrants were attracted to areas with concentrations of modern industries such as the chemical and service industries and to areas with educational opportunities. On the other hand, areas that specialized in slow-growing industries—coal mining and manufacturing—were less attractive to inmigrants. Also, the tighter a city's housing market, as measured by the number of people looking for apartments, the less attractive was the city to migrants. The effect of city size was significant after size reached the 250,000 level. At higher levels, its effect was significantly positive but declined in magnitude with increasing size. Also, the hypothesized effects of distance from another major city were demonstrated. There was a positive agglomeration effect due to proximity to another city, but this effect declined with increases in the intervening distance. A positive but weaker effect of distance beyond the pessimum distance—the hinterland effect—was also found.

The regressions explaining migration into small cities illustrated that different forces affected inmigration to small cities. Specifically, inmigration was found to be negatively related to city size. Also, no hinterland effect was observed. The only effect of increased distance from other cities was a decline in the agglomeration effect. Employment in manufacturing and in the tertiary sector positively influenced inmigration, as did local investment in infrastructure.[16]

[16] Von Böventer's results appear to have a strong implication for growth policy in depressed areas. Development efforts should combine the apparent agglomeration and hinterland effects. This could be accomplished by encouraging agglomeration in small cities through infrastructure investment which would attract inmigrants. Once the level of agglom-

In another study emphasizing structural variables, Pack (1973) analyzed the determinants of inmigration to central cities in 1955–1960. Pack (1973) postulated that economic, fiscal, and amenity characteristics of a city influence the rate of inmigration. Present economic opportunities were measured by median income and the unemployment rate, while potential economic opportunities were reflected by growth in median income and median years of education, an indicator of the city's innovativeness. Fiscal variables included per capita measures of residential taxes and public expenditures and a per recipient measure of welfare payments. The amenity variables related to the housing conditions in the central city. Presumably, migrants would prefer cities with a high-quality stock of rental housing, as measured by the proportions of rental and of sound housing units. Population was also included to assess any locational preference for small or large cities.

Using data on 20 central cities, separate equations were estimated for white and nonwhite inmigrants. For whites, all variables were of the expected sign and only two, population and median income, were insignificant. For nonwhites, the variation in inmigration rates explained by the model was much lower than it was for whites. A measure of friends and relatives, the proportion nonwhite, was subsequently included, and the additional variable proved to be the most important determinant of nonwhite inmigration. Other significant factors were the income measures, the availability of rental housing, and the local fiscal variables. The unemployment rate and the welfare measure, per recipient aid to dependent children, were insignificant.

Pack's (1973) study was criticized by Cebula and Curran (1974) for its empirical specification of the change-in-income variable.[17] In particular, since income changes are influenced by migration, a proper specification requires a simultaneous-equations model of migration and income change.

Simultaneous-Equations Models

While the simultaneous approach originated with authors of job-vacancy models (such as Mazek, who considered inmigration and unemployment to be interdependent), the focus of simultaneous-equations models of migration tends to be the role of migration in regional growth.[18]

---

eration is sufficient so that the city generatively develops such economies, it will also influence its hinterland. This would lead to growth throughout the region.

[17] See Pack (1974) for a reply.

[18] The forerunners of the simultaneous approach are Blanco (1964), Lowry (1966, pp. 36,

Muth (1968) was the first to model migration as part of a simultaneous system of regional growth. Muth's view of regional growth (1968, 1971) followed that of Borts and Stein (1964). Essentially, differential rates of employment growth are the result of differential rates of migration since the regional demand for labor is infinitely elastic beyond the point of domestic employment at a wage exogenously determined. This view competes with that of the job-vacancy approach, which derives from the export base theory. This job-vacancy approach relies implicitly upon an infinitely elastic supply of labor due to labor migration and explicitly upon exogenous differential shifts in product demand, hence labor demand, to explain differential growth rates. Whether regional growth is better explained by assuming elastic labor demand or elastic labor supply is still an issue, and the empirical evidence has not been conclusive.[19]

While studies by Muth are not reviewed here since the measure of migration was net migration rather than inmigration, we mention them for two reasons.[20] The first is to emphasize that the approach of simultaneous-equations models has been one of assessing the impact of migration on regional growth rather than the determinants of migration. The second is to provide background for the studies considered here. Studies by Olvey (1970) and Greenwood (1973, 1975b, 1976) are discussed in this section to illustrate how the simultaneous-equations work has viewed inmigration. Each of the studies separately examines inmigration and outmigration as part of a system of equations that models the regional growth process of areas. At this point, only the inmigration equations are considered.

Since inmigration affects growth in the labor force, Olvey (1970) analyzed inmigration as part of a study of the interaction of metropolitan employment growth and labor force growth. Olvey considered separate equations for short-distance inmigrants—movers from contiguous states—and for long-distance inmigrants—movers from noncontiguous states. The short-distance inmigration rate was expected to be positively related to three destination characteristics: employment growth, the wage level, and favorable climatic conditions. Negative relations were expected between the inmigration rate and two variables: wages in the rest-of-the-world, the area contiguous to the destination which includes

---

37), and Mazek (1966, Chapter III). Each author constructued a measure of unemployment that recognized the impact of migration on unemployment.

[19] For a lively interchange of the two views, see Mazek and Change (1972) and Muth (1972).

[20] Another study of the interaction of net migration and employment change that disaggregates net migration by race and employment change by whether it is agricultural employment is Persky and Kain (1970).

the origin, and the destination population. (Population was included to correct for the implicit constraint of unit elasticity imposed upon the relation between inmigration and destination populations by using their ratio as the dependent variable.) Olvey suspected that short-distance inmigration would increase less than proportionately with destination population because of the intervening effects of origin characteristics, principally wages. Long-distance inmigration was presumed to be influenced only by the destination characteristics. The inmigration rate was expected to be directly related to employment growth, wages, and climate.

In the empirical work, the two inmigration equations were simultaneously estimated using three-stage least squares. The other jointly determined endogenous variables measured other aspects of labor force growth and employment growth. The data covered 56 SMSAs in 1955–1960. The best specification used an adjusted wage variable which would correct for regional differentials in the quality of the labor force. The empirical results generally supported expectations. (The only exception was that the climate variable was typically an insignificant factor, though its coefficient was of the expected sign.) Both short- and long-distance inmigrants were most strongly influenced by the growth in employment. They were also pulled by the destination wage. For short-distance inmigrants, low wages in the rest-of-the-world led to large inmigrations, and the strength of economic pull exerted by destination characteristics was substantially less than that for long-distance inmigrants.

In a series of studies also concerned with the interaction of employment growth and population growth, Greenwood (1973, 1975b, 1976) obtained results similar to those of Olvey. In each study, Greenwood maintained a basic specification of the inmigration equation. Inmigration was considered to be related to three destination factors: economic opportunity, the population turnover, and the population or labor force size. Economic opportunity was measured by three other jointly endogenous variables—income growth, employment growth, and the change in unemployment—and by two exogenous variables—median income and the unemployment rate. The measure of turnover that would directly affect the propensity to inmigrate was outmigration, also an endogenous variable. (In the 1976 study the outmigration variable was not included in the inmigration equations.) In the 1975b and 1976 studies, regional dummy variables were also included to capture any unmeasured factors such as cost of living, climate, or social milieu that might affect the propensity to migrate.

The principal feature distinguishing each of the three studies by Greenwood is that each examines different inmigration flows. The distinctive differences among the studies by Greenwood arise from the type of migration considered. In the 1973 study, inmigration to 100 SMSAs in 1950–1960 was examined. In the 1976 work, these same inmovements were disaggregated by race, and separate equations for whites and non-whites were studied. In the 1976 analysis, the size of the labor force for whites (nonwhites) was also included as an exogenous variable in the in-migration equation for nonwhites (whites). Presumably, if each group discriminated in selecting destinations, an increasing presence of the other group would exert a negative effect on the inmigration of each group. Greenwood's 1975b study was concerned with whether the inmigrants originated in other SMSAs or in nonmetro areas. The inmigration flows from other SMSAs and from nonmetro areas were separately examined within the simultaneous-equations model using data covering 63 SMSAs in 1950–1960 and 1960–1970. In the empirical work, two-stage least squares was used in the 1975b and 1976 studies, while the 1973 study used three-stage least squares.

The empirical results for the period 1950–1960 indicated that employment growth was consistently a strong influence on each type of inmigration. Another consistent influence was outmigration, the measure of turnover; as it increased, so too did inmigration. By race, the results were mixed. Whites responded mainly to unemployment variables; decreases in unemployment and low unemployment rates both attracted whites. Nonwhites, on the other hand, were chiefly influenced by income variables. High income levels and high growth rates in income were attractions for nonwhite inmigrants. Aside from regional dummies, the only other variables that were important in the white and nonwhite equations were their respective labor force sizes. Each group responded positively to the presence of its respective group. The presence of the other group was not a significant factor in either case, though the signs were negative as expected. Also noteworthy is that neither of the racial patterns was typical of the aggregate, which appears to be an amalgam of effects. For example, both the change in unemployment and the level of income were insignificant in the aggregate, while each was alternately significant for the race groups. When the 1950–1960 inmigration flows were stratified by type of origin, metro versus nonmetro, unemployment variables were most important. For both types of inflows, the change in unemployment was the dominant influence. The only other significant relation was between inmigration from nonmetro areas and the rate of unemployment. In 1960–1970, income variables were the prominent influences, while unemployment was unimportant. For inmigrants from metro areas, the growth in employment and the level of income were significant, and for nonmetro inmigrants, both the growth in income and the income level were significant factors. Outmigration, the level of turnover, was a significant influence on inmigration from both metro and nonmetro areas.

At a general level, Greenwood's results are consistent with those of Olvey, indicating that migrants move to areas where jobs are rapidly increasing. The direction of causality is, however, elusive since inmigrants both cause and respond to increases in jobs. Also, a comparison of Greenwood's 1973 results with those of the 1976 work shows that aggregate migration patterns can mask underlying systematic differences in the behavior of subgroups.

While the simultaneous-equations models are able to account correctly for any simultaneous-equations bias arising from a more limited specification of inmigration and economic variables, their treatment of the migration decision is not their major emphasis. Indeed, Greenwood (1975b, p. 799) states that "the model employed in this study attempts to explain gross out- and gross inmigration without the explicit introduction of an individual decision function. Rather, gross out- and gross inmigration are related to a number of aggregate proxy variables." In what follows, another simultaneous-equations model of inmigration is reviewed, but because it provides a more explicit treatment of the migration decision it is considered separately.

Alternative-Opportunities Models

The inmigration study of Alperovich et al. (1977) considers alternative opportunities more fully than did Olvey. (Other alternative-opportunities models are discussed in the section beginning on page 40 entitled "Place-to-Place Models.") While the study's empirical method is a simultaneous-equations model, Alperovich et al. have strengthened the theoretical foundations of in- and outmigration models by basing their model on an analysis of place-to-place migration. Like Lowry's view of a place-to-place move, theirs was essentially a synthesized gravity perspective. The probability of migrating from one place to another depends on the economic characteristics of the origin and destination, the populations, and the intervening distance. While the Lowry formulation considers the origin and destination in isolation from other alternatives, Alperovich et al. expected that origin–destination movements depend on alternative opportunities as well as origin and destination characteristics. In particular, a move was considered to depend on the "gravity structure" between the origin and destination relative to the gravity structure existing between the origin and all other places.

Specifically, the relative frequency of an origin–destination move was hypothesized to be a linear function of the origin's and destination's attributes, where the function was weighted by the relative gravity structure—the destination's share of a weighted total population of all places. (Each of the weights in the sum of the total population is a decreasing function of the distance between each place and the origin.) The relative gravity structure expresses the attractiveness, in gravity terms, of the destination to the origin relative to that of all places in the system. Symbolically, the relative frequency of migrating from i to j is

$$\frac{M_{ij}}{P_i} = \left(\frac{P_j e^{-\theta d_{ij}}}{\Sigma_k P_k e^{-\theta d_{ik}}} \right) \cdot \left(u_0 + \sum_{s=1}^{S} u_s X_{sj} + \sum_{s=1}^{S} v_s X_{si} \right), \qquad (2.2)$$

where

M_{ij}	is the migration from i to j,
P_i, P_j, P_k	are the populations in i, j, and k,
X_{si}, X_{sj}	are the sth elements of the S attributes of i, j,
d_{ij}, d_{ik}	are the distances between i and j and between i and k,
θ	is a constant, $\theta > 0$,
k	is the kth place in the system $k = 1, \ldots, i, j, \ldots, N$,
u_s	are constants, $s = 0, \ldots, S$,
v_s	are constants, $s = 1, \ldots, S$,
e	is the exponential constant.

The first of the parenthesized expressions on the right-hand side of Eq. (2.2) is the weighting function or relative gravity structure. The second parenthesized expression is the function that assesses the attributes of the origin and destination.

The departure from the traditional or Lowry specification is clearly seen by considering the traditional approach. In the Lowry approach, economic attributes of the places are weighted by the destination's population relative to the intervening distance, and the weight is the same regardless of the sizes and distances of alternative opportunities.[21] Like von Böventer, Alperovich et al. considered the role of size and distance to be affected by the spatial structure of alternative opportunities. If alternative opportunities are large in size and close to the origin, the role of destination size and distance is reduced considerably. If alternatives were small and distant, the role afforded destination size and distance would not be diminished as much.

While based upon place-to-place movement, the empirical model was an inmigration model. The empirical model for a destination was obtained by summing the place-to-place movements to the destination over all ori-

---

[21] From (2.1) the traditional approach is expressed as $M_{ij}/P_i = (P_j/d_{ij}) \cdot f(X_i, X_j)$, where P_i, P_j are L_i, L_j; d_{ij} is D_{ij}; and $f(X_i, X_j) = k[(U_i/U_j) \cdot (W_j/W_i)]$.

gins. This procedure yields a model of the rate of inmigration to a place, IM_j:

$$IM_j = \frac{\Sigma_{i \neq j} M_{ij}}{P_j} = u_0 \sum_{i \neq j} \frac{P_i e^{-\theta d_{ij}}}{\Sigma_k P_k e^{-\theta d_{ik}}}$$

$$+ \sum_{i \neq j} \frac{P_i e^{-\theta d_{ij}}}{\Sigma_k P_k e^{-\theta d_{ik}}} \sum_{s=1}^{S} u_s X_{sj}$$

$$+ \sum_{s=1}^{S} v_s \sum_{i \neq j} \frac{P_i e^{-\theta d_{ij}}}{\Sigma_k P_k e^{-\theta d_{ik}}} X_{si}.$$

By letting

$$V_j = \sum_{i \neq j} \frac{P_i e^{-\theta d_{ij}}}{\Sigma_k P_k e^{-\theta d_{ik}}}$$

the model above is simplified to

$$IM_j = u_0 V_j + V_j \sum_s u_s X_{sj} + \sum_s v_s \sum_{i \neq j} \frac{P_i e^{-\theta d_{ij}}}{\Sigma_k P_k e^{-\theta d_{ik}}} X_{si}. \qquad (2.3)$$

Thus, the rate of inmigration depends upon three distinct groups of terms. The first group, V_j is a single measure of the combined attractive force (in gravity terms) of all other places.[22] It is conceptually similar to von Böventer's hinterland effect. The combined-attractiveness measure is relatively large when the destination is small in size and close to large-sized alternatives. It is small when the destination is large and distant from competing destinations. The second group refers to a series of weighted characteristics of the destination. The weight is the combined-attractiveness measure. The final group of terms relates to attributes of alternative opportunities. For each attribute a weighted sum over the set of alternatives is calculated. Each of the weights is the relative contribution of each of the alternative opportunities to the combined-attractiveness of all places.

Before the model was estimated, each term in Eq. (2.3) was divided by the combined-attractiveness measure, V_j,[23]

$$\frac{IM_j}{V_j} = u_0 + \sum_s u_s X_{sj} + \sum_s v_s \sum_{i \neq j} R_{ji} X_{si}, \qquad (2.4)$$

[22] The weighted sum is very similar to a weighted average of the attribute. The summation of the weights is V_j, which is, of course, the combined-attractiveness measure. The average value of V_j is reported to be .972.

[23] The authors aggregate their place-to-place model with respect to all destinations, thereby obtaining a model of outmigration as well. However, they demonstrate that estimation of the inmigration model yields an estimation of the outmigration model, and vice versa. Consequently, the empirical work is only concerned with estimating the inmigration model.

where

$$R_{ji} = \frac{P_i e^{-\theta d_{ij}}}{V_j \Sigma_k P_k e^{-\theta d_{ik}}}.$$

This complicated the nature of the dependent variable. The rate of inmigration was inflated for large isolated destinations and deflated for small destinations with neighboring alternatives. Nonetheless, the right-hand side of Eq. (2.4), the expression for the independent variables, was simplified.

In the empirical work, data covering inmigration to SMSAs in 1965–1970 were used to examine hypotheses concerning economic opportunities, amenities, and previous migration. Three variables—the unemployment rate, the growth in employment, and the wage—were used to measure economic opportunity (each variable is an average over the 5-year period). Two aspects of amenities were considered: climate (the absolute deviation in degrees from a temperate climate) and city size. Presumably, migrants would prefer city sizes of less than 1 million in population. Two variables—the log of population and its square—were used to indicate whether there was a preference for cities of less than 1 million (negative coefficient estimates for the population variables would indicate such a preference). The effect of previous migration was measured by three variables: the stock of nonmigrants (the proportion of people living in their state of birth), the rate of previous movers (the fraction of the population that changed cities during 1955–1960), and the proportion of population 65 years or older. This last variable was expected to capture any trend movement to retirement communities.

The inmigration equation was estimated along with equations for the unemployment rate and the growth in employment rate in a simultaneous-equations model using two-stage least squares. The empirical results provided general support for the hypotheses. Favorable economic conditions in destinations induced inmigration while favorable opportunities in origins reduced inmigration to a destination. Additionally, the results indicated that inmigrants are more responsive to changes in destination wages than changes in destination unemployment. Locational amenities also had strong effects on inmigration. Indeed, the elasticity of migration to temperature was found to be stronger than that with respect to unemployment. And once city size exceeded 1 million it was a negative influence on inmigration.[24]

[24] The authors report some evidence indicating that economic conditions at origins and destinations have a symmetric effect on migration, thereby supporting both the push and pull hypotheses. Alperovich *et al.* (1977, p. 40) go on to state that if regional development policy creates two new jobs in an area "one is likely to be filled by a worker who otherwise

Overview of Inmigration Models

An overview of the inmigration studies reviewed in this section is provided by Table 2.1. For each researcher, the table indicates the year, unit,
and method of analysis; the dependent variable; and the nature of the
independent variables. Some models, those by Mazek (1966), Glantz
(1973), von Böventer (1969), Pack (1973), Greenwood (1973, 1975b, 1976),
and Alperovich *et al.* (1977), explicitly or implicitly assumed that the attributes of alternatives do not vary substantially among destinations.
Hence, in empirical specifications their influence would be reflected in the
constant term. Some, notably Mazek (1966), Glantz (1973), Pack (1973),
and Greenwood (1973, 1975b, 1976), implicitly assumed that migrants
have equal information of, and access to, each destination from all possible origins. Thus, the empirical model need not consider information or
accessibility as a factor influencing inmigration. Neither of these assumptions, of course, holds. And while certain models have measured alternative opportunities directly, their attempts are less than adquate. Specifically, von Böventer's (1969) study only considered the closest large city
as an alternative, and in the study by Alperovich *et al.* (1977) economic
and amenity attributes of alternatives were not allowed a role.

OUTMIGRATION MODELS

Lowry's study was a point of departure for studies of outmigration as
well as inmigration, since many analyses of outmigration sought to investigate further Lowry's inference that migration is not influenced by origin
economic conditions. The outmigration studies reviewed here are
grouped by method and emphasis into two categroies: propensity models
and simultaneous-equations models.

Propensity Models

Four of the outmigration studies considered here are *propensity
models,*[25] so called because each study controls for differences in migra-

---

would have moved away while the other is likely to be filled by an inmigrant." Another implication for development policy is that policies designed to induce inmigration to depressed
areas are in conflict with strong traditional forces. The authors base this implication on their
finding that migrants are attracted even more strongly to regions that are growing than to
cities that are growing within regions (p. 45).

[25] An area's aggregate migration rate is like its aggregate birth rate. The birth rate depends
on the composition of the population and on fertility. Thus, an area may have a low birth rate

TABLE 2.1
Summary of Inmigration Models

Researcher (year)	Year of analysis	Unit of analysis	Method of analysis	Dependent variable
a. Job vacancy				
Mazek (1966)	1955–1960	47 SMSAs	Multiple regression	Rate of inmigration
Glantz (1973)	1955–1960 and 1965–1970	100 SMSAs and 63 SMSAs	Two-stage least squares	Inmigration rate for: a. the poor (income ≤ $4000 b. nonwhites (1955–1960) c. blacks (1965–1970)
b. Structural				
von Böventer (1969)	1959–1961 and 1961–1966	Cities	Multiple regression	Gross inmigration
Pack (1973)	1955–1960	20 Central cities	Multiple regression	Inmigration rate
c. Simultaneous equations				
Olvey (1970)	1955–1960	56 SMSAs	Three-stage least squares	Inmigration rate a. Long distance b. Short distance
Greenwood (1973)	1950–1960	100 SMSAs	Three-stage least squares double log	Gross inmigration

ABLE 2.1 (continued)

| | Independent variables (categories) | | | |
Economic opportunity	Amenities	Fiscal	Spatial structure	Propensity to migrate
Potential unemployment Regional unemployment Median income Employment potential Industrial relocation Welfare	 Population Percentage poor Percentage nonwhite			

Growth in per capita
   income
Employment structure
	Climate and
	   landscape
	Number of students
	Excess demand for
	   rental housing
	Housing rents
	Population
	   potential
		Tax receipts
		Public spending
		   on infra-
		   structure
			Hinterland effect
			   of distance
			Agglomeration ef-
			   fect of distance
			Railroad acces-
			   sibility
			Highway acces-
			   sibility	

Median income
Growth in income
Unemployment rate
Median education
	Percentage housing
	   a. Owner
	      occupied
	   b. Unsound
	Percentage
	   nonwhite
		Per capita taxes
		Educational
		   spending
		General
		   spending
		Welfare
		   payment per
		   recipient
			Population	

Growth in employment Hourly wage Per capita income Population	Climate			

Change in income
Change in employment
Change in unemploy-
   ment
Income
Unemployment
	Civilian labor
	   force
				Outmigration

(cont'd.)

TABLE 2.1 (continued)

Researcher (year)	Year of analysis	Unit of analysis	Method of analysis	Dependent variable
Greenwood (1975b)	1950–1960 and 1960–1970	63 SMSAs	Two-stage least squares double log	Gross inmigration a. From metro areas b. From nonmetro areas
Greenwood (1976)	1950–1960	100 SMSAs	Two-stage least squares double log	Gross inmigration a. Whites b. Nonwhites
d. Alternative opportunities Alperovich, Bergsman, and Ehemann (1977)	1965–1970	All SMSAs	Two-stage least squares	Inmigration rate relative to the combined-attractiveness measure.

tion propensities in assessing the responsiveness of outmigration to origin economic conditions. However, the technique used in doing so varies from one study to another.

The first is an analysis of outmigration by Miller (1973a).[26] Essentially, Miller maintained that economic variables are important determinants of outmigration, but that their effects are frequently "covered up" by a low propensity to migrate. According to Miller, the most mobile groups have already migrated from areas of low economic opportunity. The remaining population would then be concentrated in groups with low propensities to migrate, which reduces the outmigration rate. Because of the effect of the

even if its fertility is high due to population concentrations in groups with low childbearing propensities, such as males or the aged. Similarly, the migration rate in an area may be low due to concentrations of population in groups with low migratory propensities rather than unresponsive migratory behavior.

[26] Other work by Edward Miller (1973b) supports the pull of economic conditions at destinations.

TABLE 2.1 (continued)

	Independent variables (categories)			
Economic opportunity	Amenities	Fiscal	Spatial structure	Propensity to migrate
Change in income Change in employment Change in unemployment Income Unemployment	Civilian labor force		Regional dummies	Outmigration
Change in income Change in employment Change in unemployment Income Unemployment	Civilian labor force a. Own race b. Other race		Regional dummies	
Unemployment rate Growth in employment Wage Alternative opportunities (weighted sums of the economic attributes of alternatives).	Climate City size a. Log (population) b. (log (population))^2		Combined attractiveness measure (the attractive force in gravity terms of all alternatives in the system).	Stock of nonmigrants Previous migrant rate Fraction of old age (65 or older).

low migration propensity, the outmigration rate may be less than that expected solely from economic considerations.

In the empirical work, Miller considered outmigration from states to be related to economic and amenity attributes of places and to characteristics of the population which would control for the effect of the area's migration propensity. Economic attributes were measured by median income and the growth in employment rate. The amenity attributes were the average January temperature and population size. Presumably, the larger the population size of the state, the greater the chance that a migrant would find a satisfactory destination within the state, and the lower the rate of outmigration. Two measures of the area's migration propensity were also considered: the inmigration rate and the fraction of the population with at least a year of college. The inmigration rate would indicate the "footloose" who have a high propensity to move again. The education variable was also expected to affect outmigration positively, since the highly educated are one of the most mobile groups.

In the empirical analysis, Miller used data covering the 48 contiguous states and the District of Columbia in 1955–1960. To demonstrate that the effects of migration propensities can mask a relationship between outmigration and economic variables, Miller conducted two experiments. First, the outmigration rate was regressed only upon origin median income. The results indicated no relation between outmigration and income. Second, the outmigration rate was regressed upon the variables measuring the propensity to migrate along with the variables measuring economic and amenity attributes of origins. The results of this regression were generally as expected. All independent variables except population were significant factors and of the anticipated sign. Employment growth was the dominant influence. Miller therefore argued that Lowry's finding of no relationship between migration and economic characteristics of origins was attributable to misspecification bias arising from the failure to account for the effect of migration propensities.

The second propensity model is Trott's analysis of labor force outmigration (1971a). Trott maintained that including non-labor-force members in an empirical analysis would supress any relation between outmigration and economic conditions, and the suppression is most likely to occur when incomes are low and labor force participation is accordingly discouraged. Like Miller, Trott expected to observe a relation between outmigration and economic conditions upon controlling for the propensity to migrate. Trott controlled for the migration propensity directly since the data he used were for labor force participants only.

In the empirical work, Trott (1971a) examined various aspects of the importance of the job-vacancy and differential-wage hypotheses. Given the heterogeneity of labor, Trott argued that the conventional aggregate measures such as median income and the unemployment rate are not the only measures of labor market conditions relevant to potential migrants. Like Mazek, Trott considered economic variables that were specific to the potential migrant's cohort as well as aggregate measures. Since the data used by Trott (1971a), the Continuous Work History Sample (CWHS), have a micro base, outmigration streams for age–sex–race cohorts were constructed.

The economic measures examined in the analysis related to four time perspectives: base-year conditions, contemporaneous trends, and short- and long-term expectations. Five measures of base-year conditions at the origin were considered: the four-industry employment concentration ratio, the ratio of population to employment, the origin employment relative to the average employment of all places, the employment growth rate, and the cohort's share in origin employment relative to the national share. The greater the concentration ratio and the ratio of population to employment, the smaller the range of employment opportunities and the greater the excess supply of labor, respectively. In both cases, the outmigration rate would presumably be greater. The ratios of origin employment to average employment and of the origin–national cohort share measure the extent of local job opportunities relative to those elsewhere, and increases in their values would expectedly impede outmigration.

Contemporaneous conditions were measured by two variables: the origin dropout rate relative to the national average and the ratio of new labor supply entrants to the change in employment. Any slackening in employment demand reflected by an increase in the local dropout rate relative to that of the nation would presumably increase outmigration, as would increases in the number of new workers relative to that of new jobs.

Two short-term measures of expected conditions were used: industrial relocation (the ratio of the actual employment in an area relative to the predicted employment based on national growth rates for industries) and a relative wage measure (the average wage if workers in each industry were paid the national wage rate relative to the actual average wage). The greater this wage ratio, the higher wage rates for the same work elsewhere and presumably so too the rate of outmigration. The two measures of long-term expected conditions covered cohort-specific future earnings for a 5-year period and for worklife expectancy. Each variable measured the future cohort earnings at the origin relative to the expected earnings based on a national base wage and growth rate.

Since the data pertained only to those covered by Social Security employment, the analysis was able to focus upon primary workers. The cohorts were white males aged 25–34, 35–44, 45–54, and 55–64. Using data on 173 BEA areas, outmigration was examined for 1960–1963 and 1963–1966 and for two size classes of BEA areas.[27] The empirical results indicated that the 11 measures of economic opportunity were substantially able to explain the variation in outmigration rates in each of 16 regression models. This was especially the case for the period 1963–1966 and for large-sized BEA areas. In general, the results supported the job-vacancy hypothesis more strongly than the differential-wage hypothesis since the wage measures were not consistently significant. In the 1960–1963 period, migrants appeared to be concerned with employment security. High dropout rates and large excess supplies of labor caused high outmigration rates. In 1963–1966, on the other hand, the concern was with the prospects of local employment opportunities in that the vari-

---

[27] The two size classes were BEA areas with an SMSA of 250,000 to 750,000 in population, and BEA areas with an SMSA of 750,000 or more. BEA areas are economic areas defined by the Bureau of Economic Analysis "primarily from commuting patterns about an economic center, generally an SMSA . . . [Trott, 1971a, p. 4]."

able measuring relative employment size and the measure of new entrants relative to new jobs were important factors. Among the age groups, the only additional consistent relation was that the outmigration for older cohorts was stemmed by local employment opportunities as measured by the relative intensity of employment of the cohort.

While Trott's analysis (1971a) was limited in scope, it extensively examined the importance of wages and employment opportunities. Like Miller (1973a), Trott found that employment opportunities were more important determinants of outmigration than wages, and again, outmigrants were seen to respond to origin economic conditions once the propensity to migrate was taken into account.[28]

Renshaw's study (1970) also stressed the obscuring effect of differences in the propensity to migrate. Renshaw viewed the migration of labor as an extension of local labor market turnover—the matching of heterogeneous jobs to heterogeneous workers. Within this framework, Renshaw identified structural and institutional factors which can be fairly specific to labor market areas and which would affect the propensity to migrate.[29] Moreover, according to Renshaw, these factors lead to migration propensities that vary directly with past growth. That is, high propensities to migrate would tend to characterize prosperous areas and low propensities would

---

[28] In a similar study Trott (1971b, Tables 14–15) found that a measure of expected versus actual wage was the principal determinant of outmigration. However, the model employed did not include all the variables that were found to be significant in the 1971 study. The data were, nonetheless, similar except that both black and white males were studied and that a selective subset of BEA areas was covered.

[29] Turnover is an investment in human capital induced by life-cycle forces and by forces arising from changes in the composition of aggregate demand or in technology. The movement of workers within a job structure—gross turnover—is motivated by life-cycle considerations; changing tastes and technology alter a job structure requiring worker movement—net turnover.

Noting that the forces affecting net turnover are highly unpredictable by nature, Renshaw chose to examine the forces leading to gross turnover. Although most jobs are specialized, they typically involve general skills as well. Like education, movement within a job structure can enhance a worker's productivity. Turnover allows a worker to experience complementary jobs, thereby increasing the breadth of his skills and improving his productivity in any one job. Additionally, turnover enables a worker to move to a job at which he possesses a comparative advantage or that has characteristics suitable to his tastes.

The reason that turnover instead of initial job selection is the typical method of matching workers to jobs is twofold. First, randomness in the stock of job vacancies and of new entrants can cause workers to take jobs that are less than optimal, given the entrants' tastes and comparative advantages. Second, the initial job selection may often be incorrect, since job characteristics, tastes, and comparative advantages are difficult to assess prior to work experience. Thus, even with a stable job structure, there are forces causing turnover.

The strength of the forces causing turnover depends upon the skill requirements of jobs and upon the skills and tastes of workers. Renshaw (1970, p. 30) states: "Mobility, then, is

typify depressed areas.[30] Thus, it would be no surprise to find that there was no systematic relation between migration and origin economic conditions if the effects of migration propensities were not taken into account.

In the empirical work, Renshaw followed the export base tradition, and presumed that exogenous shifts in the demand for an area's exports cause corresponding increases in the area's employment of labor since wages

---

more likely to be encouraged when there is a substantial body of general knowledge which is necessary for all jobs, when differences in comparative advantages and tastes are distributed more or less randomly throughout potential entrants, and when comparative advantages are difficult to identify without actual work experience.'' Another force causing turnover is strengthened whenever the value of general skills obtained from different job experiences is high relative to the value of formalized education. There is some substitutability between the two in the process of training and selecting workers.

Clearly, in an economy with differentiated workers and jobs, mobility and turnover perform an important function. Nonetheless, the environment within which turnover decisions are made is characterized by market imperfections that can bias turnover downward and/or upward. Downward bias tends to arise from two sources: (1) the lack of a market for some turnover transactions—a worker cannot buy or sell his property rights in a job—and (2) incomplete information concerning jobs. On the other hand, external costs and benefits associated with turnover can have a bias in either direction.

The costs and benefits of turnover, voluntary and involuntary, fall upon workers and employers. Both parties have an interest in the turnover decision. Hence, there are typically explicit or implicit contractual agreements between the parties defining the manner of initial employment, tenure, and termination.

Renshaw's hypothesis is that the set of employer–employee agreements in a labor market define an institutional structure that affects gross turnover decisions. Moreover, the nature of agreements is such that turnover would be greater in prosperous, growing areas than in depressed, stagnant areas. "Production groups and social groups in growing areas may be of more recent origin and less firmly established than groups in older areas, so the external burdens of movement may be less important and the sanctions against such movement may be less important than in the older areas [Renshaw, 1970, p. 23].

In addition to the forces affecting gross turnover, there are forces arising from changing job structures affecting net turnover. One force is the overall change in jobs. If jobs are growing in an area the ratio of job vacancies to job seekers generally increases at all skill levels. Prospective job changers need not rely upon another worker's quitting to "open up" a job. Job changers are subsequently less hesitant to move, and turnover is encouraged. On the other hand, the decline of jobs in an area decreases the ratio of vacancies to seekers and turnover is discouraged.

Another important force affecting net turnover is the rate of innovation. In areas where innovation is rapid, production activities need to be adaptive, requiring an adaptable, mobile, labor force. Employees would have an interest in developing labor market institutions that imposed few restrictions on turnover. Conversely, when innovation is slow and production techniques are stable, a relatively stable and immobile labor force is advantageous. Employers would seek to establish institutions that would impose the burden of voluntary turnover on the worker.

[30] This notion is strongly supported by Ann Miller's findings (1967). Miller found that outmigration and inmigration are very highly correlated. This held generally and when the populations were stratified by occupation and by age.

are fixed at a level tied to the price of exports and since the long-run labor supply is elastic because of migration. Thus, changes in economic opportunities would be reflected by changes in employment. In the empirical model, outmigration depended on the change in employment and on time-invariant institutional and structural factors that affect migration propensities.[31]

Like Trott (1971a), Renshaw used CWHS data on workers in jobs covered by Social Security and analyzed labor force participants. From the micro observations, the outmigration rate and employment change were constructed for each of the 5 years 1961–1965 for each of 224 metropolitan areas. Like Miller (1973a), Renshaw showed that the omission of migration propensities can affect estimates of the effects of economic conditions. When outmigration rates were regressed for each of the 5 years solely upon employment change, a significant negative relation occurred only in one year, apparently supporting Lowry's finding.[32] However, upon accounting for the structural differences that cause different migration propensities, significant negative relationships between outmigration and employment change were found in each of the 5 years.

The procedure used by Renshaw to account for factors affecting migration propensities is fairly unique. Unlike Miller (1973a), who used the variables inmigration and education, Renshaw relied on the invariance of the factors over time. When one considers 5-year means of outmigration, employment change, and structural factors for each area and takes the deviations from the means in each year, the structural factors cancel since they are time invariant. Thus, the only deviations constructed were those for outmigration and employment change. The regressions of annual deviations from 5-year means of outmigration upon deviations of employment change yielded significant negative relationships for each year.[33]

---

[31] While the discussion here pertains to Renshaw's analysis of outmigration, it should be noted that his study of inmigration supports the pull hypothesis. Inmigration to an area was found to be significantly positively related to the area's employment change. See Renshaw (1970, Tables 2a, 2b, 2c, 4, 5, 7a, 7b).

[32] The results for inmigration rates were highly significant in all years; see Renshaw (1970, Table 2a).

[33] While the results indicate a relationship between outmigration and economic opportunity, there is evidence indicating an asymmetry in the overall responsiveness of migration to economic opportunity. The absolute value of the estimated coefficients in the case of outmigration was only two-thirds the value of the inmigration coefficients. Renshaw further investigated the apparent asymmetry by including as an independent variable the squared deviation of employment change from its mean in both the in- and outmigration equations. The estimated coefficients of this additional variable were found to be significantly positive in both equations. This finding further supported the asymmetry in that inmigration apparently increased at an increasing rate with employment change whereas outmigration decreased at a decreasing rate. After calculating the derivatives of inmigration and outmigration to employ-

The fourth propensity study is that by Morrision and Relles (1975). Noting the results of Lowry, Miller (1973a) and Renshaw, Morrison and Relles (1975, p. 4) concluded that migration was apparently related to origin economic conditions in the short run, once the migration propensity was accounted for (viz., Miller [1973a] and Renshaw), but insensitive to those factors over a longer period (viz., Lowry). In their work, Morrison and Relles considered the rate of outmigration to be related to the employment growth rate, characteristics of the population affecting the migration propensity, and the lagged rate of outmigration.

The mobility characteristics were threefold: the percentage of the labor force aged 18 to 32, the percentage of the labor force in professional occupations, and the percentage of the population who had inmigrated in 1955–1960. High percentages of the young, professionals, and chronic movers would expectedly lead to a high migration propensity and hence a high outmigration rate. Following Renshaw, Morrision and Relles included lagged outmigration—a moving average of outmigration in previous periods—to control for any bias that might otherwise arise from the omission of unmeasurable, structural differences affecting outmigration that are relatively time invariant.

In the empirical analysis, the data were again from the CWHS and therefore only for labor force participants. Morrison and Relles constructed annual outmigration rates and employment growth rates for 85 SMSAs for each of the 5 years, 1961–1965.[34] The regression results were contrary to expectations. The change in employment was not found to be a significant influence on outmigration. Also, the proportions of professionals and those aged 18–34 had no systematic influence on outmigration. Outmigration was, however, strongly related to the lagged rate of outmigration and measures of previous inmigration. Upon reviewing their findings, Morrison and Relles drew conclusions similar to those of Lowry. They maintained that there is an asymmetry in the response of migration to economic opportunities. Migrants are pulled to destinations where employment growth is high but are not pushed from origins where employment growth is low.

---

ment change, Renshaw stated that a metro area must grow at a rate one standard deviation below the metro average before the marginal response of outmigration becomes greater than that of inmigration.

[34] Morrison and Relles (1975) also considered a model of inmigration, which they tested along with their model of outmigration. The rate of inmigration was presumed to be positively related to the change in employment, the lagged rate of outmigration measuring jobs vacated by outmigrants, and the lagged rate of inmigration capturing any trend effect. The empirical work utilized data involving 85 metropolitan labor markets and pertaining to labor force members in employment covered by Social Security. The regression results support economic pull in that significant relations were found to hold in each of the 5 years 1961–1965.

The empirical results for the propensity models of outmigration are not totally consistent. The studies by Miller (1973a) and Renshaw show that by accounting for the effects of migration propensities, there is a systematic relation between outmigration and origin economic conditions. This was also supported by Trott's findings (1971a). The results of Morrison and Relles are the puzzle, especially since the data used by Morrison and Relles were from the same source as that used by both Trott (1971a) and Renshaw. (A high correlation between employment change and lagged outmigration, a distinct possibility, might give rise to the relationships observed by Morrison and Relles.) Nonetheless, the overall empirical evidence does support the relation between outmigration and employment change. The relation between outmigration and employment change is, however, likely to be simultaneous in nature.

Simultaneous-Equations Models

The simultaneous-equations models of inmigration discussed above also considered outmigration as a variable, like inmigration, endogenous to the region's growth. One of the early employment change–migration models is Olvey's study (1970) of the growth process in SMSAs. Like the authors of the propensity studies, Olvey was concerned with demonstrating that origin economic conditions were influences on outmigration. In particular, Olvey (1970, p. 107) considered that Lowry's failure to observe a relation between origin unemployment and migration is because Lowry's measure did not reflect the total pressure to outmigrate. According to Olvey, the proper measure of unemployment is prospective unemployment—that is, the unemployment that would have occurred had there been no outmigration.[35] The wage level and a measure of climate were also included in the outmigration equation. Olvey's empirical results supported the importance of prospective unemployment. The wage was also significant while the mean January temperature was not.

Greenwood's simultaneous-equations models of economic and population growth (1973, 1975b, 1976) extended Olvey's outmigration analysis by including measures affecting the propensity to migrate. Each of these studies by Greenwood held a basic specification of the outmigration equation. Outmigration was related to origin economic conditions (change in income, change in employment, change in unemployment, median income, and the unemployment rate), origin size (civilian labor force), and three measures of the propensity to migrate (median education, median age, and inmigration). As mentioned earlier, the differences in these

---

[35] This measure is constructed in a way similar to Mazek's measure of potential unemployment (1966) and is conceptually similar to Blanco's prospective unemployment (1964).

studies by Greenwood arise from the type of migration considered. In the 1976 study, which analyzed outmigration from SMSAs in 1950–1960 by race, the measure of labor force size was race specific. The outmigration of one group might expectedly increase with an increasing presence of the other group.

The aggregate empirical results for 1950–1960 indicated that the most important economic influences on outmigration were income measures. High income levels and growth rates reduced the outflow of migrants. The only other economic variable of importance was the unemployment rate. Two measures related to the migration propensity—median age and median education—were also significant. Increases in the civilian labor force led to increases in the outflow of migrants as well.

The aggregate results did not characterize those for the race groups. For white outmigrants, the most strongly related factors were age and education. Nonetheless, high white income levels and low rates of unemployment did lead to low outflows of white migrants; the income relation was the stronger of the two. For nonwhites, none of the economic measures was significantly related to outmigration. The most important factor was median age. Apparently, young nonwhites tend to outmigrate and old nonwhites remain behind. While the labor force size for each race was, as expected, a direct influence on each race's outflow, an increasing labor force presence of the other race also increased the outflow. This "taste for discrimination" effect was stronger for whites than for nonwhites.

When the outmigration flows were separated by whether migrants were headed for metro or nonmetro areas, the results again differed from those of the aggregate. For each of the separate outflows in 1950–1960, employment opportunities were the dominant economic variables. The most important influence was the change in unemployment. Outmigration was heavy in areas where unemployment increased. The growth in employment was also a major factor affecting outmigration. The growth in income, on the other hand, was insignificant. Additionally, low levels of income led to large outflows of metro-destined migrants, while high unemployment caused large outflows of nonmetro-destined migrants. Of lesser importance than employment considerations were the propensity measures. For each of the outflows, high levels of education and inmigration led to large outmigrations. In the case of metro-destined migrants, the age variable was significant as well.

The preceding patterns did not characterize the later period. In 1960–1970, the outflows of nonmetro-destined migrants were not affected by economic variables. The only influences were the propensity measures, median age and inmigration. While these variables also influenced the outflows of metro-destined migrants, economic measures were more

TABLE 2.2
Summary of Outmigration Models

Researcher (year)	Year of analysis	Unit of analysis	Method of analysis	Dependent variable
a. Propensity				
Miller (1973a)	1955–1960	48 States	Multiple regression	Outmigration rate
Trott (1971a)	1960–1963 and 1963–1966	173 OBEEAs	Multiple regression	Outmigration rate of White males: For: (a) Large OBEEAs (b) Small OBEEAs For: (a) Aged 25–34 (b) Aged 35–44 (c) Aged 45–54 (d) Aged 55–64 (Labor force participants)
Renshaw (1970)	1960–1961, 1961–1962, 1962–1963, 1963–1964, and 1964–1965	224 metro areas	Multiple regression	Outmigration rate (labor force participants)

TABLE 2.2 (continued)

Independent variables (categories)				
Economic opportunity	Amenities	Fiscal	Spatial structure	Propensity to migrate
Median income Employment growth rate	Mean January temperature		Log of population	Inmigration rate Percentage of population with one or more years of college

Base year conditions:
  Industrial concentration of employment
  Ratio of population to employment
  Ratio of local job opportunities to the average
  Previous growth in employment
  Relative intensity of employment of a cohort
Contemporaneous conditions:
  Dropout rate
  Excess labor demand
Expected conditions (short term):
  Industrial relocation
  Expected wage relative to the actual
Expected conditions (long term):
  Relative expected future wages of a cohort
  Relative expected five-year wages of a cohort				

Employment growth rate Employment growth rate (deviation from average) Employment size Average wage Percentage of "prime" workers	Mean January temperature Percentage of sunshine			Median education

(cont'd.)

TABLE 2.2 (continued)

Researcher (year)	Year of analysis	Unit of analysis	Method of analysis	Dependent variable
Morrison and Relles (1975)	1960–1961, 1961–1962, 1962–1963, 1963–1964, and 1964–1965	63 SMSAs	Multiple regression	Outmigration rate (labor force participants)
b. Simultaneous equations				
Olvey (1970)	1955–1960	56 SMSAs	Three-stage least squares	Outmigration rate
Greenwood (1973)	1950–1960	100 SMSAs	Three-stage least squares double log	Gross outmigration
Greenwood (1975b)	1950–1960 and 1960–1970	63 SMSAs	Two-stage least squares double log	Gross outmigration: (a) To metro areas (b) To nonmetro areas
Greenwood (1976)	1950–1960	100 SMSAs	Two-stage least squares double log	Gross outmigration: (a) Whites (b) Nonwhites

important in this case, the growth in employment being dominant. The income level was significant as well, but it was a relatively minor influence.

All in all, Greenwood's empirical results indicated that origin economic conditions generally do affect outmigration, except for certain outflows such as those of nonwhites and nonmetro-destined migrants. The relative importance of income variables and employment measures differed among the various outflows examined. And while Greenwood conducted no experiments, such as those by Miller and by Renshaw, to discern

TABLE 2.2 (continued)

Independent variables (categories)				
Economic opportunity	Amenities	Fiscal	Spatial structure	Propensity to migrate
Employment growth rate				Previous inmigration rate Previous outmigration rate Percentage of population aged 18 to 34 Percentage of population professionally employed
Prospective unemployment Average wage	Mean January temperature			
Change in income Change in employment Change in unemployment Income Unemployment	Civilian labor force			Median education Median age Inmigration
Change in income Change in employment Change in unemployment Income Unemployment	Civilian labor force		Regional dummies	Median education Median age Inmigration
Change in income Change in employment Change in unemployment Income Unemployment	Civilian labor force a. Own race b. Other race		Regional dummies	Median education Median age

whether the omission of propensity measures affected the importance of economic variables, the importance of the propensity factors was consistently demonstrated.

Overview of Outmigration Models

A summary of the outmigration models discussed in this section is provided in Table 2.2. The table depicts, for each researcher, the year, unit, and method of analysis along with the dependent and independent variables. The outmigration models have shown that migration from a place depends importantly upon the disposition of a population to move, the propensity to migrate. Also, when this is taken into account, economic considerations can be important influences. Each of the models, however, falls short of an adequate characterization of the migration decision. The shortcomings are analogous to those affecting inmigration models. Each model implicitly assumes that potential migrants regardless of origin have equal information of, and access to, all possible destinations in the system. Also, the attributes of destinations are assumed not to vary among origins. The effects of attributes of destinations would then be embodied in the constant term. These assumptions are fairly restrictive, and, as will be seen, certain of the place-to-place models reviewed in the next section demonstrate their unreasonableness.

PLACE-TO-PLACE MODELS

The place-to-place studies of migration, subsequent to Lowry's work, are numerous. While a few are directly concerned with reexamining Lowry's findings, the emphasis of most studies varies. The studies reviewed here provide an overview of the methods and issues that have concerned recent investigators. The place-to-place models considered are broadly grouped according to their fundamental method into allocation models and origin–destination models, and the studies are further categorized by either their emphasis or their view of the migration decision.

Allocation Models

Some place-to-place models analyze only the allocation of migrants among destinations. These allocation models are then concerned only with the determinants of the choice of destination. In this sense, they are similar to inmigration studies. However, the method of allocation models places the destination choice within the context of a place-to-place model that draws upon characteristics of the origin, as well as those of the destination, to explain migration. One central aspect of the allocation studies is the role of distance, and we have grouped the studies according to the approach they take in analyzing distance: the friends-and-relatives approach, the alternative-opportunities approach, and the disaggregate approach.

THE FRIENDS-AND-RELATIVES APPROACH

The basic formulation of the gravity model presumes that the only link between areas is distance. Greenwood (1969) has, however, maintained that the influence of distance on migration is affected by the information transmitted between places by friends and relatives. Greenwood considered friends and relatives to be, for the most part, previous migrants. Accordingly, previous migration is, like distance, a link between places. The omission of previous migration from an empirical model would increase the apparent importance of distance.[36] Further, the omission of previous migration would bias the effect of any variable related to current migration which was also related to previous migration. (The direction of the bias is shown by Greenwood [1969, p. 7] to depend upon the qualitative effect the variable had previously on migration.)

To evaluate the effect of friends and relatives on the effect of distance, Greenwood estimated an allocation model, changing the specification by alternately excluding and including a measure of previous migration. The allocation rate was related to economic opportunities (the destination–origin ratio of median income, the destination unemployment, and the origin unemployment), aspects of spatial structure (the destination–origin ratio of urbanization, distance, and the stock of previous migrants), amenities (the destination–origin ratio of mean temperature), and measures of the migration propensity (median education at both the origin and destination).[37] The urbanization variable was included to capture the effect of any rural–urban migration trend.

In the empirical analysis, the model was estimated using the place-to-place migration streams between the 48 states in 1955–1960. The results for the specification, which included the stock of previous migrants, indicated that the effect of distance was less when the migrant stock variable was included than when it was omitted. Indeed, the distance elasticity when the migrant stock was included was only one-third its value when the stock was omitted. Other significant variables were relative temperature, origin median education, destination median education, relative ur-

[36] The reason for this is straightforward. If previous migration were dominantly inversely related to distance, then destinations close to an origin would have high stocks of previous migrants. The information passed along by these previous migrants would counteract the effect of distance. At the same time, destinations distant from an origin would attract a small number of migrants because of their great distance and because of the small stocks of friends and relatives. The apparent effect of distance on the attractiveness of a destination would be upwardly biased, if the effect of friends and relatives had not been accounted for.

[37] The allocation rate is unique to each origin–destination combination. It is the number who migrated from the origin to a destination relative to the total number who migrated from the origin.

banization, and origin unemployment. The relative income variable and destination unemployment were not significant factors.

Greenwood's findings (1969) indicate that noneconomic variables are important determinants of migration. Locational amenities, the extent of urbanization, and the informational links formed by distance and the presence of friends and relatives are major factors in determining migration flows. Also, the distance variable will tend to reflect the effects of other linkage variables, if their effects are not directly taken into account.

THE ALTERNATIVE-OPPORTUNITIES APPROACH

A second approach to understanding the role of distance stresses the opportunity cost aspect of distance rather than the informational aspect, and two studies considered the opportunity costs of foregone alternatives in clarifying the role of distance.

The first study is an analysis of migration in Venezuela by Levy and Wadycki (1974). Levy and Wadycki found in previous work (Beals, Levy, and Moses, 1967 and Levy and Wadycki, 1972) the effect of distance to be greater than expected. Their earlier work did not, however, consider the opportunity costs of foregone alternatives, and according to Levy and Wadycki (1974) this omission upwardly biases the importance of moving cost variables, namely, distance. By directly measuring opportunity costs, Levy and Wadycki expected to eliminate this bias in assessing the importance of distance.

Like Greenwood (1969), Levy and Wadycki (1974) estimated two specifications of their allocation model. The first specification omitted measures of alternative opportunities, while the second included them. Basically, the allocation model considered the allocation rate to be related to destination economic opportunities and distance. Economic opportunities were measured by the average wage rate, the unemployment rate, and the population reflecting labor market size and diversification. Distance, road mileage between major cities of regions, presumably measured the time and money costs of moving. In the second specification, the independent variables also included alternative opportunities. In order for an alternative opportunity to be of consequence in a migration decision, it must of course be known by the potential migrant. Since information is generally inversely related to distance, Levy and Wadycki (1974) only considered alternatives that were no farther from the origin than the destination. Further, they considered only the "best" of these alternatives as the measure of foregone opportunities—the highest wage rate, the lowest unemployment rate, and the largest population.[38] Thus, these three variables

[38] The authors also tested a model that included "second-best" opportunities. The additional variables did not improve the explanatory power of the model, and each variable was

were alternately omitted and included in the estimation of the allocation model.

The empirical analysis utilized data covering the migration of males aged 15 to 54 between the 20 states of Venezuela. In comparing the results of the second specification with those of the first, the distance elasticity, when alternative opportunities were included, was roughly one-half its estimated value when they were omitted. The influences of destination opportunities were also less, once alternative opportunities were taken into account. In both specifications, all explanatory variables were highly significant and of the expected sign.

Wadycki (1974a), in a follow-up study on migration in the United States, expanded on the importance of alternative opportunities in clarifying the role of distance. To demonstrate this importance in U.S. migration, Wadycki considered four specifications of an allocation model. The first excluded alternative opportunities, while the other three utilized different formulations of alternative opportunities.

The first formulation used the best alternative opportunities in the system—the highest wage, the largest population, and the lowest unemployment (excluding those values at the destination). The second formulation was more like the formulation used by Levy and Wadycki (1974) and entailed constraining the full set of alternatives, since migrants probably do not have information on all alternatives. Only the best alternatives within a circle centered at the origin, the radius of which was the distance of the actual move, were considered. Migrants presumably had knowledge of those alternatives which were at least as close as their destination. The third formulation restricted the set of alternatives even further, in that a directional constraint was imposed as well as a distance constraint. This approach used only the best opportunities within a circle centered at the midpoint of the distance between the origin and destination. Thus, before their move migrants presumably only considered opportunities in a particular direction, which is revealed by the actual move.

The basic specification of the allocation model related the allocation rate to destination economic opportunities—median income, the unemployment rate, and population size—and distance—the time and money costs of moving. In the three alternate specifications that included different formulations of foregone opportunities the highest alternative wage, the lowest alternative unemployment rate, and the largest alternative population were also considered.

In the empirical analysis, Wadycki (1974a) used Greenwood's data on

---

insignificant. Further, the estimated elasticities of the initial variables did not change substantially. Second-best opportunities were subsequently dropped from the analysis.

interestate migration in 1955–1960 (1969). The empirical results provided additional support for the findings of Levy and Wadycki (1974). When alternative opportunities were included in any form, the estimated value of the distance elasticity was considerably below its estimated value in the basic specification.[39] Of the three formulations for alternative opportunities, the specification with the best results in terms of overall fit and significance of individual variables was the distance–direction formulation. In comparing the results of the distance–direction specification with those of the basic specification, two findings are noteworthy. First, the effect of distance, the strongest influence in the basic specification, was only one-half its former effect once alternative opportunities were considered. Second, the influences of destination income and destination population were dominant upon accounting for opportunity costs. Another interesting result was that the alternative unemployment rate was the most important of the opportunity cost measures. Low-unemployment alternatives curtailed migration between two given places.

THE DISAGGREGATE APPROACH

The distance variable reflects other factors in addition to the time and money costs of moving. It apparently also measures information flows and the opportunity costs of foregone opportunities. The two studies considered here, Greenwood and Gormely (1971) and Wadycki (1974b), examine the role of distance using disaggregated migration streams and provide additional support for the multifaceted role of distance. The purpose of the disaggregate studies was generally to assess whether the influence of certain determinants of migration, particularly distance, differed by region and/or race. Both studies used the same data. The first disaggregated migration flows by region and race, and while Wadycki (1974b) considered disaggregate flows by race only, Wadycki analyzed the role of alternative opportunities as well.

The aggregate 1955–1960 interstate migratory flows analyzed in the studies by Greenwood (1969) and Wadycki (1974a) were disaggregated by state by race by Greenwood and Gormely (1971). In their allocation model, Greenwood and Gormely related race-specific gross allocations of migrants (the number of migrations between an origin and a destination)

---

[39] The only anomalous result was the destination unemployment rate. In all four models the variable was of the wrong sign, and it was significant in all but the third modified specification. Deletion of the distance variable in the third modification resulted in a proper and significant coefficient for the destination unemployment rate. The estimated elasticities of most other variables were stable with the deletion, and the effect of the alternative unemployment rate more than doubled.

to race-specific destination measures of economic opportunity—median income, population, and distance—and destination amenities—temperature. At a general level, the empirical results of the 96 regressions (48 states by race) provided consistent support for the importance of distance. The income and temperature variables were, more often than not, significant for whites, while their influences were much less consistent for nonwhites. To assess whether these influences differed by region and by race, Greenwood and Gormely regressed the estimated elasticities on region–race dummy variables. The results indicated that distance and temperature influenced the migration of southern nonwhites less strongly than that of other groups. Greenwood and Gormely speculate that discriminatory wages in the South may account for these findings. Also, southern whites had a stronger tendency to move to temperate climates than nonsouthern whites. Apparently, differences in the ways of life in the North and the South may have been partly responsible for the different migration patterns of southern and nonsouthern whites.

Wadycki (1974b) also found different effects of distance upon examining the white and nonwhite allocations of interstate migrants. Wadycki was, as discussed above, concerned with the role of opportunity costs as well as the effect of distance. Again, Wadycki used specifications that alternatively omitted and included measures of alternative opportunities. The basic specification for each race related the allocation of migrants to destination economic opportunities—population, race-specific median income, and the unemployment rate—and to distance. The second specification also included the best alternative opportunities—the highest income, the lowest unemployment rate, and the largest population. Only opportunities at least as close as the destination were considered as alternatives.

Using Greenwood and Gormely's data, the alternate specifications were estimated, and the results for the basic specification indicated that whites and nonwhites responded differently to economic influences. In particular, distance had a greater deterrent effect on nonwhite than white migration, while whites were more strongly influenced by income than nonwhites. The unemployment variable was significant but of the wrong sign for both groups. When alternative opportunities were considered, the results were generally as expected. For both groups, the effect of distance was only about one-half its former value, and the elasticities of destination economic opportunities were somewhat reduced. Moreoever, the effects of alternative opportunities were significant and, except for nonwhite income, of the expected sign. Overall, the inclusion of alternative opportunities increased the explanatory power of the model for both races. However, the model better explained white than nonwhite migration.

On the whole, the allocation models demonstrate that economic opportunities at destinations are important determinants of migration and that these effects can vary among different groups of migrants. Further, they show the importance of considering linkages between places whether they be distances or previous migrations, since they are proxies for several factors influencing migration. And while the allocation models show the importance of alternative opportunities, their treatment of alternatives has two shortcomings. First, allocation models by construction preclude the origin as an alternative. Like inmigration models, allocation models presume that the decision to move is made without regard to economic opportunities elsewhere. Second, alternative opportunities as formulated by Levy and Wadycki (1974) and Wadycki (1974a,b) do not preserve the integrity of an alternative. While these formulations recognize the importance of the attributes (an improvement over the formulation by Alperovich *et al.*, 1977, which did not consider attributes other than the gravity variables), they only consider attributes singly instead of as a set. In actuality, each alternative has a set of attributes, that is, a wage, an unemployment rate, and a population size. To represent an alternative by the "best" of the attributes is incongruous. It is generally highly unlikely that any one alternative would simultaneously have the best of all attributes. The first of these shortcomings is remedied in the next group of models, since the origin is included as an alternative by the origin–destination models. While the second shortcoming is addressed only to a limited extent by one of the origin–destination studies, we consider it completely in our model developed in Chapter 3.

Origin–Destination Models

Origin–destination models are place-to-place models that allow the origin a role as an alternative, and many of the origin–destination models are spinoffs of Lowry's study. These models generally consider the gravity variables in human capital terms.[40] That is, population size and intervening distance are considered to be measures of job opportunities and migration costs. Other studies are more behavioral and utilize a choice-theoretic approach in analyzing the migration decision.

---

[40] The classic study that characterizes migration as an investment in human capital is by Sjaastad (1962).

THE HUMAN CAPITAL APPROACH

The models considered here are similar in both their method and their emphasis on the role of income. The first two studies examine different measures of earned income while the next two consider welfare payments as well.

Shortly after Lowry's study, Rogers (1967) used the Lowry model to study the intrastate migration streams in California. The special aspects of Rogers' study are changes in the specification of the basic Lowry model and its application to different types of metro versus nonmetro migration and to different groups of migrants. Rogers first replicated Lowry's analysis for intermetro migration between nine SMSAs in California in 1955–1960. The empirical results were generally similar to those of Lowry. Origin economic conditions, the unemployment rate and the average manufacturing wage, were insignificant. The destination wage was significant as were the civilian labor force sizes and the intervening distance. Rogers then reestimated the model using per capita wages and salaries rather than the average manufacturing wage. While the income measures were not significant, Rogers further used this specification because only the per capita measure of wages and salaries was available for nonmetro areas.

In another change in the model's specification, Rogers deleted the unemployment variables since their estimated effects were of the wrong sign. This specification, the "Rogers model," was then estimated using data on the intermetro migration between the nine SMSAs and also on the inter-SEA migration between the 19 SEAs. Once again, wages were insignificant; only the gravity variables of labor force size and distance were important. The Rogers model was then estimated using different migration streams: metro–metro, metro–nonmetro, nonmetro–nonmetro, and nonmetro–metro. The model's explanatory power was greatest for intermetro migration. The destination per capita wage was significant in the case of nonmetro-destined migration. Apparently, migrants move only to nonmetro areas where wages are relatively high. Origin wages were generally insignificant.

Rogers also examined his model for different groups of migrants. Separate regressions were estimated for whites, nonwhites, males, females, and different age groups. In each regression, the destination wage was insignificant. The origin wage was significant and of the correct sign in only two cases—for those 40–44 and 75–79 years of age. The model afforded better explanation of the migration of whites than nonwhites, males than females, and the young and middle-aged than the elderly.

Another analysis of origin–destination migration is Rabianski's study of intermetropolitan migration (1971). The focus of Rabianski's work was the income incentives to migrate. Rabianski considered three factors: the real earnings differential, the unemployment differential, and the proportion of workers in occupations with low skill levels. Other things being equal, an individual would migrate if there were a positive real earnings differential between places arising from differences in either nominal earnings or costs of living. And if there were no difference in real earnings on average, an unemployed worker would migrate in the expectation of having a better chance to earn the real wages offered at the destination, if the destination had a lower unemployment rate than the origin. The rationale of the third variable, the proportion of workers in occupations with low skill levels, is slightly more involved.

Rabianski maintained that origin unemployment reflects the unemployed who have skills but no job opportunities as well as those who have job opportunities but no skills. The latter group is more likely than others to be collecting transfer payments such as unemployment compensation and general relief benefits. Though the first group is likely to move in response to an unemployment differential, the second group will tend not to move since they would lose any welfare and unemployment benefits that are tied to residency. The proportion of workers in low skill levels at the origin reflects the presence of this relatively immobile group. An increased presence of this group would give rise to decreased migration.

In the empirical work, Rabianski related migration streams to three economic measures. Two were the origin–destination ratios of average wages and unemployment rates. The third was the origin proportion of the labor force in the occupations with the lowest skill levels. Also included in the analysis were the gravity variables of distance and employment size at the origin and destination. Using data on 11 SMSAs in 1955–1960, regressions were estimated separately for nominal and real measures of wages. The results for both specifications were as expected; all independent variables were significant and of the expected sign. The use of real wages, nominal wages deflated by a measure of the cost of living, did not substantially improve the explanatory power of the model. It is also interesting to note that, contrary to Lowry's findings, relative economic conditions are of apparent importance.

The role of relative economic conditions was also examined by Gallaway, Gilbert, and Smith (1968). Migration was viewed by Gallaway *et al.* as a response to differentials in wage rates, differentials in per capita welfare benefits, and differentials in unemployment rates. Further, potential migrants would discount these differentials because of monetary costs of moving, opportunity costs of transitory unemployment, and psychic costs of disruption. Since distance is presumably related to each of these factors, Gallaway *et al.* included it as a proxy for the discounting factors.

In the empirical analysis, the migration rate was related to differences in per capita incomes, unemployment rates, and average welfare (general assistance) payments, and to intervening distance. Using data on migration between the 48 states during 1955–1960, an overall regression and 48 state regressions were estimated. The state regressions analyzed the migration from each state to the other states, and thus the origin conditions were not a source of variation for the independent variables.

The empirical results were not entirely satisfactory. In the overall regression, relative incomes, relative unemployment rates, and the distance variable were significant factors. The measure of relative welfare benefits was insignificant. In the regressions for individual states, both relative welfare payments and relative unemployment rates were typically insignificant. The distance and relative income variables, on the other hand, were highly significant and of the anticipated sign. Nonetheless, the low explanatory power of the model in the overall regression led the authors to conclude that noneconomic factors must also be of major importance to migrants.

Like Gallaway *et al.,* Cebula, Kohn, and Vedder (1973) considered differential economic advantages to be the chief cause of migration in their analysis of black migration. Cebula *et al.* related the probability of migrating to the destination–origin ratio of per capita income for blacks, the ratio of per capita welfare (aid to families with dependent children) payments, intervening distance, and the percentage of black population at the destination. Cebula *et al.* included this last measure for two reasons : It would reflect the psychic benefits of the presence of friends and relatives and would measure the cost of labor market information more accurately for blacks than would the unemployment rate, since blacks are relatively restricted in their job searches.

In the empirical analysis, the model was estimated using black interstate migration during 1965–1970 for each of 34 states. Overall, the results indicated that distance and the presence of blacks were consistent significant influences on black migration. The welfare measure was significant in two-thirds of the regressions, while the income variable was significant in only one-half of the estimated equations. Apparently, differentials in welfare payments are a more important influence on black migration than are differentials in income.[41]

[41] The findings of Cebula *et al.* (1973) have been criticized by Zeigler (1976) on two major points. First, the data Cebula *et al.* used for black migration involved aggregating over state economic areas. This underestimates the actual figures for migration. Ziegler showed that

The findings of Rabianski, Gallaway *et al.*, and Cebula *et al.* indicate, contrary to that of Lowry, that relative economic conditions are important determinants of migration. Also in their study of the role of alternative opportunities, Levy and Wadycki considered an origin–destination model which examined origin and destination economic conditions both relatively and separately. Levy and Wadycki found that relative conditions, both origin–destination conditions and origin–alternative opportunity conditions, were highly significant factors. However, when economic conditions were allowed their separate influences, an asymmetric relationship was also found. Indeed, the estimated elasticities for each of the destination variables was at least twice the size of those for the origin variables. Moreover, origin conditions were not significant when alternative opportunities were considered. The record is then apparently mixed with regard to the importance of relative economic conditions. If Rabianski, Gallaway *et al.*, and Cebula *et al.* had assessed origin and destination conditions separately as well as relatively, more evidence could have been brought to bear on whether asymmetry is the rule or the exception.

Greenwood and Sweetland (1972) were also concerned with the role of income, and they maintained that the mixed results for destination income was due to an improper specification of the destination population. According to Greenwood and Sweetland, high levels of income in prior periods have led to large populations through inmigration, and including the destination population as an independent variable downwardly biases the effect of the destination income variable. On the other hand, if the destination population is excluded from the model, the estimated coefficient of the income variable would be upwardly biased. Greenwood and Sweetland chose a compromise and constrained the coefficient of the destination population to a value of unity by normalizing the migration streams with respect to destination populations. This procedure is atypical since the streams are conventionally normalized by origin populations, thereby measuring probabilities of migrating.

The empirical specification related the migration rate to destination and origin median incomes for males, origin population, intervening distance, the destination–origin ratio of per capita local government expenditures, and a South–non-South dummy variable. Presumably, migrants would

---

the results of the empirical analysis are less supportive of the hypotheses when better estimates of the migration data are used. Second, the relationship between welfare and migration is likely to be simultaneous in nature. For a reply to these criticisms, see Cebula *et al.* (1976).

prefer the temperate climates and the low costs of living afforded by destinations in the South.

In the empirical analysis, Greenwood and Sweetland used data on the 1955–1960 migration between 50 SMSAs with populations of 250,000 or more. To show the bias of destination population on destination income, four regression models were estimated using all 50 × 49 observations; each used a different specification of destination population and the dependent variable. In two regressions in which the destination population was omitted the income elasticities were substantially, 600%, higher than those for the two regressions in which migration was normalized by destination population. On the other hand, when destination population was unconstrained and included as an independent variable, the estimated coefficient of destination income was downwardly biased. Indeed, it was significantly negative, the incorrect sign. (This finding was not reported; rather Greenwood and Sweetland alluded to it.)

The results for the other variables generally followed expectations, and the coefficient estimates of all but the measure of government expenditures were relatively stable in the four regressions. High origin incomes and large intervening distances significantly inhibited migration. Destination incomes and high destination–origin ratios of government expenditures, on the other hand, were attractions to migrants. The effects of origin and destination incomes showed an asymmetry, but it was the reverse of that found in other studies. In particular, when migration was normalized by destination population, the absolute value of the elasticity of origin income was found to be half again as large as that for destination income.

To assess whether the estimated relationships differed among SMSAs, regressions for each of the 50 SMSAs were separately estimated. The results indicated that destination income was generally not a significant factor. On the other hand, distance and the regional dummy variable were consistently significant. The results for the government expenditure variable were mixed, it was a significant factor more often than not, however.

All in all, the results of the human capital models of origin–destination migration are mixed. On the one hand, the importance of linkages between areas, distance, and/or the presence of friends and relatives was consistently demonstrated. However, inconsistent findings were also seen, particularly the role of income. In some cases, relative incomes were found to be important. Inconsistent asymmetries in the effects of origin and destination incomes were also observed. And supplemental income such as welfare payments was found to be a factor in the migration of blacks, but it had no observable role at the aggregate level.

BEHAVIORIAL MODELS

The efforts to model the migration decision in a behavioral framework are few in number, and only two are reviewed here. The first study emphasizes uncertainty in the decision environment of the potential migrant. The second is mainly concerned with the role of alternative opportunities.

Arora and Brown (1971) viewed the migration decision as constrained utility maximization within an uncertain decision environment. The arguments of the utility function were considered to be the present discounted values of expected real income in the origin and in a destination. The income variables were assumed to be weighted by origin and destination locational amenities, respectively. The constraint was that the time spent in the origin and in a destination must equal the total time of the planning period. The problem for the potential migrant was to decide how much time to spend at the origin and at a destination.

The present discounted value of the expected real income at the jth destination $\overline{V}_j$ (only destination income was considered to be known with uncertainty) is

$$\overline{V}_j = \int_{P_i}^{P} p(\lambda_t)(\bar{y}_{jt} - C_{2ijt})e^{-\delta_j t}\, dt, \tag{2.5}$$

where $\bar{y}_{jt}$ is the real income in the destination at time t, C_{2ijt} is the fixed cost of moving between the origin i and destination j, δ_j is the discount rate at j, P_i and P are the lengths of time spent in the origin and in the total planning period, and $p(\lambda_t)$ is the probability at time t that the individual will earn the income $\bar{y}_{jt}$. This probability depends upon information λ_t, which was assumed to increase with time spent in the destination.[42]

Arora and Brown derived demand equations for time spent in the origin P_i and time spent in the destination P_j that were used to obtain relationships between the times, P_i and P_j, and the exogenous variables. Three assumptions were used to make the derivation manageable. First, real incomes in the origin and in the destination were assumed to grow at constant rates. Second, linear approximations to $\overline{V}_i$ and $\overline{V}_j$ were used to simplify their expressions. Third, the utility function was specified to be of the CES form.

By aggregating the relationships between the times P_i and P_j and the independent variables over all potential migrants, an aggregate empirical model for origin–destination migration was defined. While based on a

[42] This formulation of the probability is similar to that developed by Todaro (1969).

micro decision analysis, the aggregate model was quite similar to the empirical specification of several studies considered above. In particular, migration streams were related to the destination–origin ratio of expected income, the destination–origin ratio of government expenditures, the destination employment rate, the intervening distance, origin population, and origin and destination specific dummy variables. The measure of government expenditures reflected locational amenities, while the employment rate measured the initial information on destination labor market conditions. The dummy variables would presumably capture any unobserved influences specific to origins and destinations.

In the empirical analysis, the data pertained to 1955–1960 migration between 19 SMSAs of at least 250,000 people. The results generally supported the expected relations. Relative income was found to be the most important influence on migration. Also, the estimated elasticity of migration to origin population was close to 1, which supports the procedure of normalizing migration streams by origin population. Overall, Arora and Brown's study provides further support for the importance of relative economic conditions in the decision to migrate.

The second behavioral model is the work of Grant and Vanderkamp (1976).[43] In their approach to the migration decision, Grant and Vanderkamp assume that the potential migrant has two utility functions, one defined over the attributes of destinations and the other defined over the attributes of the origin. Each function comprised a nonstochastic part reflecting group tastes and a stochastic part reflecting deviations in individual from group tastes. Using an assumption regarding the distribution of the stochastic parts of the utility functions, Grant and Vanderkamp wrote the probability, P_j, that a potential migrant would select the jth destination as

$$P_j = \frac{e^{V(\mathbf{X}_j)}}{\sum_{j=1}^{J} e^{V(\mathbf{X}_i)} + e^{W(\mathbf{X}_i)}} \qquad (2.6)$$

where i and j are the origin and destination, $\mathbf{X}$ is the vector of attributes, $V(\mathbf{X}_j)$ is the nonstochastic part of the utility function for destinations, $W(\mathbf{X}_i)$ is the nonstochastic part of the utility function for the origin, and J is the number of destinations.

In their empirical analysis, Grant and Vanderkamp assessed the odds of moving to j over staying at i. Using the selection probabilities (2.6), the

---

[43] The study by Grant and Vanderkamp was written after I had begun my empirical analysis. Other recent examples of this approach are Fields (1979) and Schultz (1977).

odds of selecting j over i are

$$\frac{P_j}{P_i} = \frac{e^{V(\mathbf{X}_j)}}{e^{W(\mathbf{X}_i)}}$$

which by taking logs of both sides is

$$\log \frac{P_j}{P_i} = V(\mathbf{X}_j) - W(\mathbf{X}_i). \qquad (2.7)$$

Thus, although the alternative opportunities theoretically affect the selection probabilities, as is obvious in Eq. (2.6), they are not considered in the empirical analysis when the log odds formulation Eq. (2.7) is used.

To define an estimating equation, the nonstochastic parts of utility were assumed to be linear in the logarithms of the attributes,

$$\log \frac{P_j}{P_i} = (a_0 - b_0) + a_1 \log x_{j1} + \cdots + a_K \log x_{jK}$$

$$- b_1 \log x_{i1} - \cdots - b_T \log x_{iT},$$

where

$(a_0, \ldots, a_K)$ are the $K + 1$ parameters of the utility function $V(\mathbf{X}_j)$, $j = 1, \ldots, J$,

$(x_{j1}, \ldots, x_{jK})$ are the K arguments of the utility function $V(\mathbf{X}_j)$,

$(b_0, \ldots, b_T)$ are the $T + 1$ parameters of the utility function $W(\mathbf{X}_i)$,

$(x_{i1}, \ldots, x_{iT})$ are the T arguments of the utility function $W(\mathbf{X}_i)$.

The dependent variable was measured by the logarithm of the ratio of the number of migrants from i to j to the number of stayers in i. For destinations, the independent variables included economic opportunities (measures of income and the unemployment rate), locational amenities (population and the proportion of French-speaking population), and intervening distance. Measures of income, the unemployment rate, and the proportion of French-speaking population were the variables used to reflect origin attributes.

The model was estimated using data on interprovincial and interregional migration in Canada for 1968–1969 and for 1969–1970, which had been aggregated from a micro data file. In the interprovincial regression analysis, average and expected measures of income were used.[44] The ex-

---

[44] Grant and Vanderkamp also assessed whether decomposing income by income type, namely, wage income, self-employed income, and other income, improved the explanatory power of the model. The wage income was found to be the most important component of income. The other income types were typically insignificant. The use of income components did not appreciably improve the predictive power of the model.

pected income measure yielded results that consistently were of the correct sign. The overall results indicated that origin and destination incomes were the dominant factors in the migration of 1968–1969 but were less important during 1969–1970. The unemployment variables were insignificant. Intervening distance was a major factor in both periods, and destination population was also significant. Origin and destination French-speaking populations were significant and negative in both periods, suggesting that migrants are less willing to move into and from Quebec. Similar results were observed when data on Canadian regions, subregions of provinces, were used.

Grant and Vanderkamp also stratified the sample into occupation–sex groups. Males were further disaggregated by age, while females were disaggregated by marital status. In the empirical results, distance was the only consistently significant variable. Other significant results varied among the subgroups. For example, destination unemployment was a significant factor in the migration of white-collar males, while destination income was the dominant influence in the movement of blue-collar workers.

The economic model of migration developed in the next chapter is behavioral, and it extends the particular emphases of the last two models. With respect to uncertainty, our analysis treats all characteristics of places as being known with uncertainty instead of only destination income as in the work of Arora and Brown. Also, since our model is disaggregate and analyzes individual movements, it allows alternative opportunities a direct empirical role.

Overview of Place-to-Place Models

An overview of the place-to-place models reviewed in this section is portrayed in Table 2.3. The table depicts, for each researcher, the year, unit, and method of analysis; the dependent variable; and the independent variables. The models have consistently demonstrated the importance of two factors not considered by either the inmigration models or the outmigration models. First, the linkages that exist among areas, namely, distance or friends and relatives, have a substantial, and perhaps the most consistently documented, role in influencing migratory behavior. Second, alternative opportunities need to be considered in empirical analyses of migration. Potential migrants apparently do not view two places in isolation from other possible locations.

TABLE 2.3
Summary of Place-to-Place Models

Researcher (year)	Year of analysis	Unit of analysis	Method of analysis	Dependent variable
a. Allocation				
(1) *Friends and relatives*				
Greenwood (1969)	1955–1960	48 states	Multiple regression double log	Allocation rate
(2) *Alternative opportunities*				
Levy and Wadycki (1974)	1960–1961	20 states of Venezuela	Multiple regression double log	Allocation rate for males aged 15 to 54
Wadycki (1974b)	1955–1960	48 states	Multiple regression double log	Allocation rate
(3) *Disaggregative*				
Greenwood and Gormely (1971)	1955–1960	48 states	Multiple regression double log	Gross allocation for: each of the 48 states for: whites and nonwhites
Wadycki (1974b)	1955–1960	48 states	Multiple regression double log	Allocation rate for: a. Whites b. Nonwhites
b. Origin–destination				
(1) *Human capital*				
Rogers (1967)	1955–1960	19 SEAs (California)	Multiple regression double log	Migration streams for: a. SMSA vs. nonSMSA origins and destinations b. Whites and nonwhites c. Males and females d. Age groups (5-9, 20-24, 40-44, 75-79)

TABLE 2.3 (continued)

Independent variables (categories)				
Economic opportunity	Amenities	Fiscal	Spatial structure	Propensity to migrate

Relative median income
Unemployment (origin and
  destination)
	Relative average
	  temperature
			Relative urbaniza-
			  tion
			Distance
			Previous migrants
				Education (origin and
				  destination)

Average wage
Unemployment rate
Population
Alternative opportunities:
  Highest wage
  Lowest unemployment
    rate
  Largest population
			Distance	

Median income
Unemployment rate
Population
Alternative opportunities:
  Highest median income
  Lowest unemployment
    rate
  Largest population
			Distance	

Median income Population	Average tempera- ture		Distance	

Median income
Unemployment rate
Population
Alternative opportunities:
  Highest median income
  Lowest unemployment
    rate
  Largest population
			Distance	

Unemployment rates
  (origin and destination)
Per capita wages and
  salaries (origin and
  destination)
Labor force size
  (origin and destination)
			Distance	

(cont'd.)

TABLE 2.3 (continued)

Researcher (year)	Year of analysis	Unit of analysis	Method of analysis	Dependent variable
Gallaway, Gilbert, and Smith (1968)	1955–1960	48 states	Multiple regression	Migration rates for: a. All states b. Each state
Rabianski (1971)	1955–1960	11 SMSAs	Multiple regression double log	Migration streams
Greenwood and Sweetland (1972)	1955–1960	50 SMSAs	Multiple regression double log	Migration rates for: a. All SMSAs b. Each SMSA
Cebula, Kohn, and Vedder (1973)	1965–1970	48 states	Multiple regression double log	Black migration rate for each of 34 state
(2) *Behavioral* Arora and Brown (1971)	1955–1960	19 SMSAs	Multiple regression double log	Migration streams
Grant and Vanderkamp (1976)	1968–1969 and 1969–1970	10 Canadian provinces 44 Canadian regions	Multiple regression double log	The "odds" of moving to a destination rather than staying an origin for: occupations (white-collar, blue-collar, other) by males (aged 14-19, 20-24, 25-54, 55-64, 65+) by females (married and other)

MOBILITY MODELS

In addition to interregional migration, migration studies have focused upon geographic mobility—the decision to move or stay. Geographic mobility studies use disaggregate data in examining the role of personal attributes in affecting the decision to move. Five mobility studies, Ka-

ABLE 2.3 (continued)

	Independent variables (categories)			
Economic opportunity	Amenities	Fiscal	Spatial structure	Propensity to migrate
Difference in per capita incomes Difference in unemployment rates Difference in average welfare (general assistance) payments			Distance	
Relative average wages (real vs. nominal) Relative unemployment rates Employment size (origin and destination)			Distance	Fraction of origin labor force in "low" occupations
Median incomes (origin and destination) Population (origin and destination)		Ratio of per capita government expenditures	Distance South–non-South dummy	
Relative black per capita incomes Relative per capita welfare (aid to dependent children) payments	Percentage of blacks		Distance	
Relative real incomes Percent of labor force employed (destination) Origin population		Relative per capita government expenditures	Distance	

Unemployment rates (origin and destination)
Income measures:
  Expected income
  Average income
  Wage income
  Self-employed income
  Other (pension, rental, etc.) income
	Percentage of French-speaking persons
	Destination population
			Distance	

luzny (1975), Graves and Linneman (1979), Polachek and Horvath (1977), Bartel (1979), and Da Vanzo (1977), are reviewed here.[45]

An early mobility study (Kaluzny, 1975) examined the mobility of households using data from the Panel Study of Income Dynamics (PSID)

[45] Of the mobility studies, only Kaluzny's had been completed by the time I began my empirical work.

for the periods 1968–1969 and 1969–1970. Movement, migration from a metro (nonmetro) area to either a nonmetro (metro) area of the same state or an area out of state, was considered to depend on nine household characteristics—family size, home ownership, new family formation, length of residency, family income, previous migration, age of head, sex of head, education of head—and an economic variable, the expected income gain from migrating. The income measure was the differential between a weighted sum of destination incomes and the origin income relative to the origin income. The weights were relative frequencies of migration between the origin and destinations in a previous period. The empirical specification included a squared age term and a family income–age interactive term.

Two sets of regressions were estimated, one for a sample stratification by race and the other for four income groups. For both race groups, the relation between the probability of migration and age was significant and convex. Also, previous migration, new household formation, and family income were significant and positively related to mobility. The age–income term was a negative factor. Home ownership and long stays at the origin decreased the mobility of whites but were not significant factors for nonwhites. On the other hand, higher levels of education increased the probability of migrating for nonwhites, but the effect was insignificant for whites. The expected income gain was positively significant for both groups, though its effect was greater for whites than nonwhites. The effects of the sex of the household head and family size were insignificant for both race groups.

The results for the income stratifications showed considerable differences in the effects of the independent variables among the income groups. For example, the variables age, age squared, education, family size, and length of residency had their expected effects for the two lowest-income groups, but their effects were insignificant for the two highest groups. On the other hand, home ownership had a significant effect only for the two highest-income groups. For the highest-income group, the only significant factors were home ownership, previous migration, and a race variable. The effect of the race variable indicated that nonwhites were less mobile than whites in each income group. Further, the effects of the expected income gain, family income, and age–income variables were greatest for the lowest-income group.

BEHAVIORAL MOBILITY MODELS

The analysis in two of the geographic mobility studies, Graves and Linneman (1979) and Polachek and Horvath (1977), was framed in the decision calculus of utility maximization. Graves and Linneman considered the migration decision to be a derived demand for nontraded or location-specific goods, which include amenities and employment opportunities. Migration was characterized as a response to changes in the demand for, or supply of, nontraded goods and in the cost of migration.

Effects on household mobility in 1970–1971 and 1971–1972 of variables theoretically related to the changes in the demand for nontraded goods, to migration costs, and to market discrimination were examined, using data from the PSID. The variables presumed to affect demand were age of household head and changes in family composition, in family income, in health status, in unemployment, in education of household head, and in the wage. Factors related to the cost of migration were the presence of school-aged children, job tenure, religious ties, prior mobility, annual wage, and marital status. The race and sex of the household head were considered to be discriminatory factors in that the opportunity sets of nonwhites and females would be more restricted than otherwise. Such households would be expected to be less mobile.

The empirical results showed that nonwhite and female-headed households were indeed less mobile. The demand factors that consistently exhibited positive significant effects were changes in family composition, in family income, and in education of the household head. A negative effect was observed for the age variable as expected. Of the cost variables consistently significant, households with no school-aged children and with a history of previous mobility were more mobile than others. On the other hand, those with considerable job tenure, with high income, and with a spouse present were less mobile than others.

Polachek and Horvath (1977) viewed the migration decision as an investment in human capital wherein the human capital depended on locational characteristics that affect employment opportunities, wages, and place-specific information. Changes in locational characteristics would change the potential migrant's budget, hence goods consumption and lifetime utility. Consequently, the potential migrant has a derived demand for locational attributes, and changes in the demand for, and supply of, locational attributes give rise to migration.

Using an optimal control model of life-cycle mobility, Polachek and Horvath also argued that mobility has a periodicity. The periodicity results from variations in the marginal gain from moving, which is tied to one's accumulated knowledge of opportunities relative to the origin. Since this knowledge is zero immediately after a move but increases with one's length of residence, the marginal gain from movement will eventually exceed the marginal cost, which is constant, assuming a constancy of the supply of locational attributes. The periodicity will not necessarily be regular but can vary with changes in the constant marginal cost due, for example, to life-cycle phenomena.

In the empirical analysis, a simultaneous-equations model of mobility and earnings was estimated using household data from the PSID. In the earnings equation, the independent variables included a vector of personal attributes (age, annual wages, job tenure, an occupation dummy for professionals, and a dummy for 1971–1972 mobility) and a vector of interactive terms (the product of the 1971–1972 mobility dummy and the personal attribute vector). The effect of migration on earnings can be inferred from summing the observed coefficient of the mobility dummy and inner product of the interactive mobility attribute vector and the appropriate estimated coefficients. Summarily, the results showed that movers experienced greater increases in earnings than nonmovers.

In the mobility equation, the independent variables included personal attributes and an expected monetary gain from moving. The personal attributes were the age and education of the husband, the presence of nearby relatives, the number of school-aged children, the occupation and education of the wife, a dummy indicating migration in the previous year, and an interactive age–prior-migration term. Two formulations of the expected monetary gain, 5-year expected gains in earnings and in wages, were used. The results indicated that households in which the wife was highly educated and which had relatives nearby were less mobile than others. On the other hand, households that had migrated recently and had large expected wage gains from migration were more mobile than others.

MOBILITY AND EMPLOYMENT STATUS

The chief aim of Bartel's study of geographic mobility (1979) was to sort the effects of variables on mobility from their effects on the potential migrant's employment status. For example, job tenure may decrease mobility simply because it decreases job layoff and those not on layoff are less mobile. Another aim of Bartel's analysis was to sort out the separate effects of two variables, job tenure and length of residency. Each of the mobility studies discussed above analyzed the role of either job tenure or length of residency. And since these measures might be expected to be collinear, it would be important to determine whether job tenure has an effect separate from the effect of length of residency.

To isolate the effects of variables on migration from those on employment status, Bartel first considered the event of migrating, M, to be the union of three intersecting events: quitting and migrating, QM; layoff and migrating, LM; and job transfer and migrating, TM. Then when the estimates of the effects of variables on the events QM and LM were compared with those on the events of quitting and not migrating, QNM, and layoff and not migrating, LNM, the effects of variables on migration could be isolated from those on quitting or layoff.

In the empirical analysis, the effects of individual, family, and job characteristics on the events M, QM, LM, TM, QNM, and LNM were estimated. The estimates were separately computed for three samples from different data, the National Longitudinal Survey (NLS) cohort of young men aged 19–29 at the start in 1971–1973, the NLS mature men aged 45–59 at the start in 1966–1971, and men aged 26–35 at the start from the Coleman–Rossi panel file. The individual characteristics included years of education, potential experience, time remaining until retirement, age, and health status. The family attributes were labor force participation of wife, wife's annual earnings, wife's hourly wage, marital status, the presence of school-aged children, and a pure length-of-residency variable— the difference between length of residency and job tenure. The job attributes were wage, unemployment status, and job tenure.

The empirical results supported the procedure of making the estimates conditional on the potential migrant's job status. In particular, no unconditional effect of the wage on mobility was observed. Yet, the wage had a significant and positive effect on the joint event TM and a negative significant effect on the joint event QM. Further, the latter effect was too similar to the effect of the wage on the joint event QNM to permit the inference that there was any separate effect of the wage on migration in the case of job quitters. The effect of education on mobility, on the other hand, was positive and significant because of its effects on the events QM and TM. Moreover, its effect on QM was greater than its effect on QNM, indicating a separate effect of education on migration. Also, the unconditional effect of the wife's participation was observed to be negative and insignificant. However, since its effect on QNM was positive and significant as expected and its effect on QM is negative but insignificant, its effect on migration conditional upon quitting could be significant and negative.

The findings on length of residency and job tenure indicate that each can have an effect on mobility. Moreover, the effects are not necessarily reinforcing. For example, the isolated effect of job tenure on TM transfer and migrating was positive, while the pure residency effect was negative.

MOBILITY AND THE EMPLOYMENT STATUS OF WIVES

The final mobility study reviewed here is DaVanzo's analysis of the migration of married couples (1977), which emphasized the role of the employment status of wives on mobility. Like Polachek and Horvath (1977), DaVanzo considered the family migration decision as an investment in human capital. The family would then migrate when the expected real present discounted value of family income at some destination exceeded the same at the origin by more than the present discounted value of the cost of moving from the origin to the destination. Family income was interpreted broadly by DaVanzo so as to include wage, nonwage, and nonmoney factors; and costs of moving refer to search, transaction, revisit, and financing costs as well as direct moving costs. Since family income is the relevant decision variable in the migration of married couples, the partners would tend to be less mobile than if they were single. In maximizing family income, it would quite often be the case that one partner's decision would be tied to the other's. The tied partner is the one whose change in earnings from a possible move is the least of the two in absolute value.

In the empirical analysis, DaVanzo, using data from the PSID, separately examined mobility and the destination choice. The basic sample consisted of 1605 white couples with marriages intact in 1971 and 1972 and with a household head who was not a student, retired, or in the military. Since one of the novel features of DaVanzo's work is the use of personally specific measures of the present value of earnings, the principal analysis is at the census division level, the only geographic unit suitable to the estimation of DaVanzo's earnings variable. With the recognition that divisional analysis is highly aggregate, analyses without the earnings variable were undertaken for several more disaggregate geographic units, such as interstate migration, migration to noncontinguous counties, and so forth.

The explanatory variables used in the mobility analysis include several measures of labor force status, both individual (such as whether one is looking for a job and is unemployed) and regional (such as the average unemployment rate in the area). The pecuniary measure of the potential earnings gain from migrating is the maximum of the sum of the husband's and wife's differentials in the real present discounted value of lifetime earnings between the destinations and the origin deflated by the logarithm of the distances between the origin and destinations, a discounting for the costs of migrating. The lifetime-earnings measure depended on the person's age, hours worked, and wage. The wage for the origin was the actual nominal wage adjusted for the cost of living. For each destination, the nominal wage was estimated from a wage equation, specific to each census division, that made the estimate conditional on the potential migrant's age, sex, race, marital status, veteran status, and union status. Thus, the family potential-earnings variable was highly specific to the family's attributes.

Also included were several aspects of the family's income other than wages: nonwage income, total family income, wife's wage rate, husband's wage rate, wife's annual hours worked, and wife's earnings share. Location-specific assets included home ownership, presence of relatives, husband's status with respect to a professional occupation and to educational or health-related industries, and the wife's status with respect to managerial or clerical occupations and to a personal-services industry. Other personal attributes were measures of previous migration, age and education variables for the husband and the wife, and attitudinal variables regarding migration plans.

Since DaVanzo's empirical analysis was so extensive in terms of both variables examined and levels of geographic analysis, the results for each variable are not described in detail. Rather, a summary of the results for each group of variables is provided here.

Labor Force Status. Families whose heads were looking for work were more mobile than those not looking for work. And of those looking for work, the unemployed were more mobile than those with a job. Potential migrants who were looking for work were more likely to move long distances than those not looking. Recent migration experience enhanced the mobility of those potential migrants looking for work. Also the role of the unemployment rate was mixed. For unemployed potential migrants, mobility was higher when origin unemployment rates were higher. On the other hand, for others, local unemployment rates had no effect on mobility.

Lifetime Earnings. The effect of the return to migration associated with a gain in lifetime earnings was varied among the groups of potential migrants. The measure had no effect on the mobility of workers who were employed and not looking for a new job. For unemployed job seekers, the lifetime-earnings return had no systematic effect, perhaps because of the variable's inability to reflect a change in hours worked as well as a change in wages. The unemployed would be more apt to migrate in response to changes in hours than those who were already working full time. The earnings measure implicitly assumed that unemployed migrants would experience the same spell of unemployment at a destination as they had at the origin. For those who were employed but looking for work, the earnings variable was consistently a positive and significant factor.

Income. The effect of nonwage income on mobility was negative and significant for job seekers, both the unemployed and those with a job.[46] In absolute value, the effect was greater for the unemployed. The effect of total family income was less consistent, and indeed for employed job seekers the effect was positive and significant, the reverse of the effect of nonwage income. Both nonwage and total family income were insignificant factors for those not looking for work.

Wage Rates. The husband's wage rate, reflecting the opportunity cost of time spent in migration, tended to have an expected negative and significant, compensated effect on the mobility of families in which the husband was employed but looking for work. For families with unemployed husbands, the effect was positive and significant, perhaps reflecting the higher opportunity cost of not working at the origin incurred by the unem-

---

[46] Examples of nonwage income include rent, interest, dividends, transfer payments, and imputed return on autos.

ployed capable of earning higher wages. For those not looking for work, the variable exerted no influence. The wife's wage rate exerted a negative and significant, compensated effect on mobility. The effect on mobility of an uncompensated increase in the wife's wage tended to be positive if the wife's earnings share was less than the husband's. The effect tends to decrease mobility if the wife's earnings share was relatively large.

Wife's Labor Force Participation. The compensated effect of a working wife on family mobility was, as expected, negative; as the wife worked more hours per year the family's mobility decreased. On the other hand, the greater the wife's contribution to the family's total earnings, the more mobile the family, though this effect diminished as the wife's share increased. The peak effect occurred when the wife's share was between 45 and 50%. The uncompensated effect of the wife's working hours could be positive if the wife were young and the wife's wages elsewhere were higher than those at the origin or if her earnings share were relatively small. The effect would be negative if the earnings share were substantial and opportunities elsewhere were no better than local ones.

Location-Specific Capital. The effect of home ownership was consistently negative and significant, as expected.[47] The presence of nearby friends and relatives had mixed effects that were not consistently significant, though the variable was expected to be an inhibiting factor. Potential migrants, where the husband had a professional occupation and the wife a clerical or managerial one, were more apt to move long distances than were others. On the other hand, those families in which the husband was employed in education or health-related industries and the wife in personal services were less likely to make the same long-distance moves.

Prior Migration. Those potential migrants who had moved before were more mobile than those who had not. Those families who had recently moved into an area were less mobile than those who had been there for 1 or 2 years. Families that resided in areas where they were raised were less mobile than others. Further, a greater number of prior moves tended to give rise to greater mobility. Return migrants were less mobile than others. Previous migrants who were currently employed were less mobile than those who were unemployed or employed but looking for work.

Other Personal Attributes. The role of age, after controlling for other factors, was an inhibiting factor in the mobility for families with husbands 65 or older and for those with wives under age 20. The only observable effects of education were not as expected. Families with husbands who had

---

[47] Location-specific capital refers to those factors more valuable in their present location than elsewhere.

a high school degree were less mobile than others, and those with wives who had not completed high school were more mobile than others. The unusual observed effects for the age and education variables might have been due to the selection of the sample, since only married families were studied and the effects of age and education might reasonably differ for other groups of potential migrants. Also, those families indicating that they had plans to move, both for job-related and other reasons, were more mobile than others.

OVERVIEW OF MOBILITY MODELS

Overall, the geographic mobility studies have two strong points. First, since they focus on the individual decision unit, they have developed, more carefully than most other studies, a decision model for migration. Second, since they use disaggregate data, they have analyzed the role of individual, family, and job attributes on geographic mobility. The chief shortcoming, both theoretical and empirical, of the mobility studies is that either they implicitly structure the migration decision to be a sequential one of moving or not moving, with the subsequent destination choice conditioned on moving, or they simplistically consider the role of destinations. The theoretical decision models of Graves and Linneman (1979) and Polachek and Horvath (1977) do not generalize easily to the problem of destination choice, and the human capital approaches of Kaluzny (1975) and DaVanzo (1977) are fairly rigid in terms of how they treat amenity attributes. In the empirical work, the role of place attributes is limited, although Polachek and Horvath (1977) and DaVanzo (1977) do make significant contributions to examining the role of personal economic opportunities on mobility. On the whole, the mobility authors seem to recognize the shortcoming of not considering destinations explicitly; indeed, DaVanzo does analyze destination choices to a limited extent.[48] Nonetheless, the results of the mobility studies do strongly show the importance of personal attributes in migration and thereby the usefulness of disaggregate analysis.

SUMMARY OF THE REVIEW

This review has examined selected studies on the determinants of migration. The studies were purposefully chosen to indicate the various themes running through the literature of migration and to illustrate the

---

[48] DaVanzo's analysis (1977) is conceptually much like that of the allocation models discussed in the section beginning on page 40. Da Vanzo's destination analysis is distinguished from allocation models by its use of disaggregate data and of a disaggregate estimation

methods used to study the migration decision. Many early economic studies on the determinants of migration have been based on either one or both of the neoclassical arguments: the differential-wage hypothesis and the job-vacancy hypothesis. Migration was viewed as an equilibrating mechanism which would eliminate regional differentials in wages and/or unemployment rates. This view led to a conventional wisdom regarding the migration process—that migrants are pushed from areas with poor economic conditions and pulled to areas where conditions are better. The push and pull aspects of migration were understood to be complementary to one another, highlighting the importance of relative economic conditions. Initial attempts by Lowry to demonstrate this importance were not successful. Origin economic conditions were not found to be significant determinants of migration. Subsequent to Lowry's work, many migration studies have been oriented in either a destination framework (inmigration models) or origin framework (outmigration models), in part because of the apparent dichotomy in the migration decision found by Lowry.

Inmigration models have in some cases relied upon a corollary to Lowry's finding as a justification for their orientation. In particular, since origin economic variables were thought to have no role in the migration decision, it is the destination decision that is influenced by economic variables and should be the focus of economists' attention. These models have explained inmigration by using only destination measures of economic and amenity attributes. On the other hand, outmigration models have sought to investigate further the inference that migration is not influenced by origin economic conditions. Their general method has been to control for the effect of different migration propensities in assessing the responsiveness of outmigration to origin economic conditions. Each type of modeling effort, however, neglects to account for the critical importance of linkages among regions and of alternative opportunities. These modeling shortcomings have been addressed, although incompletely, by certain place-to-place models.

Place-to-place models are generally improved specifications over other migration models but they also have their shortcomings. For example, studies that consider alternative opportunities do not treat them completely. In the studies by Wadycki (1974a, 1974b) and by Levy and Wadycki (1974), the integrity of the attributes of an alternative is not maintained. In these studies the formulation of alternative opportunities only considers attributes singly, that is, the best wage, the best unemployment rate, and so on, instead of as a set. In actuality each alternative has a set

---

method, multinomial logit analysis. This estimation method is used in our empirical analysis; see Chapters 3 and 5.

of attributes. To treat an alternative opportunity as the best of the attributes is generally incongruous. Further, only one group of alternatives, the best opportunity, is considered. In work by Alperovich *et al.* (1977)—although the empirical model is a simultaneous-equations model of regional growth, the migration equation is based upon an analysis of place-to-place movement—all alternatives in the system are integrally considered. But in this work the only attributes of alternative opportunities which are afforded an influence are the gravity variables, distance and population. Most assuredly, other economic and amenity attributes of foregone alternatives influence the decision to migrate to a given destination.

An exception to this is the study of Grant and Vanderkamp (1976). All feasible alternatives and their attributes are considered theoretically. The probability of selecting an alternative is considered as the ratio of the utility associated with living at the origin relative to the sum of the utilities of living at all feasible places in the system. The empirical analysis of Grant and Vanderkamp is, however, at an aggregate level, and alternative opportunities are not allowed a role in the empirical work. The odds of moving to a destination rather than staying at the origin are regressed only upon origin and destination attributes. The model developed in the next chapter treats alternatives in a way similar to Grant and Vanderkamp's theoretical view, but we allow alternatives a role empirically as well since our analysis is disaggregate.

Another theoretical shortcoming of the place-to-place models is the notable absence of discussion pertaining to uncertainty. The work which attempts to treat uncertainty formally is that of Arora and Brown (1971). Even here, however, the discussion is incomplete. It is, for example, implicitly assumed that the expected utility defined over a place's attributes is equal to the utility of the expected value of the attributes. Also, the authors ignore uncertainty regarding attributes other than destination income.

The geographic mobility studies examine the decisions of individual potential migrants, and their modeling of the migration decision is generally more explicit than other analyses. However, since the focus of mobility studies is on the decision to move or stay rather than to move to a specific location or stay, the decision models, particularly those of Graves and Linneman (1979) and Polachek and Horvath (1977), tend not to generalize easily to the polychotomous choice problem of multiple destinations, which characterizes the interregional migration process.

DaVanzo's analysis (1977) is in the polychotomous mode, but its human capital perspective does not explicitly allow for tradeoffs between income and amenity attributes, though amenities could supposedly enter the model through location-specific assets. All the mobility models, except that of Bartel (1979), consider the role of uncertainty in the potential migrant's decision environment. However, uncertainty is typically modeled through an expected income variable or an expected budget constraint. Attributes of places, other than income, are not treated as uncertain outcomes. Our model developed in Chapter 3 frames the migration decision in a polychotomous choice setting in which there are possible tradeoffs between income and amenities. Further, uncertainty, since it is due to incomplete information regarding alternatives, is considered to affect all place attributes, and this leads to an expected utility decision model.

Like mobility studies, our empirical analysis is disaggregate and the effects of personal attributes such as job tenure and length of residency, emphasized by Bartel, on mobility are analyzed in our empirical analysis. (Indeed, in Chapter 6 the collinearity in our data is fully analyzed, and we find that job tenure and length of residency are not collinear, contrary to Bartel's conjecture.) Moreover, our study is the first disaggregate study to analyze the destination choice simultaneously with the decision to move or stay.[49] And, as in the work of Polachek and Horvath (1977) and DaVanzo (1977), personal measures of earnings are used in the empirical analysis.

Though methodological clarity is gained from a critical reading of the studies individually, other insight derives from looking at them collectively. The previous research clearly demonstrates the complexity of the migration decision. Personal economic considerations, locational amenities, and the fiscal conditions of places (alternative locations as well as the origin and destination) all enter into the potential migrant's decision. In addition, one's personal attributes and the degree of information possessed influence mobility and the response to economic and amenity attributes at alternatives. The model developed in the next chapter is considerate of these findings, and at the same time, it attempts to remedy the theoretical shortcomings of previous work.

---

[49] Note that DaVanzo's analysis of destinations (1977) only considered migrants, and thus the decision whether to stay at the origin was not analyzed along with the destination decision.

3

An Economic Theory of Migration

The review of economic studies on the determinants of migration in Chapter 2 revealed four general types of research: inmigration models, outmigration models, place-to-place models, and geographic mobility models. These studies have two major shortcomings. First, while most studies have considered economic conditions in explaining the choice behavior of migrants, few have formalized the behavioral rules of potential migrants. The link between underlying theory and the empirical specification has, therefore, been left unclear. Second, only the mobility studies have been disaggregate. Personal attributes of potential migrants have consequently been afforded little role in the interregional migration decision, which includes the destination choice as well as the choice to move, and personally relevant measures of economic factors have not typically been used.[1]

The model developed in this chapter attempts to remedy these shortcomings. The model of individual migratory choice is based on four principal considerations. First, the potential migrant is viewed as a neoclassical consumer who maximizes utility by choosing a location as well as goods. Second, special attention is paid to segmented labor market

[1] The notable exception to this is DaVanzo's study of destination choices (1977), which used individual-specific measures of income.

theories to aid in identifying personal characteristics important in the decision to migrate. Third, since the migratory choice depends importantly on unobservable tastes, the model allows for these differences among potential migrants. This gives rise to a disaggregate empirical model, the conditional multinomial logit (MNL) model. The MNL model is used to estimate the effects of personal attributes on the decision to move and the valuation of economic and amenity attributes of places. These estimates are used to assess the probability that a potential migrant will choose a particular location conditioned on the individual's observable attributes and the location's observable characteristics. Fourth, the model is framed in the context of uncertainty, which is characteristic of the potential migrant's decision environment. The theoretical model of migration is developed in the first part of this chapter. The empirical model is the subject of the section beginning on page 84.

A THEORETICAL MODEL OF MIGRATION

The migration decision involves choosing one of a set of J mutually exclusive alternatives. The choices open to the potential migrant are the alternative not to move and the alternatives to move to any of the $J - 1$ destinations. Any selected alternative eventually results in a unique consequence. The consequence, though, is multidimensional, having economic and amenity attributes. For the present, the consequence is assumed to be known by the potential migrant. Uncertainty is introduced into the decision environment in the section beginning on page 82.

The Neoclassical Potential Migrant

The neoclassical potential migrant evaluates the economic and amenity attributes of alternatives open to him in light of his endowed preferences and selects the alternative for which utility is maximized.

Economic Attributes of Alternatives. Assume M commodities and T future periods, and let b^j_{mt} be the quantity of commodity m consumed in period t at alternative j. A commodity bundle at j ($b^j_{10}, \ldots, b^j_{M0}, \ldots, b^j_{MT}$) is then the quantities of these commodities that a potential migrant might consume if he were to live at alternative j. The potential migrant is restricted by his budget constraint to a subset of the commodity space. This restricted set of commodity bundles is the economic attributes of an alternative. Letting the price associated with b^j_{mt} be P^j_{mt}, the budget constraint for the potential migrant is

$$\sum_{t=0}^{T} Y_t^j d^{-t} - C_j = \sum_{t=0}^{T} \sum_{m=1}^{M} P_{mt}^j b_{mt}^j d^{-t},$$

where Y_t^j is the income earned in period t at alternative j; C_j is the cost associated with selecting the jth alternative, typically the transport cost of migration; and d is the discount factor.[2] The budget constraint requires that the present discounted value of lifetime income net of migration costs be equal to the present discounted value of lifetime consumption expenditure.

By using composite commodity transformations the dimensionality of the economic attributes can be reduced. Assume that the rate of inflation, the discount factor, and the relative prices of commodities are constant over space. Then a commodity bundle at j $(b_{10}^j, \ldots, b_{MT}^j)$ can be represented by a scalar consumption level b_j, and the group of discounted prices $(P_0^j, P_1^j d^{-1}, \ldots, P_T^j d^{-T})$ by P_j.[3] The budget constraint is now

$$\sum_{t=0}^{T} Y_t^j d^{-t} - C_j = P_j b_j.$$

The constraint can be normalized by dividing both sides by P_j. The resultant left-hand side is the real present discounted value of lifetime income y_j:

$$y_j = \left(\sum_{t=0}^{T} Y_t^j d^{-t} - C_j \right) \Big/ P_j.$$

The budget constraint is then

$$y_j = b_j. \tag{3.1}$$

As (3.1) indicates, the economic attributes at j are equivalently the income-constrained commodity bundle at j and the real present discounted value of lifetime income net of migration costs at j.

[2] The discount factor is assumed to be constant and is equal to 1 plus the discount rate.
[3] If, for every pair of commodities in period t (b_{kt}^j, b_{mt}^j), relative prices are constant over space, then a composite commodity b_t^j, which is a transformation of the commodities $(b_{1t}^j, \ldots, b_{Mt}^j)$ can be defined. A commodity bundle at j can then be written as $(b_0^j, \ldots, b_T^j)$. P_t^j is the corresponding transformation of the prices $(P_{1t}^j, \ldots, P_{Mt}^j)$. The dimensionality can be further reduced if, for every pair of commodities (b_s^j, b_t^j), relative prices are constant over space. This occurs if the discount factor and the rate of inflation are constant over space. The commodity bundle $(b_0^j, \ldots, b_T^j)$ can then be represented by b_j, and the group of discounted prices $(P_0^j, P_1^j d^{-1}, \ldots, P_T^j d^{-T})$ by P_j. For a discussion of transformations yielding composite commodities, see Samuelson (1965, pp. 141–146).

Amenity Attributes of Alternatives. Amenity attributes are distinguished from economic attributes by the lack of a price associated with their consumption. Two groups of such attributes are locational amenities and "psychic" factors. Examples of locational amenities that may be important to a potential migrant are recreational opportunities, climatic conditions, and housing types. An important psychic factor might be the presence of persons with a similar life-style. Such persons could ease the disruptive character of migration. For some potential migrants religious or family considerations may be a factor. For others, racial conditions may be the key to lifestyle. In general, there is a vector of amenity attributes at the *j*th alternative, A_j. It is assumed that the potential migrant perceives amenity attributes as being constant over his planning horizon.

The Preference Function. Once the consequences associated with selecting the alternatives—the economic and amenity attributes—are understood, the potential migrant evaluates each consequence with respect to his preferences. It is assumed that preferences over attributes of alternatives are represented by a utility function that is used by the potential migrant to rank the *J* alternatives in order of preference. Denoting the utility function by *W*, utility at *j* is

$$W_j = W(b_j, A_j).$$

Using the budget constraint (3.1) and substituting, the potential migrant's indirect utility at alternative *j* is

$$W_j = W(y_j, A_j). \tag{3.2}$$

It is assumed that *W* is weakly cardinal, a von Neumann–Morgenstern utility function, admitting only monotonically increasing linear transforms.

By (3.2), utility depends on the real present discounted value of lifetime income net of migration costs and on amenity attributes. The potential migrant's problem is to choose an alternative for which (3.2) is maximized. The *i*th alternative is chosen if

$$W(y_i, A_i) > W(y_j, A_j), \qquad j \neq i, \quad j = 1, \ldots, J.$$

It is assumed for convenience that the probability of a "tie" is zero.

Reasons for Different Migratory Choices

The preceding characterization implies that all potential migrants of the same origin and with the same planning horizon would choose the same alternative as optimal if they had identical income opportunities at alternatives and identical tastes. Of course, these considerations do not hold, and as a rule identical choices are not observed. This section discusses three underlying reasons for different migratory choices: differences in lifetime incomes, differences in observable personal attributes affecting tastes, and differences in unobservable personal and place attributes affecting tastes.[4]

DIFFERENCES IN LIFETIME INCOMES

Earning a wage requires holding a job, and each type of job has skill requirements that the worker must possess to perform the job tasks. Workers or potential migrants vary with respect to their traits, cognitive abilities, formal and informal training, and general skill characteristics. They consequently do not have equal access to all jobs. In order for a worker to be employed, his characteristics must be suited to the job's requirements. Locational alternatives have different job structures in terms of requirements and different labor forces in terms of characteristics. Consequently, the relative wages between job types will vary over alternatives. Wages would be relatively high in jobs where the ratio of suited labor force members to job opportunities is low, and wages would be relatively low in an opposite setting.

Since potential migrants with different characteristics are not equally well suited to all jobs, the different wage structures at alternatives give rise to different migratory choices. Potential migrants expecting to work at different jobs would rank alternatives differently on the basis of their respective wages. The potential migrant's relevant wage at an alternative is that associated with his job type or industry of employment. Such personally relevant income measures are constructed for use in the empirical part of this study. To denote that the real present discounted value of lifetime income at an alternative is specific to a potential migrant, let y_{nj} be the income measure for the nth potential migrant at j.

OBSERVABLE ATTRIBUTES OF POTENTIAL MIGRANTS

Potential migrants differ in their tastes, and this in turn affects their respective rankings of alternatives. Some of these taste differences arise from different unobservable nontransport costs of migration that may be accounted for by observable differences in personal attributes. While certain nontransport costs are pecuniary, others can also be considered as costs, since they are equivalent to reductions in destination incomes.

---

[4] Uncertainty, which is considered in the section beginning on page 82, by itself does not account for dispersed choices. Differences in information or degree of uncertainty can, nonetheless, also give rise to dispersed choices by affecting a potential migrant's perception of alternatives differently.

Nontransport costs of migration impede migration by lowering the trade-off of origin attributes for those at destinations. The nontransport costs stem from job turnover and residential turnover, and the extent of these costs vary with respect to observable attributes of potential migrants.

Nontransport Costs and Job Turnover.[5] Nontransport costs of migration are borne by both employers and employees, and the employees' costs, of interest here, are of a dual nature, solicitation and separation.[6] Upon being fired or quitting, employees bear solicitation costs—the costs of job search and the opportunity cost of foregone income. There is, therefore, an incentive for employees to participate in an internal labor market where dismissal and layoff decisions are made in the context of collectively determined ground rules rather than in an environment where the employer's discretion rules. This incentive is especially strong for workers who are employed in skill-specific jobs; their skills are of little or no value to other enterprises. For such workers solicitation costs would be relatively high; they would be relatively low for workers in jobs with little skill specificity.

Nonpecuniary separation costs arise when an internal labor market institutionalizes practices that confer property rights in jobs but does not provide a market for the transaction of those rights. Seniority privileges are an example of such practices. A migrating employee bears the cost of losing his seniority privileges; whereas, if there were a market for them, he would sell them to the highest bidder, enabling him to buy back those privileges at his next place of employment. Workers facing high separation costs would tend to have a strong taste for the origin.

The solicitation and separation costs surely affect the migratory decision but are not directly observable. Nonetheless, since they are related to a worker's observable characteristics, their effects might be taken into account. One such characteristic is the type of labor market in which a potential migrant is employed. Three types of labor markets—secondary, enterprise, and craft—have been distinguished chiefly on the grounds of

[5] This discussion is drawn from Doeringer and Piore (1971, Chapter 2).

[6] Employers' costs are twofold: replacement and termination. The costs of replacement to the employer include recruitment, screening, and training costs. Each of these costs, and thus the incentive to avoid turnover, increases with the skill specificity of a production process. A specific skill is unique to a particular job type in a particular enterprise. Additionally, there are termination costs, such as employment compensation, which have caused employers to be judicious in their hiring and firing decisions and to discourage voluntary turnover. In response to these costs—most especially, high replacement costs—employers have sought to establish internal labor markets whenever such a market is a more profitable way of employing labor. The internal labor market institutionalizes practices that discourage turnover by imposing separation costs on employees who leave.

the skill specificity required by the production processes.[7] As described above, solicitation and separation costs vary with the institutional practices surrounding job turnover, and these practices are fundamentally related to the degree of skill specificity required for the job. Thus, potential migrants employed in different types of labor markets might have different tastes for the origin alternative because of underlying differences in unobservable separation costs.

In secondary markets, jobs require few skills, the markets are largely competitive, and the separation costs of migration are minimal.[8] In enterprise markets, typical of manufacturing plants, internal labor markets are specific to an individual enterprise. The production processes require job-specific skills, and separation costs are likely to be high. In craft markets, internal labor markets are organized around union jurisdictions rather than an enterprise. Skill requirements are less specific to the firm than those in the enterprise market; they are, on the other hand, more specific to the industry. Consequently, separation costs might fall somewhere between those associated with the secondary and enterprise markets. Thus, the potential migrant's taste for the origin alternative would tend to be low, moderate, or high, if he were employed in a secondary, craft, or enterprise labor market, respectively, because of the varying nontransport costs.

Other observable characteristics of potential migrants that might be tied to nontransport costs are employment tenure, frequency of job turnover, and race. Separation costs will vary directly with employment tenure. Property rights in a job and thus separation costs primarily depend on job tenure in enterprise markets and on craft tenure in craft markets.[9] Within any labor market, potential migrants with the greatest tenure would have the greatest taste for the origin alternative because of high separation costs. Because of previous experience in job search, a potential migrant with high job turnover is likely to be more efficient in his job search than

[7] The terminology *enterprise market* and *craft market* is that of Doeringer and Piore (1971). Doeringer and Piore call the secondary market the *competitive market;* the term is not used here because the labor market for professionals is also competitive to a large extent, yet the nature of the work is quite different. The markets identified as secondary, enterprise, and craft correspond to the markets termed by Clark Kerr as *unstructured, manorial,* and *guild,* and used by Alexander (1974).

[8] In the theory of the dual labor market, there are two distinct markets: the primary market and the secondary market. The primary market is predominated by internal labor markets, which the secondary market notably lacks. "Jobs in the secondary market tend to have low wages and fringe benefits, poor working conditions, high labor turnover, little chance of advancement, and often arbitrary and capricious supervision [Doeringer and Piore, 1971, p. 165]."

[9] Doeringer and Piore (1971, pp. 53–56).

one with low turnover. Efficiency in job search tends to reduce solicitation costs. Also, a history of high turnover indicates a willingness to bear separation costs. Such a potential migrant may place a lower value on the loss of property rights in a job than others, and his separation costs may indeed be relatively low. Thus, nontransport costs are likely to be low when a potential migrant has a history of high job turnover.

The race of a potential migrant may also be a factor resulting in different nontransport costs. Through discriminatory practices, whether overt or covert, economic opportunities and job securities of whites are enhanced by low opportunities and securities for nonwhites.[10] Specific traditional practices include the restriction of nonwhites to nondesirable promotion ladders. Nonwhites have been hired in jobs where there is little specific training. Consequently, little nontransferable human capital accumulates, and the separation costs incurred by migrating are relatively low for nonwhites. Thus, nonwhites may be relatively more mobile than whites.

Nontransport Costs and Residential Turnover. Nonpecuniary costs of migration also stem from residential turnover. Upon migration, a decision maker incurs costs associated with separating oneself from one's position in geographically defined social institutions.[11] Such institutions include one's family, church, and network of friends and relatives. These costs are likely to vary among potential migrants according to certain observable personal attributes such as age and length of residency.

The strength of a potential migrant's ties to social institutions is probably weakest when the potential migrant is a young adult. The young typically make major changes in their social groups and workplaces. Separation costs from prior social institutions are likely to be low for young adults as they "break away" from old ties and embark upon new ones. Young adults are expected to be more mobile than older persons.

Separation costs are also likely to increase as the potential migrant's length of residency increases. The strength of one's ties to his social institutions certainly increases with the length of time one has had to develop those ties. Potential migrants who had not recently migrated would have relatively strong ties to their origins and high separation costs. Accordingly, they would be less mobile than others.

Summary. The effect of nontransport costs of migration is to reduce mobility. Some observable personal attributes have been identified as being related to nontransport costs, and certain of these—employment

[10] Doeringer and Piore (1971, Chapter 7).
[11] These costs have been termed *psychic costs* by Sjaastad (1962).

tenure, job turnover, race, age, and length of residency—are used in our empirical analysis. In general, there are M observable personal attributes for the nth potential migrant $\mathbf{S}_{nj} = (s_{nj1}, \ldots, s_{njM})$ which are related to nontransport costs.[12] Since these attributes affect the potential migrant's ranking of alternatives, they are considered as influences upon tastes and as arguments of the potential migrant's utility function.

UNOBSERVABLE ATTRIBUTES OF POTENTIAL MIGRANTS AND ALTERNATIVES

Personal attributes such as nurture, experiences, and attitudes toward breaking traditions and social ties are unobservable empirically; yet, they certainly affect a potential migrant's ranking of alternatives. They, like observable attributes, are viewed as influences upon tastes and arguments of the potential migrant's utility function. The vector of unobservable personal attributes for the nth potential migrant is represented by $\boldsymbol{\gamma}_{nj}$. Also, there are empirically unobservable attributes of alternatives which can influence the potential migrant's utility. These factors may be specific to the potential migrant. The vector of unobservable attributes of the jth alternative specific to the nth potential migrant is represented by $\boldsymbol{\tau}_{nj}$.

The variation over potential migrants in unobservable attributes $\boldsymbol{\gamma}_j$ and $\boldsymbol{\tau}_j, j = 1, \ldots, J$, causes variation in tastes and thus in choice among potential migrants with identical observable attributes. It is necessary then to account for possible taste variation among potential migrants by considering the unobservable attributes $\boldsymbol{\gamma}_j$ and $\boldsymbol{\tau}_j, j = 1, \ldots, J$.

SUMMARY

The optimal choices of potential migrants of the same origin are not identical for two essential reasons. First, potential migrants differ with regard to the industries or occupations of their employment. They, therefore, do not all have the same income opportunities at alternatives; instead, they respond to their personally relevant incomes. Thus, all potential migrants will not rank alternatives the same, since alternatives have different earnings distributions. Second, potential migrants have different tastes, which also affects their ranking of alternatives. Part of the taste differences are due to unobservable nontransport costs of migration,

---

[12] We previously used M to denote the number of commodities (see the section beginning on page 72, entitled "The Neoclassical Potential Migrant"). Following the discussion of that section, commodities are considered only in the context of lifetime income, y. Henceforth, M is used to denote the dimension of observable personal attributes. Also, notice that $\mathbf{S}_{nj}$ carries the subscript j. Personal attributes are considered to be specific to an alternative as well as to an individual, since they reflect nontransport costs of migration. These costs are specific to the origin alternative, in that they vary between the origin and each destination but do not vary between destinations. The implication of such a specification is explained more fully in the section beginning on page 125, entitled "Empirical Specification."

which are related to observable attributes of potential migrants and can therefore be accounted for by considering the observable attributes of potential migrants. Nonetheless, the optimal choices of potential migrants with identical observable attributes facing the same incomes at alternatives will differ. This is because other factors which influence tastes, unobservable attributes of potential migrants and of alternatives, differ among potential migrants. Thus, the optimal choice of a potential migrant with given observable characteristics is indeterminate from an investigator's perspective. As seen in the following section, only the probability that a potential migrant with given observable attributes will select an alternative with given observable characteristics can be assessed.

Choice Probabilities and the Additive Disturbance Form of Utility

In the preceding section, observable personal attributes and unobservable personal and place attributes were identified as arguments of the potential migrant's utility. Using the attribute vectors, the nth potential migrant's utility at the jth alternative (3.2) is augmented as

$$W_{nj} = W(\mathbf{S}_{nj}, \mathbf{X}_{nj}, \boldsymbol{\gamma}_{nj}, \tau_{nj}), \tag{3.3}$$

where $\mathbf{X}_{nj} = (y_{nj}, \mathbf{A}_{nj})$ is a vector of R observable economic and amenity attributes at j, relevant to the nth potential migrant. Again, the potential migrant's decision problem is to choose the alternative that maximizes (3.3). The ith alternative is chosen if, as before,[13]

$$W_{ni} > W_{nj} \quad \text{for} \quad j \neq i, \quad j = 1, \ldots, J_n. \tag{3.4}$$

Since all the arguments of (3.3) are known to the nth potential migrant, his choice is deterministic.[14] The attributes $\boldsymbol{\gamma}_{nj}$ and $\tau_{nj}, j = 1, \ldots, J_n$ are, however, unknown to the investigator who observes a distribution of choices for potential migrants with identical observable attributes facing the same alternatives. The distribution of choices is due to the distribution of unobserved attributes $\boldsymbol{\gamma}_j$ and τ_j among the group of potential migrants with given observable attributes $\mathbf{S}_{nj}$ and $\mathbf{X}_{nj}, j = 1, \ldots, J_n$. Then each alternative has a relative frequency of occurrence or a choice probability for potential migrants with given observable characteristics. To the investigator, the probability that the nth potential migrant, given attributes $\mathbf{S}_{nj}$ and $\mathbf{X}_{nj}, j = 1, \ldots, J_n$, chooses the ith alternative P_{ni} is the probability

---

[13] The set of alternatives open to the potential migrant is constructed to be specific to the potential migrant (see the section beginning on page 91, entitled "Data Requirements and Sources"). That the J alternatives are specific to the nth potential migrant is denoted by J_n.

[14] This discussion closely follows that of McFadden (1975). In a concurrent study, Moss (1979) developed a migratory choice model along similar lines.

that the nth sample draw yields a potential migrant whose unobserved attributes γ_{nj} and $\tau_{nj}, j = 1, \ldots, J_n$, are such that (3.4) holds. This probability can be stated as

$$P_{ni} = P(W_{ni} > W_{nj}; j \neq i, j = 1, \cdots, J_n). \tag{3.5}$$

Taking the expectation of (3.3) with respect to the joint distribution of γ_j and τ_j over potential migrants with given observed attributes S_{nj} and X_{nj} gives

$$V_{nj} = V(S_{nj}, X_{nj}) = \underset{\{\gamma_j, \tau_j\}}{E} (W_{nj}).$$

V_{nj} is the nth potential migrant's group utility at j. The nth potential migrant's utility (3.3) is then equal to his group utility plus any deviation ξ_{nj} in his utility (3.3) from group utility. Considering ξ_{nj} as idiosyncratic utility, ξ_{nj} is

$$\xi_{nj} = \xi(S_{nj}, X_{nj}, \gamma_{nj}, \tau_{nj}) = W_{nj} - V_{nj}.$$

One can then write (3.3) as

$$W_{nj} = V_{nj} + \xi_{nj}. \tag{3.6}$$

Expression (3.6) is the additive-disturbance-term form of utility. From the investigator's standpoint, the additive term ξ_{nj} varies randomly among potential migrants with identical observable attributes. Using (3.6), the choice probability (3.5) can be rewritten as

$$P_{ni} = P(V_{ni} + \xi_{ni} > V_{nj} + \xi_{nj}; j \neq i, j = 1, \cdots, J_n)$$

or

$$P_{ni} = P(\xi_{nj} - \xi_{ni} < V_{ni} - V_{nj}; j \neq i, j = 1, \cdots, J_n). \tag{3.7}$$

Once again, the probability P_{ni} is the chance that on the nth sample draw the potential migrant with observed attributes S_{nj} and $X_{nj}, j = 1, \ldots, J_n$, views the ith alternative as optimal.

The Form of Group Utility

The selection probabilities defined by (3.7) are the base of the empirical model used to estimate the parameters of the group utility function. Before proceeding to that discussion, we first describe the form of group utility and then consider the uncertainty associated with knowing place attributes.

The nth potential migrant's group utility function at j is assumed to be the sum of a linear function of the observable personal attributes S_{nj} and a quadratic function of the observable place attributes $\mathbf{X}_{nj}$.[15] The value V_{nj} can then be expressed as

$$V_{nj} = V(\mathbf{S}_{nj}, \mathbf{X}_{nj}) = \boldsymbol{\alpha}'\mathbf{S}_{nj} + \boldsymbol{\beta}'\mathbf{X}_{nj} + \boldsymbol{\phi}'\mathbf{X}_{nj}^2, \qquad (3.8)$$

where $\boldsymbol{\alpha}, \boldsymbol{\beta}$, and $\boldsymbol{\phi}$ are parameter vectors. Following convention, presume that $X_{njr}, r = 1, \ldots, R$, are constructed such that increases in their values increase the potential migrant's utility. If the group utility function is strictly concave in the place attributes, the parameters $\boldsymbol{\beta}$ and $\boldsymbol{\phi}$ would be restricted. In particular, positive marginal utility requires

$$\beta_r + 2\phi_r X_{njr} > 0, \qquad r = 1, \ldots, R, \qquad (3.9a)$$

and strict concavity requires

$$\phi_r < 0, \qquad r = 1, \ldots, R. \qquad (3.9b)$$

The Uncertainty of Place Attributes at Alternatives

The actual consequence of selecting an alternative, the economic and amenity attributes, is not always known with certainty by the potential migrant beforehand. The degree of uncertainty associated with an alternative clearly depends on the potential migrant's information about the place. Information about places varies among potential migrants since it is not uniformly disseminated over space. Rather, information flows depend upon the structure of communication hierarchies. These hierarchies are likely to be related to the number of previous migrants from an origin to a place, who relay specific information backward, and to the number of previous migrants from a place to an origin, who relay information forward.

In the face of uncertainty, it is assumed that the nth potential migrant considers the place attributes $\mathbf{X}_{nj}$ as random. Further, he acts as if he knows the joint distribution of the attributes with means[16]

$$\boldsymbol{\mu}_{nj} = E(\mathbf{X}_{nj}), \qquad j = 1, \ldots, J_n, \qquad (3.10.\text{a})$$

and variances

$$\sigma_{nj}^2 = E(\mathbf{X}_{nj}^2) - \boldsymbol{\mu}_{nj}^2, \qquad j = 1, \ldots, J_n. \qquad (3.10.\text{b})$$

---

[15] The dissimilar treatment of personal and place attributes is due to the uncertainty, discussed below, concerning the attributes of alternatives. The quadratic utility function has often been used in decision problems involving uncertainty that characterizes the potential migrant's decision environment regarding place attributes. Strong precedents for such use of quadratic utility are Tobin (1958) and Theil (1965).

[16] The probability distribution can be objectively known or subjectively determined. See Luce and Raiffa (1967, p. 304) and Stigum (1972).

Under uncertainty, the nth potential migrant's optimal choice is that which yields the highest expected utility. Given (3.6), expected utility at j is the sum of expected group utility at j and of expected idiosyncratic utility at j:[17]

$$w_{nj} = E(W_{nj}) = E(V_{nj}) + E(\xi_{nj}) = v_{nj} + \psi_{nj}. \tag{3.11}$$

Using (3.8) and (3.11), expected group utility is expressed as

$$v_{nj} = \alpha' S_{nj} + \beta' \mu_{nj} + \phi' \mu_{nj}^2 + \phi' \sigma_{nj}^2. \tag{3.12}$$

If (3.9) holds, the potential migrant would be risk averse with respect to the place attributes. Expected group utility would depend positively on the expected values and negatively on the variances of the place attributes[18]

$$\partial v_{nj}/\partial \mu_{njr} = \beta_r + 2\phi_r \mu_{njr} > 0, \qquad r = 1, \ldots, R,$$

and

$$\partial v_{nj}/\partial \sigma_{njr}^2 = \phi_r < 0, \qquad r = 1, \ldots, R.$$

Since direct measurement of the variances of the place attributes is not possible, we assume the variance of each place attribute to be proportional to a common variance associated with the jth alternative σ_{nj}^{*2}. That is,

$$\sigma_{njr}^2 = \delta_r \sigma_{nj}^{*2}, \qquad r = 1, \ldots, R, \tag{3.13}$$

where δ_r is a nonnegative constant of proportionality for the rth place attribute. Substituting (3.13) into (3.12) yields

$$v_{nj} = \alpha' S_{nj} + \beta' \mu_{nj} + \phi' \mu_{nj}^2 + \theta \sigma_{nj}^{*2}, \tag{3.14}$$

where $\theta = \Sigma_{r=1}^{R} \delta_r \phi_r$. Thus, if (3.9) holds, increases in the common variance would lead to decreases in expected group utility, since θ would then be a sum of R nonpositive terms. The empirical specification of (3.14) is discussed in Chapter 5.

---

[17] Like ξ_{nj}, expected idiosyncratic utility ψ_{nj} is unobserved and random within a group of potential migrants with given observable attributes. The randomness is due to unobserved personal attributes and to unobserved parameters of the joint distribution of attributes of alternatives.

[18] The use of quadratic utility under uncertainty insightfully implies that of two attribute variables with the same means but different variances, the one with the smaller variance or lower risk is that which yields the higher expected utility. Nonetheless, there are criticisms of other implications of quadratic utility; for example, see Rothschild and Stiglitz (1970, pp. 225–243; 1971, pp. 66–84), and Pratt (1964, pp. 122–136).

AN EMPIRICAL MODEL OF INTERREGIONAL MIGRATION

In the first section of this chapter, the fundamentals of the migration decision were developed, and the potential migrant was seen to select the alternative for which the attributes provided him the greatest expected utility. This section discusses our empirical approach to assessing the importance of personal and place attributes to the utility of potential migrants. The discussion here is uniquely linked to the foregoing, the key being the form of the idiosyncratic component of the potential migrant's utility function.

In order to establish the link between the theoretical model of migration and the empirical model, consider the selection probabilities (3.7). In light of (3.11), the probabilities can be written as

$$P_{ni} = P(\psi_{nj} - \psi_{ni} < v_{ni} - v_{nj}; j \neq i, j = 1, \cdots, J_n)$$

and by rearranging terms inside the parentheses the selection probabilities are

$$P_{ni} = P(\psi_{nj} < v_{ni} - v_{nj} + \psi_{ni}; j \neq i, j = 1, \cdots, J_n). \qquad (3.15)$$

Expression (3.15) indicates that the relationship between the selection probabilities and the expected group utilities is determined by the joint density function of the expected idiosyncratic utilities.

The link is seen more obviously by letting ψ_{ni} equal an arbitrary t and by defining $u_{nj} = v_{ni} - v_{nj} + t$. Now, (3.15) can be written in terms of the following cumulative density defined over $\psi_{nj}, j = 1, \ldots, J_n$:

$$P_{ni} = \int_{-\infty}^{\infty} F_{ni}(u_1, \ldots, u_{i-1}, t, u_{i+1}, \ldots, u_{J_n}) \, dt. \qquad (3.16)$$

F_{ni} is the derivative of the joint cumulative distribution function with respect to its ith argument, and it is the joint probability that $\psi_{nj} < u_{nj}$, $j \neq i, j = 1, \ldots, J_n$, and that $\psi_{ni} = t$. From (3.16) it is obvious that the functional form of the probabilities is determined by a specification of the joint density function of the expected idiosyncratic utilities.

The Joint Density of the Expected Idiosyncratic Utilities

Since there is no prior information on the specification of the joint distribution of the expected idiosyncratic utilities, it is based on the tractability of the resulting expressions for the selection probabilities.[19] Compu-

---

[19] Expressions for the selection probabilities have been derived when the disturbance terms are distributed according to the multivariate normal distribution and according to the

tationally practical expressions for the probabilities result if the expected idiosyncratic utilities are independently identically distributed according to the Weibull distribution.[20]

The cumulative Weibull distribution is

$$P(\psi_{nj} < u_{nj}) = \exp[-e^{-(u_{nj}+v_{nj})}], \qquad (3.17)$$

where v is a parameter, the mode. Since the expected idiosyncratic utilities are identically distributed, v does not affect the choice probabilities. Substituting (3.17) into (3.16) and performing the integration yields the following expression for the selection probabilities:[21]

$$P_{ni} = \frac{e^{v_{ni}}}{\sum_{j=1}^{J_n} e^{v_{nj}}} \quad \text{for} \quad i = 1, \ldots, J_n. \qquad (3.18)$$

The selection probabilities defined by (3.18) are those of the MNL model, which has been used to analyze behavior of decision makers in a variety of polychotomous choice situations.[22]

The Multinomial Logit Model and Migratory Behavior

The probabilities (3.18) have two implications for migration behavior worth singling out. The first is the so-called independence of irrelevant alternatives. The role of opportunity costs is the second.

Independence of Irrelevant Alternatives. Consider the selection probabilities for two alternatives i and j and form their ratio. The ratio, the odds that the nth potential migrant selects i over j, is written as

$$P_{ni}/P_{nj} = e^{v_{ni}}/e^{v_{nj}}$$

or

$$\log(P_{ni} / P_{nj}) = v_{ni} - v_{nj}. \qquad (3.19)$$

Expression (3.19) states that the log odds of selecting one alternative over

---

independent Cauchy distribution. In the case of binary choice, the normal distribution and the Cauchy distribution give rise to the probit and arctan models, respectively. In the poly-chotomous case, the expressions are cumbersome and would be costly to use in statistical procedures. See Domencich and McFadden (1975, pp. 65–69).

[20] The Weibull distribution has the same general bell shape as the normal distribution, though it is slightly skewed to the right. Also, the Weibull distribution is distinctively characterized by the property that in the polychotomous choice setting, the difference of two Weibull-distributed random variables has the binary logistic distribution. Other features of the Weibull distribution are discussed by McFadden (1974, pp. 111, 112).

[21] The integration procedure is outlined by Domencich and McFadden, (1975, pp. 61–65).

[22] See McFadden (1976b).

another depend only on the expected group utilities of the two alternatives. In other words, the log odds are the same regardless of the choice setting—whether it is polychotomous or dichotomous. This is the independence of irrelevant alternatives (IIA) property, which derives from the observation that introducing alternatives to the choice set from outside does not influence the relative probabilities of choosing two alternatives.[23] Since $P_{nj} < 0, j = 1, \ldots, J_n$, and since $\sum_{j=1}^{J_n} P_{nj} = 1$, the IIA property requires that the introduction of a third alternative proportionately diminish each of the other probabilities, so that their ratio is unchanged.

Use of a model with the IIA property has two noteworthy analytical advantages (of course, when the assumption is valid). First, parameter estimates based upon a sample using a subset, determined by systematic or random selection, of all alternatives are asymptotically those from a sample using all alternatives. This can lead to savings in the costs of data collection and of computation. Second, choice probabilities for alternatives not in the alternative set used in estimation can be forecasted using the estimated model and the attributes of the new alternatives. Thus, the model need not be reestimated to predict the choice probabilities of new alternatives.[24]

---

[23] This assumption is the cornerstone of an alternative, but equivalent, derivation of (3.18), which requires the choice probabilities (3.15) to be consistent with certain axioms concerning selection probabilities. The derivation is detailed by McFadden (1974, pp. 109–111). It should also be noted that place-to-place migration models like that of Lowry implicitly make an assumption similar to that of the independence of irrelevant alternatives, when one considers alternative destinations. Consider a simple version of the Lowry-type model,

$$P_{ij} = \frac{M_{ij}}{N_i} = \frac{\prod_{t=1}^T X_{jt}^{\theta_{dt}} \cdot N_j^{\theta_{dN}} \cdot X_{ij}^{\theta_{od}}}{\prod_{t=1}^T X_{it}^{\theta_{ot}}},$$

where P_{ij} is the probability of migrating from i to j and is the ratio of the number of migrations from i to j, M_{ij}, to the origin population at i, N_i; X_{jt}, $t = 1, \ldots, T$ are T attributes of destination j; θ_{dt}, $t = 1, \ldots, T$ are T destination-specific parameters; X_{it}, $t = 1, \ldots, T$ are T attributes of origin i; θ_{ot}, $t = 1, \ldots, T$ are T origin-specific parameters; N_j is the destination population at j; θ_{dN} is the destination-specific parameter associated with destination population; X_{ij} is an origin–destination attribute, distance; and θ_{od} is the parameter associated with X_{ij}. The odds of moving to j from i over moving to destination k from i is then

$$\frac{P_j}{P_k} = \frac{\prod_{t=1}^T X_{jt}^{\theta_{dt}}}{\prod_{t=1}^T X_{kt}^{\theta_{dt}}} \cdot \left(\frac{N_j}{N_k}\right)^{\theta_{dN}} \cdot \left(\frac{X_{ij}}{X_{ik}}\right)^{\theta_{od}}.$$

This expression is similar to (3.19) and states that the odds of choosing j over k depend only on the attributes of j and k, although one such attribute, X_{ij}, is defined relative to a benchmark, the origin i.

[24] These advantages are discussed at length in the context of modal choice in urban transit by Domencich and McFadden (1975, pp. 69–79).

While there are analytical advantages to (3.19), there is also an important limitation. To satisfy the IIA assumption, the potential migrant must view the alternatives as being independent (i.e., as not being perfect substitutes). For example, suppose that a homogeneous group of potential migrants have the choices of staying in their eastern city of origin EAST and of migrating to a western city of destination WEST1, and suppose 75% stay at EAST and 25% migrate to WEST1. Now, suppose another western destination, WEST2, becomes a possible choice and that WEST2 has economic and amenity attributes identical to those of WEST1. Of the westward migrants, one-half will go to WEST1 and the other half to WEST2. With the IIA assumption the odds of choosing WEST1 over EAST are 1:3 regardless of whether WEST2 was in the choice set. Since the odds of selecting WEST1 over WEST2 are 1:1, the predictions of a model using the IIA assumption would allocate 60% of the potential migrants to EAST and 20% to each WEST1 and WEST2. These predictions are clearly incorrect; 75% of the potential migrants will select EAST, and WEST1 and WEST2 will each attract 12.5%.

In the preceding illustration potential migrants viewed WEST1 and WEST2 as substitutes and not as independent alternatives. Indeed, the attributes of the two destinations were identical, and the alternatives were perfect substitutes. In extreme cases such as this, when the IIA assumption totally breaks down, it is seen that predictions of such a model are biased due to inconsistent parameter estimates.[25] The extent of these problems, of course, depends upon the extent of the violation of the IIA assumption. The practicality and robustness of the MNL model in the face of violations of the IIA assumption have been advanced elsewhere with the caveats that care be used in specifying the attributes of alternatives as completely as is reasonable and that groups of potential migrants with heterogeneous behavior be segmented.

[25] Potential breakdowns in the IIA assumption can be seen by considering six conditions required for the stochastic terms to be identical, independent Weibull variables.

1. There must be no variation in taste parameters for observed attributes α, β, ϕ, θ among potential migrants.
2. Unobserved attributes of an alternative τ must be independent over alternatives.
3. The structural specification of group utility v must be valid, and the arguments of group utility, the observed attributes, must be measured without error.
4. Attributes of alternatives and the choice set must be exogenous to the choice process.
5. Composite alternatives must be properly aggregated over the true behavioral alternatives.
6. Even if the stochastic terms are independent and identical, their distribution must be of the Weibull form.

For a detailed discussion of these conditions and of tests to detect their violation, see McFadden, Tye, and Train (1976).

The Role of Opportunity Costs. A second aspect of (3.18) is that the probability of selecting an alternative depends on the conditions that prevail at all alternatives. Thus, the oftentimes neglected opportunity costs associated with foregone destinations are afforded an important role in the model (3.18) in that they enter in the denominator.[26] In other words, the probability of selecting the *i*th alternative depends directly upon the so-called strict utility at alternative *i* and inversely upon the strict utilities at other alternatives.[27]

Experimental Perspective

In Chapter 5 the model given by (3.14) and (3.18) is empirically specified and the estimation results are presented. This section describes our experimental view of the migration process and estimation method.

The sample choices of potential migrants are viewed in this study as the result of a multinomial experiment. Observing the sample choices of N potential migrants, N trials of the multinomial experiment, yields information on S_n, J_n, and i, $n = 1, \ldots, N$, where S_n is the attribute vector describing the *n*th potential migrant, J_n is the set of alternatives open to the *n*th potential migrant, and i is the chosen alternative on the *n*th trial. Although the multinomial probabilities that generate the observed choices are unknown, their form is given by (3.18). The empirical problem is, of course, to obtain maximum-likelihood estimates of the parameters α, β, ϕ, and θ using the sample information.[28]

Given the observed sample choices and the observed attributes, the likelihood function of the multinomial experiment is

$$L(\alpha,\beta,\phi,\theta) = \prod_{n=1}^{N} P_{ni} = \prod_{n=1}^{N} \frac{e^{\alpha'S_{ni}+\beta'\mu_{ni}+\phi'\mu_{ni}^2+\theta\sigma_{ni}^{*2}}}{\sum_{j=1}^{J_n} e^{\alpha'S_{nj}+\beta'\mu_{nj}+\phi'\mu_{nj}^2+\theta\sigma_{nj}^{*2}}} \tag{3.20}$$

Since an analytical solution to maximizing the likelihood function is not

---

[26] Notice that the Lowry-type model is inconsistent with regard to the role of opportunity costs. By default the probability of selecting the origin, alternative 1 (recalling footnote 23) is

$$P_{11} = \frac{M_{11}}{N_1} = 1 - \sum_{j=2}^{J} \frac{M_{1j}}{N_1} = 1 - \sum_{j=2}^{J_n} \frac{\prod_{t=1}^{T} X_{jt}^{\theta_{at}} \cdot N_j^{\theta_{aN}} \cdot X_{1j}^{\theta_{pd}}}{\prod_{t=1}^{T} X_{1t}^{\theta_{of}}}.$$

Clearly the probability of selecting the origin alternative depends on attributes of all alternatives. However, it is not symmetric for the probabilities of selecting destination alternatives.

[27] The function e^{v_i} has come to be known as the *strict utility* at alternative *i* in the literature. See Domencich and McFadden (1975, p. 69).

[28] The properties of maximum-likelihood estimators are highly desirable, especially in large samples, and are fully developed in Kendall and Stuart (1961, Chapter 18).

easily obtained, an iterative numerical method is used to determine the maximum-likelihood estimates. Under most experimental conditions, the function (3.20) is strictly concave in parameters, and standard numerical techniques that converge can be used to find the maximum-likelihood estimators.[29] The particular algorithm used in this study is the Newton–Raphson method, the principle of which is to choose successive estimates of the parameters so that the quadratic approximation to the likelihood function evaluated at those values is maximized.

SUMMARY

In this chapter an economic theory of migration that meets most of the shortcomings of previous work and an empirical model estimable at a disaggregate level were developed. The theory of the opening section of this chapter is based upon an analysis of a consumer maximizing his lifetime expected utility over space. Factors identified to be of theoretical importance in the potential migrant's decision are personal attributes, such as job tenure, that relate to unmeasurable nontransport costs of migration, the expected values of economic and amenity attributes, and the variance or degree of information one has concerning the place attributes.

Since the migration decision is dependent on both observable and unobservable (from the econometrician's perspective) attributes of places and individuals, choices will vary even among a group of potential migrants with identical observable attributes facing the same alternatives. This choice variability is accounted for by consideration of a stochastic utility function, where the random term, which is known and nonrandom to the potential migrant but is unknown and random to the investigator, is due to unobservable personal and place attributes that influence utility at an alternative. The result is that there is a probability, conditioned on observable personal and place attributes, associated with a potential migrant's selecting an alternative as optimal.

In the section beginning on page 84 an empirical model is developed, based upon the assumption of a particular distribution function for the random components of utility. The result is that the selection probabilities

[29] Problems with regard to the negative definiteness of the Hessian of the log likelihood function may arise when the number of individuals in the sample is less than the number of parameters to be estimated or when the data either do not vary over alternatives or are collinear. A detailed discussion of the existence and uniqueness of the maximum-likelihood estimators is provided by McFadden (1974, pp. 116, 117).

are analytically useful, being those of the MNL model. The migration decision is then experimentally viewed as a multinomial experiment wherein the sample migratory choices are generated by the selection probabilities. These probabilities are of the logit form by prior considerations and therefore depend upon the observed, independent arguments and the unknown parameters of a potential migrant's expected utility. Estimates of these parameters are then seen to be obtained by maximum-likelihood estimation.

4

Data Requirements and Migration Propensities

The migratory choice model developed in Chapter 3 has special data requirements. The likelihood function (3.20) requires information for each trial of the multinomial experiment, that is, for each potential migrant. This chapter first describes the data sources used in the empirical analysis in terms of how they fulfill the data requirements. The basic sample of potential migrants and their salient characteristics are then detailed. The third section discusses the manner in which mobility varies with different demographic, socioeconomic, and geographic characteristics of potential migrants.

DATA REQUIREMENTS AND SOURCES

The data requirements of the model are fivefold. First, the data on potential migrants must be at the micro level so that individual migratory choices can be observed. Second, the micro data must provide information on the socioeconomic characteristics of potential migrants. Otherwise, the influence of these characteristics could not be distinguished from that of place attributes. Third, the set of alternative locations open to each potential migrant must be specified. A consideration here is that the

91

geographic unit be such that different units approximate the true behavioral alternatives available to the potential migrant. Fourth, information is needed on the economic and amenity attributes of alternatives. Fifth, data on the informational flows between alternatives are necessary to measure the uncertainty associated with the potential migrant's knowledge of the attributes of alternatives.

THE MIGRATION MEASURE AND ATTRIBUTES OF INDIVIDUALS

The primary source of data on potential migrants is a file derived from the Social Security Administration's Continuous Work History Sample (CWHS). The file is the Longitudinal Employee–Employer Data (LEED) File, which is a work history profile of 1% of the individuals who worked at least once since 1957 in a job covered by Social Security. From a LEED file covering the years 1957 to 1969, a 1-in-10,000 sample was extracted for use in this study. The sample is then .0001% of those employed in jobs covered by Social Security and numbers 12,653 persons.

LEED is organized around individual workers, and for each worker the personal characteristics age, sex, and race are reported. And for each of the 13 years 1957–1969, characteristics of each worker's employers are reported. Each employer's characteristics include geographic location, SIC industry classification, firm identification, and wages paid to the individual. Thus, by providing personal attributes and geographic location over time LEED fills the first two data requirements listed above.

Migratory choices are taken to be changes in the location of employment. In particular, any first change in the location of employment in 1969, or any change in the location of the last employer in 1968 and the first employer in 1969, is considered a migration. The 1969 timeframe was selected for two reasons: to allow for the interfacing of LEED with other data sets, and to maximize the informational value of certain socioeconomic characteristics dependent on the length of work history at the time of decision.

Our migration measure differs from conventional measures on four counts. First, it reflects only decisions of those labor force participants in employment covered by Social Security, which well suits it to a study of labor force migration.[1] Indeed, as of 1968, 82% of the nation's employed

---

[1] In comparisons of the coverage of the CWHS data and census data on the entire population, the coverage rates of the Social Security data followed labor force participation rates and unemployment rates. The coverage of females was less than that of males, while there was little difference in the coverages of blacks and whites. While the sex differential in coverage is due to the different participation rates of males and females, the small race differential involves offsetting factors. It has been suggested that the small race differential is due to the relatively high labor force participation rate of black females and a relatively high unem-

civilians were covered by LEED.[2] There are, nonetheless, certain coverage problems. In particular, the self-employed and wage and salary employees not covered by Social Security (primarily government and railroad employees) are not represented in LEED. By industry, the impact of these reporting deficiencies is most dramatic in agriculture where Social Security coverage is only 11% that of the census. Other undercovered industries in which Social Security coverage is roughly 75% that of the census are construction, transportation, services, and government.

Coverage is not uniform with respect to annual wages as well. At annual wage levels less than $7000, Social Security coverage exceeds census coverage. However, as annual wages increase beyond $7000, Social Security coverage relative to census coverage falls below 100%. Coverage is lowest, 60% for workers earning $25,000 or more. Thus, the CWHS data report more workers earning small incomes and fewer workers earning large incomes than do the census data. This is probably because the Social Security Administration must estimate annual wages once a worker has earned a certain amount.[3]

A second feature of our migration measure is that it registers "job" migration instead of "residence" migration. While there are some job migrations that do not entail a change in residency, job migration is a useful surrogate for residence migration.[4] The findings of any study employing a job migration measure must, nonetheless, be considered in light of the measure's tendency to overstate residence migration.

A third difference is the length of the migration period. The measure used here is an annual measure, that is, migration in 1969. Standard measures of migration are derived from the census question, "Where did you live 5 years ago?" This question does not allow the registration of multiple movements or return movements, and it underestimates the true movement. The measure used in this study is less apt to miss such movement and is, in this regard, an improvement over quinquennial measures.

---

ployment rate of black males. The first factor increases the coverage of blacks relative to whites, while the second decreases it. The CWHS also unevenly covers different age groups of the population. The young, less than 20 years of age, and the old, 60 or older, are undercovered. This, again, reflects the low labor force participation rates of these groups. For details, see Nelson (1975, Table 2).

[2] See Social Security Administration (1971, Table 1.).

[3] For example, in 1968 firms did not need to report to Social Security any wages earned by an employee in excess of $7800. In cases where the taxable limit is reached in a year, the Social Security Administration estimates the value for annual wages. Apparently, the estimates are low. See Social Security Administration (1971, pp. 5, 6).

[4] A discussion of the comparability of the two measures is provided by U.S. Department of Commerce (1970, Table A).

The fourth distinctive feature of our migration measure is its geographic level. Since the location of employment is coded in LEED at the county level, the migration measure is of county-level movements. This level of disaggregation for directional or stream movements is only available through panel data such as LEED.[5] An advantage of using the county in our analysis is that the true behavioral alternatives facing the decision maker are closely approximated.

ATTRIBUTES OF ALTERNATIVES

Data on the economic and amenity attributes of alternatives are mainly from the County and City Data Book, 1972 (CCDB) and the County Business Patterns, 1972 (CBP). CCDB provides information on many relevant attributes for each of the over 3000 U.S. counties for 1969 or 1970, and CBP details wage information by county by indutry. Since the potential migrant's industry of employment is available from LEED, CBP is used to construct individual-specific measures of income for each of the alternatives.

THE ALTERNATIVE SET

Part of the information required to estimate the model (3.20) is knowledge of the nth potential migrant's alternative set. LEED, unfortunately, does not provide any direct information on which counties are considered by the potential migrant as feasible alternatives, other than the origin and destination. In the absence of information on alternative sets, a default strategy, in which each potential migrant's alternative set comprises all the U.S. counties, is inefficient.[6] For each potential migrant, many counties would be zero-probability alternatives, and their inclusion would presumably provide little information relative to the added costs of computation. Two procedures have, nonetheless, been used for determining alternative sets so that zero-probability alternatives are not included: the distance–radius and sample–choice approaches. Our approach combines aspects of both of these procedures and shares with them the feature that each potential migrant's alternative set is constructed so that it is unique to the potential migrant's origin.

Distance–Radius Approach. The first procedure, the distance–radius approach, restricts the alternative set geographically. By selecting a reasonable distance or radius, a circle centered at the origin would be con-

---

[5] Net migration figures are, of course, available at the county level but net migration provides no information on where migrants originate or are destined. The most disaggregate census data on migration streams are for state economic areas or for SMSAs.

[6] Consistent estimates of the parameters of (3.20) can be obtained by using a subset, random or otherwise, of alternatives from the full choice set. See McFadden (1977).

structed. All counties within the circle's circumference would be considered as feasible. The implicit assumptions here are twofold. First, potential migrants have information on alternatives in close proximity to the origin. Alternatives beyond a certain distance are not feasible since there is no knowledge of them (prohibitive migration costs are not as relevant here since the concern is internal migration in the United States). Second, information depends only on distance, not direction. That is, information is uniform over space within the circumference. While neither assumption holds strictly, alternatives "close by" are probably more relevant than those "far away."[7]

Sample-Choice Approach. The second procedure, the sample-choice approach, uses the sample choices to reveal nonzero-probability alternatives. By identifying the sample choices of all potential migrants of the same origin, a set of alternatives to the origin is constructed. Thus, if a potential migrant at an origin selected a particular alternative, the alternative was a nonzero-probability alternative to all potential migrants of the same origin. The alternatives selected by migrants from the same origin are then considered as the feasible set, the nonzero-probability alternatives. A shortcoming of the sample-choice approach is that the alternative set is likely not to include some nonzero-probability alternatives, since the set is determined by the choices of a limited sample of a population. Nonetheless, the most important alternatives are likely to be in the set.

A Combined Approach. Our approach to the problem of determining alternative sets combines the above two procedures, preserving their useful aspects but remedying their shortcomings. Essentially, each origin's alternative set is constructed so as to include not only all the sample choices of migrants from the same origin, but also any high, nonzero-probability alternatives not selected by the migrants in the sample. Our procedure is a two-step process: the identification of the "primary" alternatives of each set, and the inclusion of any "nonprimary" choices.

Primary alternatives are identified by examining the aggregate migratory behavior of potential migrants during 1965 to 1970. This reveals the relative frequency that potential migrants of a particular origin select alternatives. The primary alternatives are those destinations with high relative frequencies. This procedure captures the effect of the information one has of alternatives in a more refined way than the distance-radius approach. In Chapter 2 it was seen that the relative frequency of migration is strongly related to distance. Yet, like information, it is not uniform with

---

[7] This is consistent with the notion of an expanding web of perception, which maintains that information over space is most detailed in the immediate region of the origin and is less complete and more aggregate at greater distances from the origin. See Adler (1975, p. 98).

respect to direction. Again like information, the relative frequency is not uniform up to some distance and nonexistent beyond. Rather, relative frequencies of migration occur over distance and direction along the pattern through which information channels itself. This pattern is, of course, along the pattern through which people interchange, which is reflected by the relative frequencies of migration. So then, the relative-frequency approach identifies more accurately the alternatives for which potential migrants have information than does the distance-radius approach. Further, the relative-frequency approach indicates the degree of information rather than merely whether or not information about alternatives exists, as is characteristic of the distance-radius approach.

The primary alternatives are then those alternatives revealed as most relevant by the aggregate migratory choice behavior of the population. Since they are not directly available, the relative frequencies of movement between counties are obtained from census data covering migratory interchanges between state economic areas (SEAs). Because counties are unique to an SEA, the matrix of SEA interchanges can be expanded into a matrix of migratory interchanges between counties. The necessary assumption of this procedure is that the migratory behavior of each county in an SEA is approximately that of the SEA in the aggregate. Since the average number of counties in an SEA is less than six and since SEAs are constructed by grouping characteristically homogeneous counties, this assumption is not likely to result in the inclusion of many zero-probability alternatives in the alternative set. On the other hand, its use effectively provides a basis for eliminating most zero-probability alternatives and hence for identifying the primary alternatives.

In the interest of minimizing computational cost and maximizing the informational value of the included alternatives, the primary alternatives to an origin are taken to be those for which the relative frequency of movement between the origin and the alternative counties is greater than some critical level. For each of the 3141 possible origins, a set of primary alternatives was constructed using a critical level of .001 for the relative frequency. The average number of primary alternatives per set is 36.

Once the set of primary alternatives is in hand, it needs to be augmented by any nonprimary alternatives. Since the choices observed in the sample are influenced by chance, it is quite likely that some sample potential migrants would select alternatives that are not primary. The chosen alternative could be one for which the relative frequency of movement was below the critical level and hence not a member of the feasible set as yet defined. To accommodate any such choices, the sample-choice approach discussed above is used to augment the set of primary alternatives. The choices of all potential migrants of the same origin are identified. Each choice is then checked against the appropriate set of primary alternatives. If any choice is not a member of the primary set, then the set is augmented to include the choice. Following this procedure for each choice for each origin, the feasible set unique to each origin was constructed. The primary sets in this study were augmented by a total of 648 nonprimary alternatives, and the resulting sets of alternatives average 37 counties.

INFORMATIONAL LINKAGES

The migration streams between SEAs also provide a basis for constructing a measure of information or uncertainty that potential migrants have of alternatives. While the specification of this variable is not discussed until Chapter 5, note again that use of SEA data as a base for county-level informational linkages assumes that county patterns closely resemble SEA patterns. The practical value of this assumption greatly outweighs the restrictions it imposes on the data.

THE LEED SAMPLE

In this section, we first discuss how a sample of potental migrants was selected from LEED for the purpose of analysis. Then the characteristics of this sample are considered.

Selection Criteria

Our LEED file covers over 12,000 potential migrants. However, for one reason or another, only about half these observations were suitable for use in the empirical work. In total, 6327 observations were deleted; the remaining 6326 LEED observations constitute the sample for this study. The criteria for deleting an observation and the number of observations deleted by each criterion are detailed in Table 4.1. The most frequent reason was the inability to observe migratory choice behavior in 1969, because this required both a 1968 and a 1969 employer record for an individual. Over 4000 observations failed to meet this criterion and were consequently deleted. The next most frequent reason for deleting an observation was military enlistment. Since choice on the part of the military is institutionally constrained, only civilian potential migrants are considered in this study, so that the observed migratory behavior will presumably be more responsive to economic motives.

Other reasons for deleting observations arose from three consider-

TABLE 4.1
Deletions from LEED File and Reasons for Deletion[a]

	Number	Percentage
LEED file		
Selected observations	6,326	50.00
Deleted observations	6,327	50.00
Total	12,653	100.00
Reason for deletion		
Unknown race	198	
Not white, not black race	181	
Unknown sex	0	
Unknown age	0	
No 1968 employer record	1,041	
No 1969 employer record	3,986	
Unknown employment	108	
Military employment	898	
Statewide employment	585	
Unknown location of employment	4	
Location of employment in Alaska	22	
Location of employment in		
American Samoa, Hawaii, Puerto Rico, Virgin Islands, or Guam	191	
Location of employment in ships at sea or international operations	43	
Total	7,257	

[a] Notice that the reasons for deletion are not mutually exclusive. For example, if an individual died prior to 1968, there would be no 1968 employer record and there would be no 1969 employer record. Thus, the total reasons for deletion exceed the total deleted observations.

ations. The first was unidentified characteristics of the individual—unknown race, sex, age, or employment. The second was an inability to identify characteristics of the chosen alternative—a statewide or unknown location of employment. Third, any individual whose place of employment was beyond the contiguous United States was deleted.

Since some demographic groups are more affected by deleting observations than others, the demographics of the sample are different from that of LEED. A comparison of the demographics of LEED and the sample is provided in Table 4.2. In terms of race and sex, the sample has somewhat greater fractions of whites and males than LEED. The most notable difference pertains to age, particularly the aged. Since the chief reason for deleting observations was the absence of 1968–1969 employer records, any worker leaving the labor force, either through retirement or death prior to 1969, would not be in the sample. Since the incidence of leaving the labor force increases with age after one's middle years, the age composition of the sample would expectedly be younger than that of LEED. Table 4.2 shows that this is the case. The aged, those 66 years or older,

TABLE 4.2
Demographic Characteristics of LEED File and Selected Sample

Characteristic	LEED file Number	LEED file Percentage	Selected sample Number	Selected sample Percentage
Total persons	12,653	—	6,326	—
Percentage of total	—	100.00	—	50.00
Race				
Unknown	198	1.56	0	0.00
White	10,892	85.08	5,675	89.71
Black	1,382	10.92	651	10.29
Other	181	1.43	0	0.00
Total	12,653	100.00	6,326	100.00
Sex				
Male	7,050	55.72	3,764	59.50
Female	5,603	44.28	2,562	40.50
Total	12,653	100.00	6,326	100.00
Age (years)				
20 or less	1,505	11.89	657	10.39
21 to 25	1,667	13.17	810	12.80
26 to 30	1,374	10.86	723	11.43
31 to 35	1,182	9.34	609	9.63
36 to 40	1,040	8.22	603	9.53
41 to 45	1,109	8.76	692	10.94
46 to 50	999	7.90	602	9.52
51 to 55	994	7.86	616	9.74
56 to 60	849	6.71	476	7.52
61 to 65	646	5.11	317	5.01
66 or more	2,576	20.36	221	3.49
Total	12,653	100.00	6,326	100.00

TABLE 4.3
Demographic Characteristics of the Sample, Nonmigrants, and Migrants

Demographic characteristic	Total Number	Total Percentage	Nonmigrants Number	Nonmigrants Percentage	Migrants Number	Migrants Percentage
Total	6326	100.0	4715	100.0	1611	100.0
Sex						
Male	3764	59.5	2696	57.2	1068	66.3
Female	2562	40.5	2019	42.8	543	33.7
Race						
White	5675	89.7	4254	90.2	1421	88.2
Black	651	10.3	461	9.8	190	11.8
Sex and race						
White male	3368	53.2	2435	51.6	933	57.9
White female	2307	36.5	1819	38.6	488	30.3
Black male	396	6.3	261	5.5	135	8.4
Black female	255	4.0	200	4.2	55	3.4

accounted for 20.4% of the total in LEED and only 3.5% of the sample. In other words, over 90% of the aged in LEED were deleted from the sample. Other differences in the age composition are less dramatic and they generally follow the pattern of labor force participation. The fraction of those deleted is greater than average for those aged 20 years or less and for those above 60 years of age. For those in the middle years, 36 to 60 years, the fraction deleted is considerably below average.

Characteristics of the Sample

The next chapter discusses results of using the sample data in estimating the model (3.20). While the estimation results ultimately reflect the sample in the aggregate, they do not offer much of an overview of the sample. To provide such an understanding, this section summarizes the sample in terms of important characteristics—demographic, economic, mobility, and geographic.

DEMOGRAPHIC CHARACTERISTICS

The demographic characteristics of the sample are portrayed in two tables. Table 4.3 presents the sex and race distributions for the total sample, migrants, and nonmigrants, and Table 4.4 details the age distribution. In the sample, males outnumber females by $3:2$; this ratio is $2:1$ for migrants. With regard to race, the sample is predominantly white; both the nonmigrant and the migrant groups are approximately 90% white.

The age distribution of the sample follows the expected pattern of labor force participation rates. The proportions of the young and the old in the sample are small. The proportions of those in the middle years are large, as are labor force participation rates. Indeed, 50% of the black females in the sample are between the ages of 21 and 35. This age pattern does not, however, characterize the migrant and nonmigrant groups. For migrants, 60% are under 35 years of age, the fraction is 80% for black female migrants. For nonmigrants, the proportion of those under 25 years of age is only one-half the fraction for migrants, whereas the fraction greater than 55 years is twice that for migrants. This last feature is most striking in the case of black males aged 55 years or more, for whom the ratio of nonmigrants to migrants is about $4:1$.

The total sample is then dominated by white males in the prime ages 25 to 45, and this is even more so for migrants. The smallest race–sex–age group in the sample is black females aged 55 years or more.

ECONOMIC CHARACTERISTICS

The chief economic characteristic of potential migrants identifiable from LEED is estimated annual wage and salary income. The income dis-

TABLE 4.4
Age Distribution (Percentage) by Race, Sex, and Migrant Status

	Total									Nonmigrants									Migrants								
	Sex			Race						Sex			Race						Sex			Race					
				White			Black						White			Black						White			Black		
Age (years)	Total	Male	Female	Total	Male	Female	Total	Male	Female	Total	Male	Female	Total	Male	Female	Total	Male	Female	Total	Male	Female	Total	Male	Female	Total	Male	Female
Total persons	6326	3764	2562	5675	3368	2307	651	396	255	4715	2696	2019	4254	2435	1819	461	261	200	1611	1068	543	1421	933	488	190	135	55
Percentage of total	100.0	59.5	40.5	89.7	53.2	36.5	10.3	6.3	4.0	74.5	42.6	31.9	67.2	38.5	28.8	7.3	4.1	3.2	25.5	16.9	8.6	22.5	14.7	7.7	3.0	2.1	.9
20 or less	10.4	9.2	11.8	10.3	9.2	11.9	10.9	10.6	11.4	8.5	7.2	10.2	8.4	7.3	10.0	8.9	6.9	11.5	16.0	14.9	18.0	16.0	14.5	18.9	15.8	17.8	10.9
21 to 25	12.8	10.1	16.8	12.4	9.7	16.4	16.0	13.1	20.4	10.3	7.4	14.3	10.1	7.1	14.0	13.0	10.3	16.5	20.0	16.8	26.3	19.6	16.5	25.4	23.2	18.5	34.5
26 to 30	11.4	12.3	10.2	11.4	12.6	9.7	11.7	9.3	15.3	10.3	11.3	9.1	10.3	11.5	8.7	11.1	10.0	12.5	14.6	14.6	14.5	14.8	15.5	13.3	13.2	8.1	25.5
31 to 35	9.6	10.8	7.9	9.4	10.8	7.3	11.8	11.1	12.9	9.1	9.9	7.9	8.9	10.1	7.3	10.6	8.0	14.0	11.2	13.0	7.7	10.8	12.4	7.6	14.7	17.0	9.1
36 to 40	9.5	10.0	8.8	9.4	9.7	9.0	10.4	12.6	7.1	9.7	10.1	9.3	9.7	9.9	9.5	10.0	11.9	7.5	8.9	9.9	7.0	8.6	9.3	7.2	11.6	14.1	5.5
41 to 45	10.9	11.2	10.6	11.2	11.5	10.9	8.1	8.6	8.2	11.6	11.8	11.4	11.9	12.1	11.6	9.3	8.8	10.0	8.9	9.6	7.6	9.3	9.9	8.2	6.3	8.1	1.8
46 to 50	9.5	9.4	9.7	9.6	9.5	9.7	8.8	8.1	9.8	10.6	10.5	10.7	10.6	10.6	10.6	10.6	9.6	12.0	6.3	6.6	5.9	6.6	6.8	6.4	4.2	5.2	1.8
51 to 55	9.7	10.1	9.1	9.7	10.1	9.2	9.8	10.6	8.6	10.6	11.2	9.8	10.6	11.1	9.8	11.1	12.3	9.5	7.2	7.4	6.8	7.2	7.4	7.0	6.8	7.4	5.5
56 to 60	7.5	7.7	7.3	7.7	7.5	7.9	6.3	8.8	2.4	9.0	9.3	8.6	9.1	9.0	9.2	8.0	12.3	2.5	3.2	3.4	2.8	3.3	3.5	2.9	2.1	2.2	1.8
61 to 65	5.0	5.4	4.4	5.3	5.7	4.8	2.5	3.0	1.6	5.9	6.4	5.2	6.2	6.7	5.6	3.0	4.2	1.5	2.4	2.8	1.7	2.6	3.1	1.6	1.1	.7	1.8
66 or more	3.5	3.7	3.2	3.5	3.7	3.3	3.4	4.0	2.4	4.3	4.7	3.6	4.3	4.6	3.7	4.3	5.7	2.5	1.2	1.0	1.7	1.3	1.1	1.6	1.1	.7	1.8

tributions of the total sample, migrants, and nonmigrants are presented in Table 4.5. For the total sample, the income distribution follows a general inverted U pattern. Earnings in 1969 were less than $2000 for 18% of the sample, and 30% earned income between $2000 and $5000, 25% earned between $5000 and $8000, 12% earned between $10,000 and $20,000, and 4% earned over $20,000.

The general pattern does not, however, characterize the income distributions of different race–sex groups. For females, 75% earned less than $6000 in 1969; on the other hand, 63% of males earned more than $6000. The black–white difference is almost as great. And the joint effect of the sex and race differences is seen in the case of black females, 92% of whom earned less than $6000.

The differences in the income distributions of migrants and nonmigrants are less striking than the race and sex differences. For each race–sex group, migrants are slightly more concentrated in the lower income levels than nonmigrants. On the whole, 57% of the migrants and 45% of the nonmigrants earned less than $5000.

MOBILITY CHARACTERISTICS

Four mobility characteristics defined over the potential migrant's work history at the time of the decision were constructed from LEED: industrial tenure (the length of time the potential migrant has been employed in the same industry), job tenure (the length of employment with the same firm), length of residency (the length of employment in the same county), and job turnover (the average number of jobs per year the potential migrant has held over his work history). The distributions of the sample data by each characteristic are provided in Tables 4.6, 4.7, 4.8, and 4.9. For the first three characteristics the length of time truncates at 12 years because the work history extends only from 1957 to 1969.

Industrial Tenure. Over 40% of the potential migrants had only 1 year of industrial tenure at the time of the migration decision. A mere 10% had 2 years of tenure, and the fraction steadily declines as industrial tenure increases. Males generally held less industrial tenure than females, and blacks held less than whites. Black males held the least tenure; 55% of black males had 1 year of tenure or less. White females, on the other hand, held the most tenure; 47% had 3 years or more.

This general pattern characterizes both migrant and nonmigrant groups. But while the patterns for the two groups are the same, the levels are noticeably different. Over 75% of the migrants have 1 year of tenure or less; the figure for nonmigrants is only 36%. Similarly, 26% of nonmigrants have 7 years of tenure or more, and for migrants the figure is only 6%.

TABLE 4.5

Income Distribution (Percentage) by Race, Sex, and Migrant Status

Note: The table is organized in three major panels — **Total**, **Nonmigrants**, and **Migrants** — each subdivided by **Sex** (Total, Male, Female) and **Race** [**White** (Total, Male, Female) and **Black** (Total, Male, Female)].

Income	Total – Sex Total	Sex Male	Sex Female	White Total	White Male	White Female	Black Total	Black Male	Black Female	Nonmig. Sex Total	Sex Male	Sex Female	White Total	White Male	White Female	Black Total	Black Male	Black Female	Migr. Sex Total	Sex Male	Sex Female	White Total	White Male	White Female	Black Total	Black Male	Black Female
Total persons	6326	3764	2562	5675	3368	2307	651	396	255	4715	2696	2019	4254	2435	1819	461	261	200	1611	1068	543	1421	933	488	190	135	55
Percentage of total	100.0	59.5	40.5	89.7	53.2	36.5	10.3	6.3	4.0	74.5	42.6	31.9	67.2	38.5	28.8	7.3	4.1	3.2	25.5	16.9	8.6	22.5	14.7	7.7	3.0	2.1	.9
$999 or less	7.7	4.9	11.9	7.6	4.5	12.2	8.4	8.3	8.6	7.0	4.3	10.5	6.8	3.9	10.7	8.5	8.0	9.0	10.1	6.5	16.8	10.1	6.1	17.8	8.4	8.9	7.3
$1,000 to $1,999	9.9	7.2	13.9	9.6	6.9	13.4	12.7	9.1	18.4	8.8	5.5	13.2	8.5	5.5	9.4	11.1	3.0	18.5	12.7	11.5	16.6	12.0	10.8	16.4	16.8	16.3	18.2
$2,000 to $2,999	9.7	6.1	15.0	9.0	5.4	14.2	15.7	11.6	22.0	9.2	5.3	14.3	8.6	4.8	10.2	14.3	10.0	20.0	10.1	7.8	17.7	9.6	6.8	16.4	18.9	14.8	29.1
$3,000 to $3,999	11.0	6.2	18.0	10.4	5.6	17.5	15.7	11.6	22.0	10.6	5.3	17.5	9.9	4.7	12.7	16.3	11.5	22.5	12.0	8.5	19.9	11.8	8.0	19.5	15.3	11.9	23.6
$4,000 to $4,999	10.4	7.4	14.8	10.0	6.4	15.2	13.8	15.7	11.0	10.0	6.5	14.7	9.7	5.5	11.4	13.2	15.7	10.0	11.0	9.7	14.9	10.8	8.9	15.0	15.3	15.6	14.5
$5,000 to $5,999	8.9	7.8	10.4	8.8	7.6	10.5	9.5	9.3	9.8	9.4	7.5	11.8	9.2	7.3	8.9	10.4	11.5	11.0	7.5	8.5	5.3	7.4	8.6	5.3	6.3	8.1	5.6
$6,000 to $6,999	7.8	8.6	6.5	7.8	8.5	6.9	7.2	10.1	2.7	8.1	8.8	7.1	8.1	8.5	5.7	7.6	11.1	2.5	7.0	8.2	4.4	6.9	7.1	4.5	3.7	7.4	3.6
$7,000 to $7,999	8.2	10.8	4.4	8.4	11.1	4.5	6.9	8.8	3.9	9.0	11.9	5.1	9.1	12.0	5.2	8.2	7.7	4.5	6.3	8.1	1.8	6.1	6.5	1.8	3.7	4.4	1.8
$8,000 to $8,999	6.2	8.7	2.6	6.5	8.9	2.9	4.3	6.8	.4	6.6	9.5	2.8	6.8	9.7	3.0	4.6	4.2	.5	5.4	6.5	2.0	5.5	6.5	2.3	1.6	2.2	0.0
$9,000 to $9,999	4.7	7.1	1.1	4.9	7.5	1.0	2.6	3.5	1.2	4.8	7.6	1.2	5.0	7.9	1.2	3.0	1.5	1.5	4.5	6.0	.6	4.9	3.5	.6	.5	.7	0.0
$10,000 to $10,999	2.3	3.6	.3	2.4	3.9	.3	.8	1.3	.0	2.3	3.8	.4	2.5	4.0	.4	.9	.0	.0	2.3	3.2	.0	2.5	2.8	.0	1.1	1.5	0.0
$11,000 to $11,999	.7	1.2	.0	.8	1.2	.0	.2	.5	.0	.7	.6	.0	.4	.7	.0	.0	.0	.0	1.9	2.6	.2	2.1	1.3	.2	.5	.7	0.0
$12,000 to $12,999	.4	.7	.0	.5	.8	.0	.2	.3	.0	.4	.5	.0	.3	.6	.0	.0	.0	.0	.8	1.2	.0	.9	.3	.0	.0	.0	0.0
$13,000 to $13,999	.5	.9	.0	.6	1.0	.0	.2	.3	.0	.5	1.1	.0	.7	.7	.0	.2	.4	.0	.2	.3	.0	.2	.3	.0	.5	.7	0.0
$14,000 to $14,999	2.0	3.1	.4	2.2	3.4	.4	.5	.8	.0	2.2	3.4	.5	2.4	3.7	.5	2.2	.8	.0	1.7	2.3	.0	1.8	2.6	.0	.5	.7	0.0
$15,000 to $15,999	1.4	2.3	.1	1.6	2.5	.1	.3	.5	.0	1.6	2.6	.2	1.7	2.9	.2	.7	.4	.0	1.1	1.5	.0	1.1	1.6	.0	.5	.7	0.0
$16,000 to $16,999	1.4	2.4	.1	1.6	2.6	.1	.3	.5	.0	1.6	2.8	.1	1.8	3.0	.1	.4	.4	.0	.9	1.3	.0	1.0	1.4	.0	.5	.7	0.0
$17,000 to $17,999	1.1	1.7	.1	1.1	1.8	.1	.5	.8	.0	1.3	2.2	.1	1.3	2.3	.1	.4	1.1	.0	.5	.7	.0	.5	.8	.0	.0	.0	0.0
$18,000 to $18,999	.9	1.4	.2	1.0	1.5	.3	.2	.3	.0	.6	1.0	.3	.7	1.8	.3	1.3	.4	.0	.4	.6	.0	.5	.6	.0	.0	.0	0.0
$19,000 to $19,999	.6	1.0	.0	.7	1.1	.0	.0	.0	.0	.6	1.0	.0	.7	1.1	.0	.0	.0	.0	.7	1.1	.0	.8	1.1	.0	.0	.0	0.0
$20,000 or more	4.1	6.7	.2	4.5	7.5	.3	.0	.0	.0	4.6	7.9	.2	5.1	8.7	.3	1.1	.0	.0	2.8	3.7	.2	2.8	4.2	.2	.0	.0	0.0

TABLE 4.6

Industrial Tenure (Percentage Distribution) by Race, Sex, and Migrant Status

Industrial tenure (years)	Total									Nonmigrants									Migrants								
	Sex			Race						Sex			Race						Sex			Race					
				White			Black						White			Black						White			Black		
	Total	Male	Female	Total	Male	Female	Total	Male	Female	Total	Male	Female	Total	Male	Female	Total	Male	Female	Total	Male	Female	Total	Male	Female	Total	Male	Female
Total persons	6326	3764	2562	5675	3368	2307	651	396	255	4715	2696	2019	4254	2435	1819	461	261	200	1611	1068	543	1421	933	488	190	135	55
Percentage of total	100.0	59.5	40.5	89.7	53.2	36.5	10.3	6.3	4.0	74.5	42.6	31.9	67.2	38.5	28.8	7.3	4.1	3.2	25.5	16.9	8.6	22.5	14.7	7.7	3.0	2.1	.9
0	5.5	6.1	4.5	5.3	5.8	4.6	6.6	8.6	3.5	0.0	0.0	0.0	0.0	0.0	0.0	.2	0.0	.5	21.4	21.5	21.2	21.3	21.0	21.9	22.1	25.2	14.5
1	41.1	42.6	38.8	40.6	42.2	38.4	44.9	46.2	42.7	36.2	37.0	35.1	35.7	36.6	34.4	41.0	40.6	41.5	55.4	56.8	52.5	55.5	56.8	53.1	54.2	57.0	47.3
2	10.2	9.7	10.9	10.0	9.4	10.7	12.1	11.6	12.9	11.2	10.9	11.7	11.0	10.5	11.7	13.7	14.9	12.0	7.1	6.6	7.9	6.9	6.9	7.0	8.4	5.2	16.4
3	7.4	6.9	8.1	7.3	6.9	7.8	7.8	6.1	10.6	8.7	8.5	9.1	8.7	8.5	8.9	9.5	8.0	11.5	3.4	2.8	4.4	3.3	2.9	4.1	3.7	2.2	7.3
4	5.9	5.3	6.7	5.8	5.2	6.6	6.6	6.1	7.5	6.7	6.2	7.4	6.6	6.2	7.3	7.8	6.9	9.0	3.3	2.8	4.1	3.2	2.7	4.3	3.7	4.4	1.8
5	5.6	5.3	6.1	5.9	5.7	6.2	3.2	2.0	5.1	6.9	6.8	7.0	7.3	7.3	7.2	3.5	2.3	5.0	2.0	1.5	2.9	1.9	1.5	2.7	2.1	1.5	5.5
6	3.1	2.7	3.7	3.1	2.7	3.8	2.8	2.5	3.1	3.6	3.2	4.2	3.6	3.1	4.3	3.0	3.4	2.5	1.7	1.5	2.0	1.6	1.6	1.6	2.1	.7	5.5
7	2.5	2.3	2.8	2.6	2.4	2.9	2.3	2.0	2.7	3.1	2.9	3.5	3.1	2.9	3.5	3.0	2.9	3.5	.8	.9	.6	.8	1.0	.6	.5	.7	0.0
8	2.5	2.4	2.6	2.6	2.5	2.8	1.7	1.8	1.6	3.1	3.0	3.4	3.2	3.1	3.4	2.0	1.9	2.0	.9	1.1	.6	.9	1.1	.6	1.1	1.5	0.0
9	2.6	2.2	3.1	2.7	2.3	3.2	1.7	1.5	2.0	3.2	2.8	3.8	3.3	2.9	3.9	2.2	1.9	2.5	.7	.8	.6	.8	.9	.6	.5	.7	0.0
10	2.0	1.9	2.2	2.0	1.9	2.3	1.8	1.8	2.0	2.5	2.4	2.7	2.5	2.4	2.7	2.6	2.9	2.5	.6	.6	.6	.6	.6	.6	0.0	0.0	0.0
11	1.7	1.8	1.6	1.8	1.9	1.6	1.1	1.0	1.2	1.8	2.0	1.5	1.8	2.1	1.5	1.3	1.1	1.5	1.6	1.5	1.7	1.7	1.6	1.8	.5	.7	0.0
12 or more	9.9	10.7	8.7	10.2	11.0	9.1	7.4	8.8	5.1	12.9	14.4	10.7	13.1	14.5	11.3	10.2	13.4	6.0	1.2	1.3	1.1	1.3	1.5	1.0	.5	0.0	1.8

TABLE 4.7
Job Tenure (Percentage Distribution) by Race, Sex, and Migrant Status

Job tenure (years)	Total									Nonmigrants									Migrants								
	Sex			Race						Sex			Race						Sex			Race					
				White			Black						White			Black						White			Black		
	Total	Male	Female	Total	Male	Female	Total	Male	Female	Total	Male	Female	Total	Male	Female	Total	Male	Female	Total	Male	Female	Total	Male	Female	Total	Male	Female
Total persons	6326	3764	2562	5675	3368	2307	651	396	255	4715	2696	2019	4254	2435	1819	461	261	200	1611	1068	543	1421	933	488	190	135	55
Percentage of total	100.0	59.5	40.5	89.7	53.2	36.5	10.3	6.3	4.0	74.5	42.6	31.9	67.2	38.5	28.8	7.3	4.1	3.2	25.5	16.9	8.6	22.5	14.7	7.7	3.0	2.1	.9
0	37.1	23.7	11.0	36.5	38.9	32.9	43.0	47.5	36.1	22.6	23.7	21.1	22.1	23.2	20.6	27.1	28.4	25.5	79.8	80.5	78.3	79.5	80.0	78.7	81.2	84.4	74.5
1	17.8	15.4	21.2	17.5	15.1	21.1	19.8	18.2	22.4	21.0	18.4	24.5	20.4	17.9	23.9	24.3	23.8	30.0	8.9	7.8	11.0	8.9	7.8	10.9	8.9	7.4	12.7
2	9.2	8.3	10.5	9.1	8.2	10.5	9.5	8.8	10.6	11.4	10.6	12.3	11.3	10.3	12.6	12.1	12.6	11.5	2.6	2.4	2.9	2.5	2.6	2.5	3.2	1.5	7.3
3	6.8	6.2	7.7	7.0	6.5	7.6	5.2	3.5	7.8	8.3	7.8	8.8	8.4	8.1	8.7	7.2	5.0	10.0	2.6	2.2	3.3	2.8	2.4	3.7	.5	.7	0.0
4	4.8	4.4	5.4	4.7	4.4	5.2	5.4	4.5	6.7	6.0	5.6	6.4	3.6	5.7	6.3	6.3	5.4	7.5	1.3	1.2	1.7	1.1	1.0	1.4	3.2	3.0	3.6
5	3.2	3.2	3.3	3.4	3.3	3.5	2.2	2.5	1.6	4.1	4.1	4.1	4.2	4.2	4.3	2.8	3.4	2.0	.7	.9	.4	.8	1.0	.4	.5	.5	0.0
6	2.6	2.4	3.0	2.7	2.5	3.1	1.8	1.5	2.4	3.3	3.0	3.6	3.4	3.1	3.7	2.4	2.3	2.5	.8	.8	.7	.8	1.0	.6	.5	.7	1.8
7	2.6	2.6	2.7	2.7	2.7	2.7	2.0	1.8	2.4	3.4	3.4	3.3	3.5	3.5	3.4	2.4	1.9	3.0	.6	.7	.4	.5	.5	.4	.5	0.0	0.0
8	2.5	2.4	2.7	2.7	2.6	2.8	.9	.5	1.6	3.2	3.0	3.3	3.4	3.3	3.5	1.1	.4	2.0	.7	.8	.4	.7	.9	.4	1.1	1.5	0.0
9	2.4	2.4	2.3	2.5	2.6	2.4	1.0	1.0	1.2	3.1	3.3	2.8	3.2	3.4	2.9	1.5	1.5	1.5	.4	.5	.4	.4	.5	.4	.5	.7	0.0
10	1.4	1.5	1.1	1.4	1.6	1.2	1.1	1.3	.8	1.7	2.0	1.4	1.8	2.0	1.5	1.5	1.9	1.0	.3	.5	0.0	.4	.5	0.0	0.0	0.0	0.0
11	1.2	1.5	.7	1.3	1.7	.7	.3	0.0	.8	1.3	1.6	.8	1.3	1.8	.8	.4	0.0	1.0	1.1	1.4	.6	1.3	1.6	.6	0.0	0.0	0.0
12 or more	8.3	9.8	6.2	8.4	9.9	6.3	7.7	8.8	5.9	11.1	13.5	7.9	11.1	13.5	8.0	10.8	13.4	7.5	.2	.4	0.0	.3	.4	0.0	0.0	0.0	0.0

TABLE 4.8
Length of Residency (Percentage Distribution) by Race, Sex, and Migrant Status

Locational tenure (years)	Total									Nonmigrants									Migrants								
		Sex		Race							Sex		Race							Sex		Race					
				White			Black						White			Black						White			Black		
	Total	Male	Female	Total	Male	Female	Total	Male	Female	Total	Male	Female	Total	Male	Female	Total	Male	Female	Total	Male	Female	Total	Male	Female	Total	Male	Female
Total persons	6326	3764	2562	5675	3368	2307	651	396	255	4715	2696	2019	4254	2435	1819	461	261	200	1611	1068	543	1421	933	488	190	135	55
Percentage of total	100.0	59.5	40.5	89.7	53.2	36.5	10.3	6.3	4.0	74.5	42.6	31.9	67.2	38.5	28.8	7.3	4.1	3.2	25.5	16.9	8.6	22.5	14.7	7.7	3.0	2.1	.9
0	5.5	6.1	4.7	5.4	5.7	4.9	6.6	9.1	2.7	0.0	0.0	0.0	0.0	0.0	0.0	.2	0.0	.5	21.7	21.4	22.1	21.6	20.7	23.4	22.1	26.7	10.9
1	22.7	23.9	21.0	22.3	23.7	20.4	25.8	25.8	25.9	12.0	11.6	12.6	11.7	11.4	12.1	15.0	13.4	17.0	53.9	54.9	52.1	54.2	55.6	51.4	52.1	49.6	58.2
2	12.1	12.5	11.4	11.9	12.3	11.5	13.2	14.9	10.6	13.6	14.4	12.5	13.4	14.0	12.7	14.5	17.6	10.5	7.8	8.0	7.4	7.5	7.7	7.0	10.0	9.6	10.9
3	8.3	8.0	8.8	8.4	8.3	8.5	8.0	5.6	11.8	9.7	9.6	9.9	9.6	9.8	9.5	10.4	7.7	14.0	4.2	3.9	4.8	4.5	4.3	4.9	2.1	1.5	3.6
4	6.5	5.7	7.6	6.4	5.8	7.3	7.2	5.1	10.6	7.6	6.8	8.7	7.5	6.8	8.4	8.5	6.5	11.0	3.2	3.0	3.7	3.1	3.1	3.1	3.7	2.2	7.3
5	8.0	7.5	8.5	8.1	7.7	8.8	6.6	6.6	6.7	8.9	8.5	9.5	9.1	8.6	9.7	7.4	7.7	7.0	5.1	5.1	5.2	5.1	5.1	5.1	5.8	4.4	9.1
6	33.2	34.5	31.3	33.9	35.0	32.1	27.5	30.0	23.9	43.4	46.7	38.9	44.1	47.2	40.0	36.9	42.1	30.0	3.4	3.6	3.1	3.2	3.2	3.3	4.7	5.9	1.8
7	1.2	.7	1.9	1.1	.6	1.9	1.5	1.0	2.4	1.5	.9	2.4	1.5	.8	2.3	2.2	1.5	3.0	.1	.1	.2	.1	.1	.2	0.0	0.0	0.0
8	.7	.3	1.2	.7	.3	1.2	.8	.8	.8	.8	.4	1.4	.8	.3	1.5	1.1	1.1	1.0	.1	.1	.2	.1	.1	.2	0.0	0.0	0.0
9	.7	.4	1.1	.6	.4	1.0	1.2	.5	2.4	.9	.6	1.4	.8	.6	1.2	1.7	.8	3.0	0.0	0.0	0.0	0.0	0.0	0.0	0.0	0.0	0.0
10	.5	.1	1.1	.5	.1	1.1	.8	.3	1.6	.7	.1	1.3	.6	.1	1.3	1.1	.4	2.0	.1	0.0	.4	.1	0.0	.4	0.0	0.0	0.0
11	.3	.1	.7	.4	.1	.7	.2	.3	0.0	.4	.2	.6	.2	.2	.7	.2	.4	0.0	.2	0.0	.7	.2	0.0	.8	0.0	0.0	0.0
12 or more	.3	.2	.7	.3	.1	.7	.3	.5	.8	.5	.2	.8	.4	.2	.8	.9	.8	1.0	.1	0.0	.2	0.0	0.0	.2	0.0	0.0	0.0

TABLE 4.9
Job Turnover (Percentage) by Race, Sex, and Migrant Status

Job turnover (jobs per year)	Total: Sex Total	Sex Male	Sex Female	White Total	White Male	White Female	Black Total	Black Male	Black Female	Nonmigrants: Sex Total	Sex Male	Sex Female	White Total	White Male	White Female	Black Total	Black Male	Black Female	Migrants: Sex Total	Sex Male	Sex Female	White Total	White Male	White Female	Black Total	Black Male	Black Female
Total persons	6326	3764	2562	5675	3368	2307	651	396	255	4715	2696	2019	4254	2435	1819	461	261	200	1611	1068	543	1421	933	488	190	135	55
Percentage of total	100.0	59.5	40.5	89.7	53.2	36.5	10.3	6.3	4.0	74.5	42.6	31.9	67.2	38.5	28.8	7.3	4.1	3.2	25.5	16.9	8.6	22.5	14.7	7.7	3.0	2.1	.9
1.00 or less	21.6	18.8	25.7	21.9	19.3	25.8	18.7	14.9	24.7	27.1	24.5	30.6	27.4	25.0	30.6	20.3	20.3	30.0	5.5	4.4	7.7	5.6	4.4	8.0	4.7	4.4	5.5
1.01 to 1.50	42.0	22.9	47.2	42.7	39.3	47.6	36.3	31.3	43.9	45.0	42.2	48.8	45.7	43.0	49.3	39.0	34.9	44.5	33.3	29.2	41.3	33.8	29.9	41.2	29.5	24.4	41.8
1.51 to 2.00	21.7	14.1	18.8	21.5	23.7	18.4	23.2	23.5	22.7	19.3	21.9	15.8	18.9	21.5	15.4	23.0	25.7	19.5	28.7	28.0	30.0	29.3	29.3	29.5	23.7	19.3	34.5
2.01 to 2.50	7.7	5.6	5.0	7.5	9.2	5.0	9.1	11.6	5.1	5.1	6.5	3.1	5.0	6.3	3.1	6.1	8.4	3.0	15.2	16.9	12.0	15.1	16.7	11.9	16.3	17.8	12.7
2.51 to 3.00	3.4	2.6	1.9	3.0	3.8	1.9	6.6	9.6	2.0	1.8	2.6	.9	1.6	2.2	.8	3.9	5.7	1.5	8.0	9.2	5.7	7.3	8.0	5.9	13.2	17.0	3.6
3.01 to 3.50	1.6	1.3	.8	1.5	2.0	.9	2.3	3.5	.4	.8	1.0	.5	.8	.9	.5	1.3	1.9	.5	4.0	5.0	2.0	3.9	4.7	2.3	4.7	6.7	0.0
3.51 or more	2.2	1.9	.8	2.0	2.8	.7	4.0	5.8	1.8	.9	1.3	.5	.8	1.1	.4	2.2	3.1	1.0	5.8	7.9	1.8	5.5	7.4	1.8	8.4	11.1	1.8

That nonmigrants have more industrial tenure than migrants generally holds for each of the race–sex groups as well.

Job Tenure and Length of Residency. The distributions of the sample by job tenure and length of residency are similar to those by industrial tenure. Females hold more job tenure and greater length of residency than males, and whites more than blacks. Black males have the least tenure and shortest length of residency and white females hold the most of both. In general, these patterns also characterize both migrant and nonmigrant groups.

The distinctive difference between the distributions by job tenure and those by length of residency is the level. Potential migrants generally have a shorter job tenure than length of residency. In particular, 55% of the sample have less than 2 years of experience with the same firm (65% for black males), whereas only 28% of the sample have less than 2 years residency at the origin.

Nonmigrants hold more of both job tenure and length of residency at the time of decision than do migrants. Indeed, 90% of migrants have less than 2 years of job tenure; the figure for nonmigrants is only 44%. And 75% of migrants have 1 year of residency or less, while only 1% have more than 6 years of residency. These figures are 12 and 5% for nonmigrants.

Job Turnover. The general pattern of the distribution of potential migrants by job turnover is an inverted U. One-fifth of the potential migrants have, on average, one job per year, 40% average between one and one and one-half jobs per year, 20% average between one and one-half and two jobs, and the fraction tails off gradually as job turnover increases beyond two jobs per year.

There are notable variations in this general pattern, however, for different race–sex groups. In particular, males experience higher job turnover than females. The fraction of males having two and one-half or more jobs per year is considerably higher than that for females. The differential in turnover between males and females is greater for blacks than for whites. The upper tail of the distribution by turnover for black males is relatively thick; substantial proportions of black males experience high job turnover.

While the general inverted-U pattern holds for migrants and nonmigrants, the upper tail of the turnover distribution is thicker for migrants than nonmigrants. This holds for each of the race–sex groups as well. The group with the highest turnover is black male migrants; 34% have an average of two and one-half or more jobs per year.

REGIONAL CHARACTERISTICS

The geographic distribution of the total sample, migrants, and nonmigrants is displayed in Table 4.10 for census divisions and states. The more industrialized regions, the East North Central and the Middle Atlantic, have the largest representation, accounting for 42% of the sample. The regions with small shares of the sample are Mountain, East South Central, and New England. This general pattern does not vary much by sex or migrant status. Nonetheless, there are the expected differences by race. The proportions of blacks in New England, Pacific, Mountain, and West North Central regions are substantially below the sample averages. On the other hand, the proportions of blacks in the southern regions, especially the South Atlantic, are above average.

The least populous states have, as expected, the smallest shares of the sample. In particular, New Hampshire, Vermont, Delaware, the Dakotas, Montana, Wyoming, New Mexico, Nevada, and Idaho each have 3% or less of the potential migrants. The most populous states, New York and California, have the highest fractions. To assess whether regions are adequately represented by the sample, the ratio of the region's share of the sample to the region's share of total population was calculated for each area. This measure is portrayed in Table 4.11, and it is apparent that coverage is fairly uniform. Twenty-seven states had shares of potential migrants that were within 15% of their shares of total population. Only three states, Vermont, New York, and the District of Columbia, are somewhat overrepresented in the sample. A slightly greater number of states, generally in the more rural and less industrialized regions, are somewhat underrepresented.

MIGRATION PROPENSITIES

In this section, the migration propensities for different groups of potential migrants are presented. (While certain mobility patterns considered here have been consistently observed, the patterns by race and sex have not usually been assessed.)[8] Examination of the aggregate migration propensities has two principal benefits. First, it provides an overview of the migratory process and an improved understanding of the mobility of a local population. Second, the insight gained from this overview aids in specifying our model of migratory choice, a task undertaken in the next chapter. The discussion of migration propensities follows that of the last

[8] An extensive review of research on migration propensities is provided by Parnes (1970).

TABLE 4.10
Geographic Distribution (Percentage) by Race, Sex, and Migrant Status

Geographic area	Total									Nonmigrants									Migrants								
	Sex			Race						Sex			Race						Sex			Race					
				White			Black						White			Black						White			Black		
	Total	Male	Female	Total	Male	Female	Total	Male	Female	Total	Male	Female	Total	Male	Female	Total	Male	Female	Total	Male	Female	Total	Male	Female	Total	Male	Female
Contiguous United States	6326	3764	2562	5675	3368	2307	651	396	255	4715	2696	2019	4254	2435	1819	461	261	200	1611	1068	543	1421	933	488	190	135	55
Percentage of total	100.0	59.5	40.5	89.7	53.2	36.5	10.3	6.3	4.0	74.5	42.6	31.9	67.2	38.5	28.8	7.3	4.1	3.2	25.5	16.9	8.6	22.5	14.7	7.7	3.0	2.1	.9
New England	6.4	6.0	6.9	6.8	6.4	7.4	2.6	2.3	3.1	6.3	5.9	6.9	6.8	6.3	7.4	2.4	2.3	2.5	6.5	6.2	7.2	7.0	6.8	7.4	3.2	2.2	5.4
Maine	.5	.5	.5	.5	.5	.5	.2	.0	.4	.4	.4	.5	.4	.4	.5	.2	.0	.5	.6	.7	.4	.7	.9	.4	0.0	0.0	0.0
New Hampshire	.3	.3	.4	.4	.3	.4	.0	.0	.0	.3	.3	.3	.3	.3	.3	.0	.0	.0	.4	.4	.2	.4	.2	.8	0.0	0.0	0.0
Vermont	.3	.2	.4	.4	.2	.4	.0	.0	.0	.3	.1	.4	.3	.2	.5	.0	.0	.0	.2	.3	.2	.3	.3	.2	0.0	0.0	0.0
Massachusetts	3.1	2.8	3.5	3.3	3.0	3.8	.9	1.0	.8	3.1	2.8	3.4	3.3	3.0	3.7	.7	1.1	.0	3.2	2.7	4.1	3.4	3.0	4.1	1.6	.7	3.6
Connecticut	1.8	1.7	1.8	1.8	1.8	1.8	1.4	1.0	2.0	1.9	1.9	2.0	2.0	2.0	1.9	1.5	1.1	2.0	1.4	1.3	1.5	1.4	1.4	1.4	1.1	.7	1.8
Rhode Island	.5	.6	.4	.5	.6	.4	.2	.3	.0	.4	.4	.3	.4	.5	.4	.0	.0	.0	.7	.9	.4	.8	1.0	.4	.5	.7	0.0
Middle Atlantic	21.8	21.5	22.1	21.9	21.7	22.1	21.0	20.2	22.4	21.9	21.7	22.3	22.2	21.9	22.5	19.5	19.2	20.0	21.4	21.3	21.5	20.9	21.1	20.5	24.7	22.2	30.9
New York	11.4	11.0	12.1	11.2	10.9	11.6	13.4	11.4	16.5	11.4	10.9	12.1	11.2	11.0	11.9	11.7	11.1	14.0	11.4	11.1	12.0	10.6	10.7	10.5	17.4	14.1	25.5
Pennsylvania	6.7	6.8	6.5	6.9	7.0	6.8	3.2	4.0	3.9	7.1	7.2	6.8	7.2	7.3	7.1	5.4	6.5	4.0	6.0	5.6	5.5	6.0	6.2	5.5	2.1	1.5	3.6
New Jersey	3.7	3.8	3.6	3.7	3.7	3.7	4.4	4.8	2.0	3.4	3.5	3.4	3.5	3.6	3.5	2.4	2.7	2.0	4.4	4.5	4.5	4.3	4.2	4.5	5.3	6.7	1.8
East North Central	21.4	22.3	19.9	21.5	22.6	19.9	20.4	20.5	20.4	22.1	23.3	20.6	22.0	23.3	20.3	23.0	23.0	23.0	19.2	20.0	17.7	19.9	20.7	18.4	14.2	15.6	10.9
Ohio	5.3	6.0	4.4	5.4	6.1	4.4	4.5	4.5	3.9	5.4	6.2	4.5	5.5	6.2	4.6	3.5	3.5	3.5	5.0	5.5	4.1	5.1	5.8	3.9	4.2	3.7	5.4
Michigan	4.8	5.6	3.7	4.8	5.6	3.6	5.4	5.8	4.7	4.8	5.6	3.8	4.7	5.6	3.6	6.0	5.7	6.0	4.8	5.5	3.5	4.9	5.5	3.9	4.2	5.9	0.0
Indiana	2.8	2.6	3.1	2.9	2.8	3.2	1.7	1.5	2.0	3.0	2.8	3.3	3.2	2.9	3.5	1.5	1.9	1.5	2.2	2.2	2.3	2.3	2.4	2.0	1.6	.7	3.6
Illinois	5.9	5.7	6.2	5.6	5.5	5.8	8.1	7.3	9.4	6.3	6.1	6.5	5.9	5.8	5.9	10.0	8.8	11.5	4.8	4.7	4.9	4.9	4.7	5.3	3.7	4.4	1.8
Wisconsin	2.5	2.5	2.5	2.8	2.6	2.8	.8	1.0	.4	2.5	2.6	2.5	2.7	2.8	2.7	.9	1.1	.5	2.4	2.2	2.9	2.7	2.4	3.3	.5	.7	0.0
West North Central	7.4	7.0	8.1	7.9	7.4	8.8	2.9	3.3	2.4	7.6	7.2	8.2	8.2	7.7	8.8	2.2	1.9	2.5	6.9	6.5	7.9	7.2	6.5	8.6	4.7	5.9	1.8
Missouri	2.3	2.1	2.5	2.4	2.1	2.8	1.5	1.8	1.2	2.2	2.0	2.4	2.3	2.1	2.5	1.3	1.1	1.5	2.6	2.3	3.1	2.7	2.3	3.5	2.1	3.0	0.0
Iowa	1.5	1.4	1.6	1.6	1.5	1.8	.3	.3	.4	1.6	1.5	1.8	1.7	1.6	1.9	.4	.4	.5	1.1	1.1	.9	1.2	1.3	1.0	0.0	0.0	0.0
Minnesota	1.6	1.6	1.5	1.7	1.8	1.6	.2	.3	.3	1.8	1.8	1.7	2.0	2.0	1.9	.0	.0	.0	1.1	1.2	.7	1.1	1.3	.8	.5	.7	0.0
North Dakota	.2	.2	.2	.2	.3	.2	0.0	0.0	0.0	.2	.2	.1	.3	.3	.2	0.0	0.0	0.0	.2	.2	.3	.3	.3	.2	0.0	0.0	0.0
South Dakota	.3	.2	.4	.4	.3	.4	0.0	0.0	0.0	.3	.2	.3	.3	.2	.3	0.0	0.0	0.0	.6	.3	.6	.6	.6	.6	0.0	0.0	0.0
Nebraska	.7	.6	.8	.9	.7	.9	.2	.0	.4	.7	.6	.8	.8	.7	.8	.2	.0	.5	.7	.6	.9	.8	.8	1.0	0.0	0.0	0.0
Kansas	.9	.8	1.1	1.2	.9	.7	.8	1.0	.4	.9	.9	1.0	1.0	.9	1.2	.2	.2	.4	.9	.9	.6	1.4	.3	.3	2.1	2.2	1.8

South Atlantic	14.4	13.1	16.5	12.5	11.9	14.7	30.6	28.8	35.3	13.7	13.3	14.3	11.9	11.7	12.2	30.2	30.0	33.0	16.2	14.5	19.5	14.1	12.2	17.8	31.6	30.4	34.5
Delaware	.3	1.5	.2	.2	.3	.2	.6	.5	.8	.3	.3	.1	.3	.3	.2	.2	.4	0.0	.4	.3	.6	.2	.2	.2	1.6	.7	3.6
Maryland	1.6	1.8	1.8	1.4	1.3	1.6	3.7	3.3	4.3	1.7	1.6	1.8	1.5	1.5	1.5	3.7	3.1	4.5	1.4	1.2	1.8	1.1	.9	1.6	3.7	3.7	3.6
District of Columbia	.5	.4	.7	.4	.4	.5	1.5		2.4	.3	.3	.3	.3	.2	.3	1.1	.8	1.5	.7	.4	1.5	.8	.6	.8	2.6	1.5	5.5
Virginia	1.9	1.9	1.8	1.7	1.7	1.8	3.5	4.3	2.4	1.6	1.9	1.2	1.4	1.6	1.1	3.7	4.6	2.5	2.8	2.2	4.1	2.7	1.9	4.3	3.2	3.7	1.8
West Virginia	.6	.7	.6	.7	.7	.7	0.0	0.0	0.0	.7	.7	.6	.8	.8	.7	0.0	0.0	0.0	.5	.6	.4	.6	.6	.4	0.0	0.0	0.0
North Carolina	2.8	2.5	3.1	2.3	2.2	2.5	6.6	5.3	8.6	2.8	2.5	3.2	2.4	2.2	2.5	6.9	5.0	9.5	2.7	2.6	2.8	2.3	2.1	2.5	5.8	5.9	5.5
South Carolina	1.2	1.1	1.4	1.0	1.0	1.0	3.5	2.8	4.7	1.2	1.1	1.3	.9	.9	1.0	3.7	3.4	4.0	1.3	1.1	1.7	1.1	1.1	1.0	3.2	1.5	7.3
Georgia	2.5	2.4	2.7	2.2	1.9	2.6	5.2	6.1	3.9	2.4	2.2	2.6	2.1	1.8	2.5	4.8	5.7	3.5	2.9	2.9	2.9	2.5	2.4	2.7	6.3	6.7	5.5
Florida	2.9	2.8	3.0	2.5	2.4	2.7	5.8	5.6	6.3	2.8	2.7	2.8	2.4	2.5	2.3	6.1		7.5	3.2	2.9	3.9	3.0	2.4	4.1	5.3	6.7	1.8
East South Central	5.6	5.4	6.0	5.3	4.9	5.9	8.4	9.8	6.3	5.8	5.6	6.0	5.4	5.1	5.9	8.9	10.7	6.5	5.3	5.0	5.9	5.0	4.5	5.9	7.4	8.1	5.5
Alabama	1.5	1.4	1.8	1.4	1.2	1.7	2.3	2.5	2.0	1.5	1.3	1.7	1.5	1.3	1.8	1.5	1.9	1.0	1.6	1.4	2.0	1.3	1.1	1.6	4.2	3.7	5.5
Mississippi	.8	.9	.6	.6	.6	.5	2.5	3.0	1.6	.7	.8	.6	.5	.5	.4	2.8	3.4	2.0	.9	1.1	.6	.8	1.0	.6	1.6	2.2	0.0
Tennessee	1.9	1.8	2.1	1.9	1.8	2.1	2.3	2.3	2.4	2.2	2.1	2.3	2.1	2.0	2.3	2.8	2.7	3.0	1.2	1.2	1.3	1.3	1.2	1.4	1.1	1.5	0.0
Kentucky	1.4	1.4	1.5	1.4	1.3	1.6	1.4	2.0	.4	1.4	1.4	1.4	1.4	1.3	1.5	1.7	2.7	.5	1.5	1.2	2.0	1.6	1.3	2.3	.5	.7	0.0
West South Central	7.8	7.9	7.6	7.7	7.8	7.5	8.3	8.6	7.8	7.6	7.5	7.8	7.6	7.5	7.8	7.6	7.3	8.0	6.8	9.0	8.7	8.0	6.7	6.7	10.0	11.1	7.3
Arkansas	.6	.5	.8	.7	.6	.8	.1	.3	.4	.7	.6	.9	.8	.6	.9	.4	.4	.5	.5	.4	.4	.4	.4	1.4	0.0	0.0	0.0
Louisiana	1.2	1.4	.9	1.0	1.1	.8	2.9	3.5	2.0	1.0	1.3	.7	.9	1.1	.6	2.4	3.1	1.5	1.6	1.5	1.7	1.2	1.1	1.2	4.2	4.4	3.6
Oklahoma	1.0	.9	1.2	1.2	1.0	1.3	0.0	0.0	0.0	1.0	.9	1.2	1.2	1.0	1.4	0.0	0.0	0.0	1.0	.9	1.1	1.1	1.1		0.0	0.0	0.0
Texas	4.9	5.1	4.7	4.9	5.1	4.6	5.1	4.8	5.5	4.8	4.6	5.0	4.8	4.7	4.8	4.8	3.8	6.0	5.3	6.2	3.7	5.3	6.1	3.7	5.8	6.7	3.6
Mountain	3.6	3.8	3.3	3.9	4.1	3.6	.6	1.0	.4	3.3	3.4	3.1	3.6	3.7	3.4	.4	.8	0.0	4.5	4.7	4.1	4.9	5.1	4.3	1.6	1.5	1.8
Montana	.3	.3	.4	.4	.4	.4	0.0	0.0	0.0	.3	.2	.3	.3	.2	.4	0.0	0.0	0.0	.6	.6	.6	.7	.8	.6	0.0	0.0	0.0
Wyoming	.2	.1	.2	.2	.1	.3	0.0	0.0	0.0	.2	.1	.3	.2	.1	.3	0.0	0.0	0.0	.1	.2	0.0	.8	.2	0.0	0.0	0.0	0.0
Colorado	.8	.7	1.0	.9	.8	1.0	.1	0.0	.4	.8	.7	.8	.8	.8	.9	0.0	0.0	0.0	1.1	.7	1.7	1.1	.9	1.6	.5	0.0	1.8
New Mexico	.3	.4	.2	.4	.4	.3	0.0	0.0	0.0	.3	.4	.3	.4	.4	.3	0.0	0.0	0.0	.3	.5	0.0	.4	.5	0.0	0.0	0.0	0.0
Arizona	.8	1.0	.7	.9	1.0	.7	.3	.5	0.0	.9	1.0	.8	.9	1.0	.2	.4	.8	0.0	.7	.8	.4	.8	1.0	.4	0.0	0.0	0.0
Utah	.5	.6	.3	.5	.7	.3	.1	.3	0.0	.4	.5	.1	.5	.5	.4	0.0	0.0	0.0	.7	1.0	.2	.8	1.1	.2	.5	0.0	0.0
Nevada	.2	.2	.2	.3	.3	.3	0.0	.3	0.0	.2	.2	.1	.2	.3	.1	0.0	0.0	0.0	.3	.6	.7	.4	.1	.8	0.0	0.0	0.0
Idaho	.3	.3	.2	.3	.4	.3	.1	.3	0.0	.2	.3	.2	.2	.2	.2	0.0	0.0	0.0	.6	.6	.6	.6	.6	.6	.5	.7	0.0
Pacific	11.7	12.4	10.7	12.5	13.2	11.4	4.9	5.6	3.9	11.7	12.2	11.0	12.3	12.8	11.7	5.9	6.9	4.5	11.7	12.9	9.4	12.9	14.4	10.2	2.6	3.0	1.8
Washington	1.4	1.4	1.2	1.5	1.6	1.4	.1	.3	3.9	1.4	1.5	1.3	1.6	1.6	1.4	.2	.4	0.0	1.2	1.2	1.1	1.3	1.4	1.2	0.0	0.0	0.0
Oregon	1.2	1.4	1.1	1.4	1.5	1.2	0.0	0.0	0.0	1.1	1.1	1.1	1.3	1.3	1.3	0.0	0.0	0.0	1.5	1.9	.7	1.7	2.1	.8	0.0	0.0	0.0
California	9.1	9.6	8.4	9.6	10.1	8.8	4.8	5.3	3.9	9.1	9.5	8.6	9.5	9.9	9.0	5.6	6.5	4.5	9.1	9.8	7.6	9.9	10.8	8.2	2.6	3.0	1.8

TABLE 4.11
Coverage Ratio of the Sample to the Population by Geographic Area

Geographic area	Coverage ratio[a]	Geographic area	Coverage ratio[a]
Contiguous United States	1.00	*South Atlantic (cont.)*	
New England	*1.08*	Virginia	.83
Maine	1.00	West Virginia	.67
New Hampshire	.75	North Carolina	1.12
Vermont	1.50	South Carolina	.92
Massachusetts	1.11	Georgia	1.09
Connecticut	1.20	Florida	1.26
Rhode Island	1.00	*East South Central*	*.89*
Middle Atlantic	*1.19*	Alabama	.88
New York	1.27	Mississippi	.73
Pennsylvania	1.16	Tennessee	1.00
New Jersey	1.06	Kentucky	.88
East North Central	*1.08*	*West South Central*	*.82*
Ohio	1.02	Arkansas	.67
Michigan	1.09	Louisiana	.67
Indiana	1.08	Oklahoma	.77
Illinois	1.07	Texas	.89
Wisconsin	1.14	*Mountain*	*.88*
West North Central	*.93*	Montana	1.00
Missouri	1.00	Wyoming	1.00
Iowa	1.07	Colorado	.73
Minnesota	.84	New Mexico	.60
North Dakota	.67	Arizona	.89
South Dakota	1.00	Utah	1.00
Nebraska	1.00	Nevada	1.00
Kansas	.82	Idaho	.75
South Atlantic	*.95*	*Pacific*	*.89*
Delaware	1.00	Washington	1.00
Maryland	.84	Oregon	.82
District of Columbia	1.25	California	1.20

[a] The coverage ratio for each area is the fraction of potential migrants in the sample relative to the fraction of the total census

section, in that the propensities are considered by different characteristics of potential migrants—demographic, economic, mobility, and regional.

DEMOGRAPHIC PROPENSITIES

The migration rates of those in the sample are presented by sex, race, and age in Table 4.12. Overall, the sample migration rate is 25%, and there are some general mobility patterns among demographic groups. Blacks have a slightly higher tendency to move than whites, the mobility rates of males are higher than those for females, and mobility declines with age.

Race and Sex. The first pattern, that of blacks being more mobile than whites, holds for each age group, but in the aggregate it masks underlying differences. On the whole, black males are more mobile than white males, whereas the patterns by race for females are roughly the same. The race pattern for males holds for ages up to 55 years; in the ages beyond 55, white males have greater mobility rates than black males.

For females, the similarity in the migration rates of whites and blacks is primarily due to offsetting mobility rates of different age groups. Black females aged 21 to 30 years are more mobile than white females (35% of black females in the sample are aged 21 to 30; only 25% of white females are in those ages). For all other age groups, except the 55-or-older group, white females are more mobile than black females. On the whole, white

TABLE 4.12
Migration Rates by Age, by Sex and Race

	Migrants as a percentage of the total								
				Race					
		Sex		White			Black		
Age (years)	Total	Male	Female	Total	Male	Female	Total	Male	Female
Total persons	25.5	28.4	21.2	25.0	27.7	21.2	29.2	34.1	21.6
20 or less	39.1	46.1	32.3	38.7	43.3	33.6	42.3	57.1	20.7
21 to 25	39.8	37.1	33.2	39.4	47.1	32.7	42.3	48.1	36.5
26 to 30	32.5	33.8	30.2	32.5	34.2	29.1	32.9	29.7	35.9
31 to 35	29.7	34.2	20.8	28.8	32.0	21.9	36.4	52.3	15.2
36 to 40	23.9	28.0	16.9	22.8	26.5	16.9	32.4	38.0	16.7
41 to 45	20.8	24.5	15.1	20.7	23.8	15.9	22.6	32.4	4.8
46 to 50	16.9	19.8	12.9	17.2	19.6	13.8	14.0	21.9	4.0
51 to 55	18.8	20.7	15.8	18.7	20.3	16.0	20.3	23.8	13.6
56 to 60	10.7	12.5	8.0	10.8	13.0	7.7	9.8	8.6	16.7
61 to 65	12.3	14.8	7.9	12.3	15.2	7.3	12.5	8.3	25.0
66 or more	9.0	7.9	11.0	9.0	8.1	10.5	9.1	6.3	16.7

females, except for those in their twenties, are more mobile than black females.

That females move less than males is consistent with previous findings and with the general observation that labor market experiences differ between the two groups.[9] Females are likely to have different perspectives on migration than males due to acclimatization to different social roles in the culture and to different economic roles in the household. That their behavior is different is expected. An insight into the relatively low migration propensity of women is provided by the so-called crowding hypothesis.[10] Essentially, the scope of jobs open to women is restricted, and since the opportunities elsewhere are less different for women than for men, women might be less likely to move than men.

The finding that black males have a greater propensity to migrate than white males and that the black–white differential for females is unsubstantial has some consistency with previous work. The consistency apparently depends upon the type of mobility studied in that our finding is consistent with studies of job mobility, but is inconsistent with findings on geographic mobility.[11] Since the mobility measure here is job migration instead of either job turnover or residence migration, the observed propensity reflects both kinds of mobility. The effect of job turnover apparently dominates.

The black–white differential in the propensity to migrate may reflect, in part, the effect of discrimination in labor markets. Through discriminatory practices, economic opportunities and securities of whites are enhanced by low opportunities and securities for blacks.[12] Specific traditional practices include the restriction of blacks to nondesirable promotion ladders. Blacks tend, more than whites, to be hired in jobs where there is little specific training. Consequently, little nontransferable human capital accumulates, and the separation costs incurred by migrating are relatively low. Also, blacks tend, more than whites, to be employed in temporary labor pools and in entry-level positions of job ladders. Persons in these positions are the first to be laid off, and migration is more likely to occur if one has just been laid off than otherwise. When separation costs and involuntary job changes are considered, blacks might well be expected to have a greater tendency to migrate than whites.

---

[9] The specific mobility differential noted here is supported by other work; see Parnes (1970, p. 46). A discussion of how labor market experiences vary is provided by Kahne (1975).

[10] Women are crowded into certain occupations by men, which results in low marginal productivity for female work and consequently in low wages (Kahne, 1975, p. 1257).

[11] See Parnes (1970, pp. 46, 47).

[12] See Doeringer and Piore (1971, Chapter 7).

Age. With respect to age, the most mobile group is aged 21 to 25 years, and the least mobile is aged 66 or more years. Among the race–sex groups, there are some exceptions, but for each case declining mobility with increased age is the rule. Most notable is the high mobility of young black males; the migration rate of black males under 20 years of age is 57%, over twice the sample average.

The pattern of declining mobility rates with age is well documented.[13] The young and those in their twenties are typically in the midst of major adjustments in both their life-cycle and their work history. Many are breaking old family ties and starting new ones, finishing educational commitments, and searching for preferred jobs. Also, the benefits from moving persist longer for the young than for others, which provides them with greater incentives to move. It is therefore no surprise that the young are the most mobile.

ECONOMIC PROPENSITIES

As portrayed in Table 4.13, the migration rates vary with respect to the income of potential migrants in a reverse J-shaped pattern. Mobility rates are highest among those with low incomes, and the rates generally fall as incomes rise. Declining mobility is the rule up to the highest levels of income, where mobility rates rise.

For potential migrants in the same income group, there are differences in mobility for different race–sex groups. In particular, males have higher mobility rates than females. And in the low income levels black males are more mobile than white males, while at income levels about $3000, the mobility rates for white males consistently exceed those for black males. White and black females have roughly the same mobility rates.

The general reverse J-shaped pattern may represent two opposite effects of income. Since potential migrants with little income may value a gain in income from a move more highly than persons with high incomes, the likelihood of moving in response to a given income differential may fall as incomes rise. On the other hand, since migration disrupts social contexts, high incomes might be a reward for the migratory demands of certain jobs. Migration might be a necessary characteristic of a job and workers might receive high incomes as compensation for migratory disruptions. Thus, the migration rates might be higher at high levels of income because higher incomes accrue to those willing to migrate.

MOBILITY PROPENSITIES

Since three of the mobility characteristics—job tenure, industrial tenure, and length of residency—are fundamentally related, the mobility

---

[13] See Parnes (1970, p. 45).

TABLE 4.13
Migration Rates by Income, by Sex and Race

	Migrants as a percentage of the total								
				Race					
		Sex		White			Black		
Income	Total	Male	Female	Total	Male	Female	Total	Male	Female
Total persons	25.5	28.4	21.2	25.0	27.7	21.2	29.2	34.1	21.6
$999 or less	32.7	37.3	29.9	33.2	37.5	30.9	29.1	36.4	18.2
$1,000 to $1,999	34.0	45.6	25.3	33.3	43.2	25.9	38.6	61.1	21.3
$2,000 to $2,999	29.3	36.6	25.0	28.1	34.8	24.4	35.3	43.5	28.6
$3,000 to $3,999	28.6	38.7	23.5	28.7	39.7	23.4	28.4	34.8	23.2
$4,000 to $4,999	28.2	37.3	21.4	27.5	38.2	20.9	32.2	33.9	28.6
$5,000 to $5,999	21.4	31.0	10.9	21.2	31.1	10.7	22.6	29.7	12.0
$6,000 to $6,999	22.8	27.1	14.4	22.5	27.4	13.8	25.5	25.0	28.6
$7,000 to $7,999	18.5	21.1	8.8	18.7	21.5	8.7	15.6	17.1	10.0
$8,000 to $8,999	21.3	22.3	16.4	21.0	21.9	16.7	25.0	25.9	0.0
$9,000 to $9,999	22.7	23.9	11.1	23.0	24.0	12.5	17.6	21.4	0.0
$10,000 to $10,999	23.6	25.0	0.0	23.7	25.2	0.0	20.0	20.0	—
$11,000 to $11,999	64.4	63.6	100.0	62.8	61.9	100.0	100.0	100.0	—
$12,000 to $12,999	48.1	48.1	—	46.2	46.2	—	100.0	100.0	—
$13,000 to $13,999	8.8	9.1	0.0	9.1	9.4	0.0	0.0	0.0	—
$14,000 to $14,999	19.5	21.2	0.0	19.2	20.9	0.0	33.3	33.3	—
$15,000 to $15,999	17.8	18.4	0.0	17.0	17.6	0.0	50.0	50.0	—
$16,000 to $16,999	15.4	15.7	0.0	14.6	14.9	0.0	50.0	50.0	—
$17,000 to $17,999	10.4	10.8	0.0	10.9	11.3	0.0	0.0	0.0	—
$18,000 to $18,999	10.3	11.5	0.0	10.5	11.8	0.0	0.0	0.0	—
$19,000 to $19,999	26.3	26.3	—	26.3	26.3	—	—	—	—
$20,000 or more	15.5	15.5	16.7	15.5	15.5	16.7	—	—	—

patterns for these variables are similar and are portrayed in Tables 4.14, 4.15, and 4.16. The pattern of mobility by job turnover is shown in Table 4.17.

Job Tenure. As job tenure increases, mobility generally declines (Table 14.4). (The major exception to this is for those with 11 years of tenure. However, only 77 potential migrants, 1.2% of the sample, are in this category, and this sample group may be less than representative of the population with 11 years of tenure.)[14] Indeed, after one has been on the job for at least 4 years, the chance of migrating is only about one-fourth of that for

[14] The pattern observed here is consistent with the findings of work relating tenure to turnover in other countries. See Hunter and Reid (1968, pp. 102, 103).

TABLE 4.14
Migration Rates by Job Tenure, by Sex and Race

	Migrants as a percentage of the total								
				Race					
		Sex		White			Black		
Job tenure (years)	Total	Male	Female	Total	Male	Female	Total	Male	Female
Total persons	25.5	28.4	21.2	25.0	27.7	21.2	29.2	34.1	21.6
0	54.7	57.4	50.0	54.6	56.9	50.7	55.4	60.6	44.6
1	12.7	14.3	11.0	12.7	14.4	10.9	13.2	13.9	12.3
2	7.2	8.4	5.9	13.0	8.7	5.0	9.7	5.7	14.8
3	9.5	9.8	9.2	10.1	10.0	10.2	2.9	7.1	0.0
4	6.9	7.9	6.5	6.0	6.1	5.8	17.1	22.2	11.8
5	5.6	8.3	2.4	5.8	8.1	2.5	7.1	10.0	0.0
6	7.8	10.0	5.2	7.7	10.7	4.2	8.3	0.0	16.7
7	5.4	7.1	2.9	4.5	5.5	3.2	15.4	28.6	0.0
8	6.9	10.0	2.9	6.5	9.0	3.1	16.7	50.0	0.0
9	4.0	4.3	3.4	4.2	4.5	3.6	0.0	0.0	0.0
10	5.7	8.6	0.0	6.3	9.4	0.0	0.0	0.0	0.0
11	23.4	25.9	15.8	24.0	25.9	17.6	0.0	0.0	0.0
12 or more	0.8	1.1	0.0	0.8	1.2	0.0	0.0	0.0	0.0

TABLE 4.15
Migration Rates by Industrial Tenure, by Sex and Race

	Migrants as a percentage of the total								
				Race					
		Sex		White			Black		
Industrial tenure (years)	Total	Male	Female	Total	Male	Female	Total	Male	Female
Total persons	25.5	28.4	21.2	25.0	27.7	21.2	29.2	34.1	21.6
0	100.0	100.0	99.1	100.0	100.0	100.0	97.7	100.0	88.9
1	34.3	37.8	28.7	34.2	37.3	29.3	35.3	42.1	23.9
2	17.7	19.5	15.4	17.3	20.1	13.8	20.3	15.2	27.3
3	11.6	11.6	11.5	11.3	11.5	11.0	13.7	12.5	14.8
4	14.3	15.6	12.8	14.0	14.3	13.7	16.3	25.0	5.3
5	9.0	8.0	10.2	8.0	7.3	9.0	19.0	25.0	23.1
6	13.8	15.8	11.6	12.9	16.5	9.2	22.2	10.0	37.5
7	8.1	11.4	4.1	8.2	11.3	4.5	6.7	12.5	0.0
8	9.3	13.0	4.3	8.7	11.8	4.6	18.2	25.0	0.0
9	7.4	10.7	3.8	7.2	10.3	4.1	9.1	16.7	0.0
10	7.0	8.5	5.3	7.8	9.4	5.8	0.0	0.0	0.0
11	22.9	23.2	22.5	23.5	23.1	24.3	14.3	25.0	33.3
12 or more	3.2	3.5	2.7	3.3	3.8	2.4	2.1	0.0	7.7

TABLE 4.16
Migration Rates by Length of Residency, by Sex and Race

	Migrants as a percentage of the total								
				Race					
		Sex		White			Black		
Length of residency (years)	Total	Male	Female	Total	Male	Female	Total	Male	Female
Total persons	25.5	28.4	21.2	25.0	27.7	21.2	29.2	34.1	21.6
0	99.7	100.0	99.2	100.0	100.0	100.0	97.7	100.0	85.7
1	60.5	65.2	52.7	60.7	65.1	53.3	58.9	65.7	48.5
2	16.4	18.0	13.7	15.6	17.4	12.8	22.1	22.0	22.2
3	12.9	14.0	11.5	13.5	14.4	12.2	7.7	9.1	6.7
4	12.7	15.0	10.3	12.2	14.9	8.9	14.9	15.0	14.8
5	16.3	19.0	12.8	15.9	18.6	12.4	25.6	23.1	29.4
6	2.6	2.9	2.1	2.4	2.5	2.2	5.0	6.8	1.6
7	2.7	4.0	2.0	3.1	4.8	2.3	0.0	0.0	0.0
8	4.8	8.3	3.3	5.4	11.1	3.6	0.0	0.0	0.0
9	0.0	0.0	0.0	0.0	0.0	0.0	0.0	0.0	0.0
10	6.1	0.0	6.9	7.1	0.0	8.0	0.0	0.0	0.0
11	18.2	0.0	23.5	19.0	0.0	23.5	0.0	0.0	0.0
12 or more	4.3	0.0	5.9	5.3	0.0	6.7	0.0	0.0	0.0

TABLE 4.17
Migration Rates by Job Turnover, by Sex and Race

	Migrants as a percentage of the total								
				Race					
		Sex		White			Black		
Job turnover (jobs per year)	Total	Male	Female	Total	Male	Female	Total	Male	Female
Total persons	25.5	28.4	21.2	25.0	27.7	21.2	29.2	34.1	21.6
1.00 or less	6.5	6.6	6.4	6.4	6.3	6.5	7.4	10.2	4.8
1.01 to 1.50	20.2	21.5	18.5	19.8	21.1	18.3	23.7	26.6	20.5
1.51 to 2.00	33.7	33.6	33.8	34.2	34.3	34.0	29.8	28.0	32.8
2.01 to 2.50	50.6	50.6	50.8	50.4	50.3	50.4	52.5	52.2	53.8
2.51 to 3.00	59.7	58.7	63.3	60.1	58.1	65.9	58.1	60.5	40.0
3.01 to 3.50	62.7	65.4	52.4	63.2	50.6	55.0	60.0	64.3	0.0
3.51 or more	68.1	71.2	50.0	69.6	69.6	52.9	61.5	65.2	33.3

the sample as a whole. For those with tenure of 12 or more years, the migration propensity is a mere 4% of the sample average.

At all levels of job tenure, males are more mobile than females. And mobility rates for blacks are generally greater than those for whites. On the whole, black males are more mobile than white males, primarily because of high concentrations of black males at the lowest levels of tenure, where mobility is greatest. In the case of females, whites with no job tenure are more likely to migrate than blacks. Black females are consistently more mobile than whites at levels of tenure other than that of no job tenure, in which case white females are more mobile.

Industrial Tenure. The general pattern of mobility by industrial tenure is the same as that of job tenure. However, as Table 4.15 shows, the levels of the migration rates differ. Potential migrants with any given amount of industrial tenure are more mobile than those with the same amount of job tenure. This holds consistently for each of the race–sex groups. Nonetheless, the mobility patterns by industrial tenure are otherwise similar to those in the case of job tenure for the race–sex groups. In particular, white females are more mobile than black females at the lowest levels of industrial tenure; black females are more mobile at the higher levels. And black males are more mobile than white males.

Length of Residency. As Table 4.16 shows, the general pattern of mobility by length of residency is, again, like that by job tenure. Mobility declines as residency increases. However, migration rates for potential migrants with 5 years of residency or less exceed those associated with 5 years of job tenure or less by a wide margin and are, on average, above those of industrial tenure. The reverse pattern characterizes higher levels of tenure, 6 years or more. For the race–sex groups, the mobility patterns by length of residency are similar to those by job tenure and industrial tenure. For females, whites are more mobile at the lowest levels of length of residency, whereas blacks are more mobile at the higher levels. Also, black males have higher overall mobility than white males, mainly because of the relatively short length of residency blacks hold as a group.

The general pattern of declining mobility as length of residency increases was expected. The greater the stay at the origin, the greater the psychic costs incurred by migrating and, subsequently, the lower the mobility. Similarly, as job tenure and industrial tenure accumulate, the separation costs incurred by migrating increase and the propensity to migrate would be expected to decline.

Since the three variables—length of residency, job tenure, and industrial tenure—are related, one would also expect to observe consistent patterns among the mobility rates. The key to the difference in mobility patterns by residency versus job tenure is that a job change need not imply a migration, but a job change generally coincides with migration. That is, giving up one's job tenure does not generally entail being uprooted from one's residency, but giving up one's residency does generally require losing job tenure as well. For any given number of years, say 5, for both job tenure and length of residency, chances are that those with 5 years of job tenure would have at least that long of a stay at the origin, whereas those with 5 years of residency would have at most 5 years of job tenure. Thus, the migration rate for those with 5 years of job tenure would tend to be lower than that for those with 5 years of residency.

A similar pattern is expected to characterize mobility rates by job tenure versus industrial tenure. While a migrant tends to lose job tenure, he need not also lose industrial tenure. If a migrant is able to obtain employment at the destination in the same industry of his origin employment, he might not lose industry or craft tenure, nor would he lose the value of his industry-specific skills. Considering job versus industrial tenure, the industrial tenure is more inclusive. That is, potential migrants with any level of job tenure have at least that much industrial tenure. At any level of tenure, the difference between the number of potential migrants having that amount of job tenure and the number having the same level of industrial tenure is attributable to those who have changed jobs but remained in the same industry. For this last group—job changers in the same industry—separation costs from the job are likely to be less than those for job changers who also change their industry. Thus, when job changers in the same industry migrate, only psychic costs associated with the uprooting of one's residency tend to be incurred, provided the migrants are employed in a job of their industry at the destination. It is expected, then, that those with a high level of industrial tenure would be more inclined to migrate than those with the same level of job tenure because of the differential in separation costs. That migration rates by industrial tenure exceed those by job tenure for given levels of tenure is therefore no surprise.

The pattern of mobility rates by industrial tenure versus length of residency is more difficult to assess a priori. Migrants can change their place of residency without changing their industry of employment, and they can change their industry without changing their residency. Thus, it is difficult to judge whether the separation and psychic costs of moving are greater for those with a given level of industrial tenure or for those with the same length of stay at the origin. Notice that Tables 4.15 and 4.16 suggest that the migration rates by the two characteristics are fairly similar.

Job Turnover. The general pattern of mobility by job turnover (Table 4.17) is that mobility increases steadily with job turnover. Indeed, those with an average of three and one-half or more jobs per year have a propensity to migrate 10 times that for those with only one job per year. The general pattern of steadily increasing mobility holds for males of each race. For females, however, peak migration rates occur for those with two to three jobs per year; mobility declines as turnover increases further. This inverted-U pattern holds for females of each race. For the race groups, the most notable difference in the mobility patterns is that between white and black males with low turnover rates. Black males are much more mobile than white males. At higher turnover rates, mobility for the two groups is roughly the same.[15]

That mobility increases with the frequency of job turnover is not surprising. Potential migrants with more experience in turnover are simply more apt to migrate. A worker is more inclined to be seeking a job elsewhere, if he has been frequently dismissed from employment or if he has few sanctions against changing his work environment. As turnover increases due to either voluntary or involuntary causes, it understandably follows that migration increases.[15]

REGIONAL PROPENSITIES

Migration rates by census divisions and states are portrayed in Table 4.18. Regional differences in mobility are, as a rule, not substantial. Nonetheless, areas in the North Central and the Northeast regions generally have mobility rates slightly below average. Potential migrants in the South and the West are slightly more mobile than average. Among the states, there are some notable propensities to migrate. Idaho, Montana, and the District of Columbia have migration rates roughly twice the average. Arkansas, Tennessee, Minnesota, Iowa, and Wyoming, on the other hand, have relative low migration propensities.

The mobility differentials between the race–sex groups noted above generally characterize geographic patterns as well. Males are more mobile than females and blacks more mobile than whites in most states. Black males typically have greater mobility rates than white males. And except for certain states in the Northeast, white females are more mobile than black females.

[15] While there is no previous empirical work assessing this particular variable, work that has found that migration rates for an area are directly related to previous gross migration in an area is consistent with the observed relation here (see Chapter 2).

TABLE 4.18
Migration Rates by State, by Sex and Race

	Geographic total		Sex		White			Black		
		Total	Male	Female	Total	Male	Female	Total	Male	Female
Contiguous United States		25.5	28.4	21.2	25.0	27.7	21.2	29.2	34.1	21.6
New England		*26.0*	*29.2*	*21.9*	*25.6*	*29.0*	*21.2*	*35.3*	*33.3*	*37.5*
Maine		33.3	44.4	16.6	34.5	14.4	18.2	0.0	—	0.0
New Hampshire		30.0	20.0	40.0	30.0	20.0	40.0	—	—	—
Vermont		23.5	42.9	10.0	23.5	42.9	10.0	—	—	—
Massachusetts		26.2	27.6	24.4	25.4	27.7	22.7	50.0	25.0	100.0
Connecticut		19.6	21.5	17.0	19.4	21.3	16.7	22.2	25.0	20.0
Rhode Island		40.0	47.6	22.2	37.9	45.0	22.2	100.0	100.0	—
Middle Atlantic		*25.0*	*28.0*	*20.6*	*23.9*	*26.9*	*19.6*	*34.3*	*37.5*	*29.8*
New York		25.4	28.7	21.0	23.7	27.1	19.1	37.9	42.2	33.3
Pennsylvania		21.1	23.5	17.4	21.6	24.6	17.2	13.8	10.5	20.0
New Jersey		30.4	33.8	25.3	28.8	31.0	25.6	47.6	56.3	20.0
East North Central		*22.9*	*25.4*	*18.8*	*23.2*	*25.4*	*19.6*	*20.3*	*25.9*	*11.5*
Ohio		24.0	26.2	19.6	23.7	26.2	18.6	27.6	26.3	30.0
Michigan		25.5	28.1	19.8	25.8	27.3	22.6	22.9	34.8	0.0
Indiana		19.7	23.2	15.2	19.2	23.7	13.5	27.3	16.7	40.0
Illinois		20.7	23.4	17.1	21.9	23.8	19.4	13.2	20.7	4.2
Wisconsin		24.5	24.7	24.2	24.7	24.7	24.6	20.0	25.0	0.0
West North Central		*23.8*	*26.3*	*20.7*	*22.8*	*24.5*	*20.8*	*47.4*	*61.5*	*16.7*
Missouri		29.2	31.6	26.2	28.4	29.2	27.4	40.0	57.1	0.0
Iowa		18.3	23.1	12.2	18.7	23.5	12.5	0.0	0.0	0.0
Minnesota		17.0	21.0	10.5	16.2	19.7	10.5	100.0	100.0	—
North Dakota		30.8	33.3	25.0	30.8	33.3	25.0	—	—	—
South Dakota		31.6	33.3	30.0	31.6	33.3	30.0	—	—	—
Nebraska		27.9	31.8	23.8	28.6	31.8	25.0	0.0	—	0.0
Kansas		24.1	20.7	27.6	18.9	12.0	25.0	80.0	75.0	100.0
South Atlantic		*28.7*	*30.2*	*25.0*	*28.3*	*28.5*	*25.7*	*30.2*	*36.0*	*22.4*
Delaware		33.3	25.0	50.0	21.4	20.0	25.0	75.0	50.0	100.0
Maryland		22.1	22.8	21.3	20.0	18.2	22.2	29.2	38.5	18.2
District of Columbia		48.5	50.0	47.1	47.8	50.0	45.5	50.0	50.0	50.0
Virginia		37.5	31.5	46.8	40.2	32.1	51.2	26.1	29.4	16.7
West Virginia		20.0	24.0	13.3	20.0	24.0	13.3	—	—	—
North Carolina		24.6	29.5	18.8	24.2	27.0	20.7	25.6	38.1	13.6
South Carolina		26.9	27.9	25.7	27.3	31.3	21.7	26.1	18.2	33.3
Georgia		29.7	34.8	23.2	28.2	33.8	22.0	35.3	37.5	30.0
Florida		28.6	29.8	26.9	29.2	26.8	32.3	26.3	40.9	6.3
East South Central		*23.8*	*26.0*	*20.9*	*23.5*	*25.5*	*21.2*	*25.5*	*28.2*	*18.8*
Alabama		27.1	29.4	24.4	22.2	24.4	20.0	53.3	50.0	60.0
Mississippi		31.3	36.4	20.0	37.5	42.9	27.3	18.8	25.0	0.0
Tennessee		16.3	18.8	13.0	16.7	18.3	14.6	13.3	22.2	0.0
Kentucky		26.7	25.5	28.2	28.4	27.9	28.9	11.1	12.5	0.0

TABLE 4.18 (continued)

Migrants as a percentage of the total

Geographic total	Total	Sex		White			Black		
		Male	Female	Total	Male	Female	Total	Male	Female
West South Central	*27.1*	*32.3*	*19.1*	*26.1*	*30.8*	*19.0*	*35.2*	*44.1*	*20.0*
Arkansas	15.0	20.0	10.0	15.8	21.1	10.5	0.0	0.0	0.0
Louisiana	33.8	31.4	39.1	30.9	27.0	38.9	42.1	42.9	40.0
Oklahoma	24.2	28.6	19.4	24.2	28.6	19.4	—	—	—
Texas	27.7	34.6	16.7	27.3	33.1	17.0	33.3	47.4	14.3
Mountain	*31.9*	*35.2*	*26.2*	*31.2*	*34.8*	*25.3*	*75.0*	*50.0*	*100.0*
Montana	45.5	58.3	30.0	45.5	58.3	30.0	—	—	—
Wyoming	18.2	40.0	0.0	18.2	40.0	0.0	—	—	—
Colorado	32.1	28.6	36.0	30.8	28.6	33.3	100.0	—	100.0
New Mexico	23.8	33.3	0.0	23.8	33.3	0.0	—	—	—
Arizona	20.8	25.0	11.8	21.6	26.5	11.8	0.0	0.0	—
Utah	37.5	45.8	12.5	35.5	43.5	12.5	100.0	100.0	—
Nevada	33.3	11.1	66.6	33.3	11.1	66.6	—	—	—
Idaho	52.6	53.8	50.0	50.0	50.0	50.0	100.0	100.0	—
Pacific	*25.5*	*29.6*	*18.7*	*26.0*	*30.1*	*19.0*	*15.6*	*18.2*	*10.0*
Washington	22.1	24.1	18.8	22.4	24.5	18.8	0.0	0.0	—
Oregon	30.8	39.2	14.8	30.8	39.2	14.8	—	—	—
California	25.3	29.0	19.2	25.9	29.6	19.6	16.1	19.0	10.0

SUMMARY

The next two chapters discuss our empirical investigation of the migration model developed in Chapter 3. This chapter serves as the link between the model development and the empirical work by describing the data used in the study and the procedures employed to assemble them functionally. Additionally, this chapter explored the sample of potential migrants by examining its demographic, economic, mobility, and geographic characteristics. Mobility patterns by the same salient characteristics were also assessed. The observed patterns were, for the most part, consistent with expectations concerning how the personal characteristics would influence the decision to migrate.

5

Empirical Specification
and Results

In Chapter 3 an economic theory of migratory choice was developed that identified possibly important factors in a worker's decision to migrate, and an empirical model estimable at a disaggregate level was considered for use in evaluating the theory. The data used in the empirical work and the aggregate characteristics of the sample were described in Chapter 4. The purpose of this chapter is essentially twofold: to detail the empirical specification of the potential migrant's expected group utility and to discuss the results of estimating the model (3.20).

EMPIRICAL SPECIFICATION

We first discuss how personal attributes are specified so that they vary over alternatives, as do the separation costs of migration. Second, the variables used to measure the personal attributes, place attributes, and variances associated with place attributes are specified, along with a discussion of how these variables might affect the potential migrant's expected utility. A third concern is the use of counties as the choice alternatives, since they are possibly aggregates of the true alternatives. Under mildly restrictive conditions the estimates obtained using aggregate alternatives are those obtained using the true alternatives.

PERSONAL ATTRIBUTES, NONGENERIC VARIABLES, AND SEPARATION COSTS

Since the values of personal attributes such as sex do not vary over alternatives, they are not of the genre of the alternatives. Such variables have been termed *nongeneric*, and they must be carefully specified in order to make any empirical influence observable.[1] In particular, we specify the personal attributes so as to have alternative-specific values. That is, they assume their values for a specific alternative, in particular the origin, and take upon zero values for the other alternatives (this is analogous to a dummy slope variable in regression analysis). The estimated coefficients of variables so specified are then considered as effects upon the origin utility.

In Chapter 3 the personal attributes S_{nj}—job turnover, job tenure, length of residency, race, and age—were defined to be origin specific. This was because they were identified to be related to separation costs of migration that vary between the origin and each destination but not between destination alternatives. This specification also permits the empirical effects of personal attributes to be discerned from those of place attributes.

VARIABLES AFFECTING EXPECTED GROUP UTILITY

Three sets of variables were identified in Chapter 3 as relevant in the migration decision: personal attributes of potential migrants, expected values of place attributes, and the variance associated with place attributes. Table 5.1 is a summary list of the variables used in our analysis. Each measure is discussed in turn in the following.

[1] A more complete discussion of generic and nongeneric variables is provided by Domencich and McFadden (1975). It is easily seen that without careful specification the influence of nongeneric variables is not identifiable. Recalling (3.18) and letting $v_{ni} = \boldsymbol{\theta}'\mathbf{z}_{ni}$ for convenience, since v is linear in parameters, the selection probability of alternative i by the nth potential migrant is

$$P_{ni} = \frac{\exp\left(\sum_{k=1}^{K} \theta_k z_{nik}\right)}{\sum_{j=1}^{J_n} \exp\left(\sum_{k=1}^{K} \theta_k z_{njk}\right)}.$$

Suppose that the first variable is a personal attribute. Its value then does not vary over alternatives. That is, $z_{ni1} = z_{nj1}, i, j = 1, \ldots, J_n$. The selection probability can be rewritten as

$$P_{ni} = \frac{\exp(\theta_1 z_{ni1}) \exp\left(\sum_{k=2}^{K} \theta_k z_{nik}\right)}{\exp(\theta_1 z_{ni1}) \sum_{j=1}^{J_n} \exp\left(\sum_{k=2}^{K} \theta_k z_{njk}\right)} = \frac{\exp\left(\sum_{k=2}^{K} \theta_k z_{nik}\right)}{\sum_{j=1}^{J_n} \exp\left(\sum_{k=2}^{K} \theta_k z_{njk}\right)}.$$

In the right-hand equality above, it is clear that the personal attribute z_{ni1} has no effect on the selection probabilities.

TABLE 5.1
Variable Description

Variable[a]	Description	Hypothesized effect on Expected group utility
Personal attributes		
6 TRN	Job turnover, average number of jobs per year	minus
7 JT	Job tenure, consecutive years on the job	plus
3 NW	Dummy = 1 for nonwhites	minus
4 YNG	Dummy = 1 for those aged 20-25	minus
5 OLD	Dummy = 1 for those aged 56 or more	plus
8 LR	Length of residency, consecutive years at the origin	plus
2 FM	Dummy = 1 for females	plus
Place attributes: Mean values		
39 WAG	Lifetime earnings	plus
10 ER	Employment rate	plus
38 DI	Employment in one's industry	plus
9 UR	Percent of population urban	plus
14 DN	Residential density	plus
16 HC	Rate of change in housing stock	plus
17 P50	Percentage of housing built before 1950	plus
18 VO	Percentage of homeowner housing vacant	plus
19 VR	Percentage of rental housing vacant	plus
20 UH	Percentage of housing uncrowded	plus
21 OH	Percentage of housing owner occupied	plus
22 GS	Per capita government expenditures on public services	plus
13 NFN	Percentage of population nonwhite for nonwhites	plus
12 WFW	Percentage of population white for whites	plus
15 CG	Percentage of adults completed college	plus
11 AP	Percentage of families above the low income level	plus
Place attributes: Squared values		
40 WAG2	Square of WAG	minus
24 ER2	Square of ER	minus
23 UR2	Square of UR	minus
28 DN2	Square of DN	minus
30 HC2	Square of HC	minus
31 P502	Square of P50	minus
32 VO2	Square of VO	minus
33 VR2	Square of VR	minus
34 UH2	Square of UH	minus
35 OH2	Square of OH	minus
36 GS2	Square of GS	minus
27 NFN2	Square of NFN	minus
26 WFW2	Square of WFW	minus
29 CG2	Square of CG	minus
25 AP2	Square of AP	minus
Variance of place attributes		
41 VA	Common variance, an indirect function of common information	minus
Alternative-specific variables		
1 DO	Origin-specific constant	plus
Size of alternatives		
37 LP	Logarithm of population	plus

[a] The variable number refers to the variable's column position in Table 6.1.

Personal Attributes. One of the advantages of a disaggregate study of interregional migration is that the effects of personal attributes of potential migrants on migration choices can be assessed. As the geographic mobility studies show (see the section beginning on page 58 entitled "Mobility Models"), a host of personal attributes ranging from family to job characteristics should be analyzed. The LEED data emphasize the potential migrant's work history, and we analyzed the importance of seven variables. When interpreting the signs of Table 5.1 indicating the expected effects of personal attributes, again note that personal attributes assume zero values for alternatives other than the origin. That is, the effects of personal attributes are specific to the potential migrant's origin utility. Thus, factors enhancing mobility would negatively affect origin utility.

Previous experiences of job turnover, TRN, indicate a willingness to bear separation costs, which lessens the ties to the origin. On the other hand, increased job tenure, JT, and prolonged lengths of residency, LR, raise separation costs and ties to the origin by enhancing property rights in jobs and social involvements in the community, respectively. The age variables YNG and OLD are commonly associated with stages of the life-cycle affecting mobility. The young are more apt to migrate than the old, since they are more likely to undergo other social changes, such as starting new households, which lower origin ties. NW is included since through practices, intentional or otherwise, nonwhites have tended, more so than whites, to be hired in jobs where there is little specific training and little accumulation of nontransferable human capital.[2] Separation costs would then be lower for nonwhites than whites, and one would expected nonwhites to be more mobile than whites.

The other personal attribute FM is considered for two reasons. First, labor market experiences of women are thought to be different from those of men, in part because of a "crowding" phenomenon, whereby labor market practices limit the scope of occupations open to women.[3] Thus, opportunities "elsewhere" are likely to be less different for women than for men, and women may accordingly be less mobile. Second, nonheads of households are more likely to bear separation costs from the household upon migration than are household heads. Thus, female potential migrants might be expected to be less mobile than males.[4]

Table 5.1 also lists an alternative-specific variable, DO, which in addi-

---

[2] Specific traditional practices include the restriction of nonwhites to nondesirable promotion ladders. See Doeringer and Piore (1971, Chapter 7).

[3] For a review discussion of how labor markets differ and of the crowding hypothesis, see Kahne (1975).

[4] In 1969, about 96% of women in the labor force were not household heads; see U.S. Department of Commerce (1974a, 1976).

tion to the personal attributes reflects nontransport costs of migration. DO is an origin-specific constant and is specified to be 1 for the origin alternative and 0 for the others. The effects of any costs of migration not otherwise captured by the personal attributes are likely to be measured by DO. Its effect on origin utility is expected to be positive.

Place Attributes. Since it is impossible to know the subjective probability distributions potential migrants have of place attributes, their expected values are represented by the measured actual values of the variables at the alternatives.[5] As indicated in Table 5.1 the place attributes were conventionally constructed so that potential migrants might view the attributes as "goods" (in which case [3.9a] would hold).

The economic place attributes include two personally specific variables, WAG and DI. From the theoretical considerations of Chapter 3, WAG is an age–industry–place specific estimate of the potential migrant's discounted earnings up to the retirement age of 65.[6] More precisely, WAG_{nj} is the measure of lifetime earnings at alternative j specific to the nth potential migrant,

$$WAG_{nj} = Y_{onj} \int_0^{65-a_n} \exp[(g_j - d)t] \, dt.$$

Y_{onj} is an estimate of the annual income the nth potential migrant might earn at alternative j at $t = 0$, 1969, and is the 1969 base income Y^*_{onj} weighted by the average employment rate at j. The base measure Y^*_{onj} is the annual wage prevailing at alternative j in the nth potential migrant's industry classification, either firstly 4-digit SIC or secondly 3-digit SIC, if there was employment in that industry at the alternative. Otherwise, Y^*_{onj} is the average annual wage at alternative j weighted by the ratio of the nth potential migrant's industry-specific wage at the origin to the average wage at the origin. The industry–county specific wages are from CBP. The rate of growth in average nominal wages at the jth alternative is g_j, and it is based upon the 1965–1971 change in average wages reported in CBP. The discount rate d is assumed to equal 14% at all alternatives. The nth potential migrant's age in 1969 is a_n.

DI indicates whether there was employment at an alternative in the industry, 4-digit or 3-digit SIC, of the potential migrant's employment prior

---

[5] All place attributes expressed as percentages have been multiplied by 10.

[6] WAG does not adjust for cost-of-living differences, since the data were inappropriate to the task. Cost-of-living data are published for only about 65 metro areas in the United States. Since these figures would need to be imputed to the 3141 counties, little variation in WAG would be introduced using this procedure, especially given that most alternative sets are largely composed of nearby counties, which would have the same inputed cost of living. And

to the migration decision. Presumably, potential migrants would be attracted to places where they might obtain employment in the industry of their present employment. The third economic variable, ER, is the average employment rate at an alternative.

Two of the amenity place attributes—the percentage urban UR and the residential density DN—are likely to reflect the extent of a place's household agglomeration economies. Since certain activities such as cultural opportunities are only available when threshold levels of population concentration are attained, potential migrants might be expected to be attracted to dense and highly urbanized places where such activities are provided. Also, to the extent that any trend in migration favoring urban over rural areas persists, UR should capture the effect.

Several variables measuring local housing conditions are also among the amenity place attributes. The change in the housing stock, HC, and the vacancy rate variables, VO and VR, can indicate the availability of local housing, certainly a concern to potential migrants assessing alternatives as places to live. The other variables measure characteristics of the housing stock—the age, P50; the commodiousness, UH; and the status of occupancy, OH. New arrivals to a place might be attracted to the older, more centrally located neighborhoods, since such areas may provide better access to the area's job locations than a less central neighborhood. Other things equal, potential migrants are expected to be attracted to neighborhoods offering spacious housing and the special maintenance provided by owner–occupants. Another amenity attribute is the level of government expenditures on public services, GS. Since expenditure levels are thought to be related to levels of services, GS is expected to exert a positive influence on the potential migrant's decision.

The percentages of nonwhites, NFN, and whites, WFW, were included for nonwhite and white potential migrants, respectively. Nonwhites are expected to migrate to areas where there are other nonwhites and whites to predominately white areas for two reasons. First, potential migrants might prefer neighborhoods where social and cultural identifications are reinforced. And second, practices in housing markets may result in non-whites locating in predominately nonwhite neighborhoods, and similarly for whites.

The final two amenity variables, CG and AP, reflect an area's general

---

while many migration studies use a distance term as a proxy for transportation costs as well as information, we have used an information measure that has advantages over a distance term since it is a two-way interchange. Moreover, the information measure can be considered as a general measure of accessibility, spatial as well as informational, since it is based on prior migration flows which reflect distance between areas in addition to the channel of information.

well-being by measuring its educational level and its economic prosperity.[7] Potential migrants might be attracted to more well-off areas.

Variance of Place Attributes. The common variance σ_{nj}^{*2} reflects the uncertain knowledge the nth potential migrant has of the jth place that affects all place attributes. Since this uncertainty is considered a result of imperfect information, rather than an inherent randomness in the attribute variables, we assume that the common variance is a negative exponential function of the information one has of the place I_{nj}. That is,

$$\sigma_{nj}^{*2} = e^{-I_{nj}}.$$

When no information is at hand, the common variance is 1, its maximal value. And as information becomes available, the uncertainty decreases at a decreasing rate—the variance approaches 0 as information becomes infinite.

We specify the information I_{nj} to be the recent two-way migration flow between the nth potential migrant's origin i and the jth alternative, deflated by the origin population P_i.[8]

$$I_{nj} = \frac{M_{ij} + M_{ji}}{P_i}.$$

Recent migrants from the origin to the destination M_{ij} relay information backward concerning j.[9] The reverse flow, M_{ji}, relays information about j forward. Thus, the measure of common variance, VA in Table 5.1, is

$$\mathrm{VA}_{nj} = \exp - \left(\frac{M_{ij} + M_{ji}}{P_i} \right).$$

Potential migrants are expected to favor alternatives with low variances, those for which they have a relatively good amount of information.

GROUPED ALTERNATIVES

The variable list (Table 5.1) includes one additional variable, the logarithm of population, LP. This variable in effect controls for the size of alternatives by serving as a proxy for the number of true alternatives within the county alternatives. Since a county may be an aggregate of the

[7] The poverty threshold level differs among places, as do characteristics of the populations, namely, age, family size, sex of head, and farm or nonfarm residency.

[8] Information also varies among potential migrants of the same origin, since potential migrants differ in their ability to obtain and perceive informative messages through formal and informal signals. In our empirical analysis we, however, do not examine this aspect of information. Our data on personal attributes do not include measures such as educational attainment needed to study this additional variation in information.

[9] The data on intercounty migratory flows are from migration streams between SEAs; see the section beginning on page 91, entitled "Data Requirements and Sources."

true behavioral alternatives, it is seen in the following that proper estimation of the model requires such a measure to be included.

The model of choice probabilities (3.18) implicitly assumes that data on the attributes of the J alternatives are available. However, data available for migration study typically pertain to geographic areas encompassing more than one distinct alternative. Regions, states, SEAs, and even counties are likely to be collections of distinct alternatives. The interesting question, then, is whether data on groups of true alternatives provide good estimates of the model (3.20).[10] In the following, we state the problem and then show that under mildly restrictive conditions (namely, that attributes of alternatives within counties be homogeneous), reasonable estimates are obtained by using aggregate alternatives, provided the logarithm of population or group size is included. We also discuss the problem of a potential breakdown in the IIA assumption (see the section beginning on page 84, entitled "An Empirical Model of Interregional Migration") for the alternatives in the groups.

Let the T true alternatives open to the potential migrant (the subscript n is suppressed here for convenience) be grouped into J mutually exclusive counties, $J < T$. The probability that the jth county is selected is the sum of the probabilities of selecting the alternatives within j. This is expressed, recalling (3.18), as

$$P_j = \sum_{i \in j} P_i = \sum_{i \in j} \frac{e^{v_i}}{\Sigma_{t=1}^{T} e^{v_t}} = \frac{e^{v_j}}{\Sigma_{k=1}^{J} e^{v_k}}, \tag{5.1}$$

where

$$v_j = \ln \sum_{i \in j} e^{v_i} \qquad j = 1, \ldots, j, k, \ldots, J.$$

The model of choice probabilities for county alternatives (5.1) is of MNL form and theoretically estimable. However, the data on attributes of the T true alternatives needed for estimating (5.1) are not available. Data are only available at the county level. Nonetheless, if the attributes of alternatives within the counties are relatively homogeneous, reasonable estimates of the potential migrant's expected utility function are obtainable by using the average, county-level values of the attribute variables in place of values for the alternatives within each county.

Consider the average value, $\bar{v}_j$, of the utilities of the jth county.

$$\bar{v}_j = \frac{1}{S_j} \sum_{i \in j} v_i = \frac{1}{S_j} \sum_{i \in j} \boldsymbol{\theta}' \mathbf{z}_i = \boldsymbol{\theta}' \bar{\mathbf{z}}_j,$$

where S_j is group size, the number of alternatives in the jth county, and $\bar{\mathbf{z}}_j$ is the vector of average values for the variables in the jth county. (For

[10] This problem was pointed out by Steven Lerman, and the discussion that follows is primarily taken from his work (1975, pp. 155–165).

convenience, we have here considered $v_j = \boldsymbol{\theta}'\mathbf{z}_j$, where $\boldsymbol{\theta}$ is a parameter vector and $\mathbf{z}$ is an attribute vector, since (3.14) is linear in parameters.) If the attributes of alternatives within a county are relatively homogeneous, then $\mathbf{z}_i \cong \bar{\mathbf{z}}_j$, $i \in j$, and $v_i \cong \bar{v}_j$, $i \in j$.[11] Substituting the approximations into the expression for v_j yields

$$v_j = \ln \sum_{i \in j} e^{\bar{v}_j} = \ln (e^{\bar{v}_j} \cdot S_j) = \bar{v}_j + \ln S_j,$$

and (5.1) can be written as

$$P_j = \frac{e^{\bar{v}_j + \ln S_j}}{\sum_{k=1}^{J} e^{\bar{v}_k + \ln S_k}}. \tag{5.2}$$

The choice probabilities for county alternatives (5.2) is of MNL form, and the parameters are those associated with the model for the true alternatives.

Estimation of (5.2) requires data on the county-level values of the attribute variables and on the number of alternatives in the county or group size. Since the variables listed in Table 5.1 pertain to county-level measures, the list only needs to include a measure of county size, which we take as county population. The logarithm of county population is then LP.

The preceding discussion assumes that the alternatives within a county satisfy the IIA assumption. It is possible, however, that the alternatives within a group have so-called nested dependence, that is, some unobserved identical group attributes which can cause a breakdown in the IIA assumption. The extent of nested dependence can nonetheless easily be examined. The procedure is to obtain an unconstrained coefficient estimate of LP (note that [5.2] implies that the coefficient of LP is 1). The estimate provides a measure of how similar alternatives within a county are perceived. If the estimate is significantly different from both 0 and 1, nested dependence exists and has been properly taken into account.[12] In the empirical analysis, the coefficient of LP is not constrained, thereby controlling for the effects of both aggregating true alternatives and any nested dependence.

ESTIMATION RESULTS

This section discusses the results of estimating the migratory choice model (3.20) specified in the previous section. The results are first pre-

---

[11] The approximations are not likely to be too restrictive in the case of this study since the geographic units are counties, which are highly disaggregate relative to other geographic units used in migration analysis.

[12] See McFadden (1977, pp. 25–30).

sented for the total sample of potential migrants and then for stratifications of the sample by race, sex, and income since our work with the stratifications shows differences in the behavior of the subgroups.

The high cost of estimating large MNL models precluded the use of all
6326 sample observations available to us, as described in the section
beginning on page 97, entitled "The LEED Sample." [13] A large subset, 1996
potential migrants, was used in the estimation, and with respect to other
studies using MNL analysis this sample size is still quite large. In all results reported, the convergence criterion was that the change in each
parameter estimate be no more than .5%.

In each of the tables presenting results, the estimated coefficient and
the asymptotic t statistic are presented for each variable. For place attributes, an indication is provided concerning whether the estimated coefficients for the linear and quadratic terms are consistent with positive
marginal utility, using the average values of the attributes. [14] Also reported
are five summary measures:

1. K is the number of parameters.
2. χ_K^2 is a chi-squared variable with K degrees of freedom, $\chi_K^2 = -2[L(0) - L(\hat{\theta})]$. $L(\hat{\theta})$ is the log likelihood function evaluated at
   the estimated parameter values, and $L(0)$ is the log likelihood
   evaluated at parameter values of zero. χ_K^2 can be used to test the
   null hypothesis that all parameters are simultaneously zero. That
   is, alternatives are equally likely to be chosen. [15]
3. ρ^2 is a "goodness of fit" measure analogous to R^2, $\rho^2 = 1 - [L(\hat{\theta})/L(0)]$.

[13] Since the computation costs of using the estimation procedure are also directly related
to how "far away" the initial values for the estimators are from the convergent values, it has
been useful to begin by separately estimating the subsets of the coefficients. The selection
probability can easily be written as the product of conditional and marginal probabilities,
that is, the probability of a particular destination given a move and the probability of
moving. Each probability is the basis of a multinomial logit model that can be estimated. Estimation of the conditional probability model provides parameter estimates for variables
that vary over destinations, and estimation of the marginal probability model yields estimates for variables varying between the origin and all destinations. Together, the estimates
so obtained provide initial values for the full set of parameters that would in all likelihood be
closer to the convergent values than the default values of zero. Thus, it can be considerably
less expensive to use such a technique than to estimate the full model using initial values of
zero. See Ben-Akiva (1973, pp. 191–203), McFadden (1976, p. 106), and Lerman (1975, pp.
150–155).

[14] Only an indication is provided because the national averages are only approximations
to the actual averages for the alternatives used in the analysis. This is because for some potential migrants the alternative sets may comprise alternatives with attributes below the national average, while others may have above-average attributes.

[15] Failure to reject the hypothesis of equally likely alternatives would indicate a serious
misspecification of the model.

4. N is the sample number of potential migrants used in the estimation.

5. C is the number of cases used in the estimation and is the sum over the potential migrants of the unselected alternatives.

Because the data refer only to members of the labor force and then only to those working in the periods immediately before and after the migration decision, the decisions of potential migrants not in the labor force and of labor force members unable to find destination employment are not part of the analysis.

RESULTS FOR THE TOTAL SAMPLE

Estimates of the potential migrant's expected group utility function (3.14) are presented in Table 5.2 for the total sample. Considering the results, columns (1), the estimates compare reasonably well to the expectations presented in Table 5.1. The effects of the personal attributes are all of the anticipated sign. Two, job turnover and length of residency, are highly significant; job tenure is marginally so. That job tenure JT and length of residency LR have separate effects are consistent with Bartel's findings (1979). Further, our diagnosis of collinearity presented in Chapter 6 indicates that JT and LR are not involved in a collinear relation. Suspicion of such a relation led Bartel to consider a pure residence variable, the difference between the length of residency and job tenure, along with the job tenure variable. Of the other personal attributes, only old age is a significant factor.

The results for the place economic attributes are not as uniform. Two of the economic attributes, WAG and ER, are of the wrong sign and insignificant. The third, DI, is, as expected, a positive significant influence. The poor performances of the first two economic measures are disconcerting at first glance. However, WAG may not be as precise an income measure as desired. The income data were industry specific rather than occupation specific (recall that data from LEED and CBP pertain only to industries and not occupations). The intra-industry variation in incomes over occupations may render the industry-specific income variable to be a less precise measure than, perhaps, an occupation-specific variable. To such extent, the income variable WAG may be inadequate to examining the importance of personally relevant incomes.

With regard to ER, recall that the sample consists only of individuals who were employed both before and after the migration decision. Those able to obtain employment after the decision are indeed those least likely to be adversely affected by high unemployment at places. Had the sample included those unable to find work after the decision, ER may have exerted a positive influence. Even so, decisions were conditioned by the

TABLE 5.2
Estimates for the Migratory Choice Model: All Potential Migrants

Variable	1[a,b]	1[c]	2[a,b]	2[c]	3[a,b]	3[c]
TRN	-.65E-02	-5.96	-.50E-02	-4.84	-.65E-02	-5.97
JT	.71E-01	1.60	.85E-01	1.86	.71E-01	1.60
NW	-.33E-01	- .15	-.11E-01	-.05	-.29E-01	- .13
YNG	-.16E 00	- .98	-.82E-01	- .49	-.16E 00	- .98
OLD	.49E 00	1.90	.63E 00	2.41	.48E 00	1.87
LR	.69E 00	13.46	.75E 00	14.26	.69E 00	13.47
FM	.43E-01	.30	.21E 00	1.42	.41E-01	.28
WAG	-.20E-05	- .97	-.17E-05	- .87	-.20E-05	- .99
ER	-.21E 00	-1.04	-.81E 00	-6.02	-.20E 00	-1.00
DI	.25E 00	2.28	.26E 00	2.35	.25E 00	2.27
UR	.85E-03	1.11	.11E-02	1.51		
DN	.69E-04*	2.62	.82E-04*	3.13	.66E-04*	2.54
HC	-.13E-02	-1.84	-.20E-02*	-3.02	-.12E-02*	-1.76
P50	.66E-02*	3.40	.46E-02*	2.49	.69E-02*	3.58
VO	-.54E-02	- .42	-.18E-01*	-1.41	-.47E-02*	- .37
VR	.11E-01*	2.12	.95E-02*	2.08	.11E-01*	2.08
UH	-.56E-02	- .23	-.58E-02	- .25	-.55E-02*	- .23
OH	.59E-02	1.69	.74E-02*	2.15	.59E-02*	1.71
GS	-.13E-02	- .53	-.10E-02*	- .38	-.15E-02*	- .61
NFN	.90E-02*	3.35	.88E-02*	3.14	.88E-02*	3.31
WFW	.16E-02	.50	-.17E-02	- .53	.15E-02*	.46
CG	.81E-02*	1.97	.77E-02*	1.90	.80E-02*	1.94
AP	-.11E-02	- .13	.54E-02*	.64	.68E-06	.01
WAG2	.55E-11	.13	.10E-10	.25	.56E-11	.13
ER2	.12E-03	1.06	.43E-03	5.96	.11E-03	1.03
UR2	-.58E-06	- .85	-.87E-06	-1.29		
DN2	-.56E-09	-1.78	-.63E-09	-1.99	-.52E-09	-1.67
HC2	.85E-06	2.25	.11E-05	3.32	.82E-06	2.16
P502	-.49E-05	-2.91	-.38E-05	-2.32	-.51E-05	-3.06
VO2	.92E-05	.82	.12E-03	1.06	.88E-04	.77
VR2	-.40E-04	-1.59	-.22E-04	-1.10	-.40E-04	-1.58
UH2	.30E-05	.21	.37E-05	.27	.28E-05	.20
OH2	-.40E-05	-1.40	-.58E-05	-2.04	-.40E-05	-1.41
GS2	.19E-05	.47	.60E-06	.13	.21E-05	.53
NFN2	-.13E-04	-3.09	-.12E-04	-2.79	-.13E-04	-3.06
WFW2	-.96E-06	- .44	.14E-05	.67	-.83E-06	- .38
CG2	-.94E-05	- .77	-.90E-05	- .76	-.91E-05	- .75
AP2	-.39E-07	- .01	-.39E-05	- .70	-.71E-06	- .13
VA	-.11E-05	-1.07	-.53E-05	-11.85	-.10E-05	-1.06
DO	.27E 01	5.42			.27E 01	5.44
LP	.17E 00	3.06	.16E 00	2.94	.15E 00	2.95
RUR					.27E-03	.77
K		41		40		40
χ^2_K		8,454		8,400		8,453
ρ^2		.66		.66		.66
N		1,996		1,996		1,996
C		54,441		54,441		54,441

[a]Coefficient estimates.

[b] Asterisk denotes place attributes for which the estimates of the coefficients of the linear and quadratic terms are such that the marginal utility of the attribute is positive, (3.9.a) holds, when evaluated at the national-average attribute.

[c]Asymptotic t statistics.

presence of employment in one's industry, DI. This suggests that the overall employment rate may not be a good barometer of the employment possibilities in any specific industry. It should also be noted that our diagnosis of collinearity reveals that ER is highly collinear with its square and that when ER2 is omitted the effect of ER is positive and marginally significant.

The estimates for the amenity variables are, on the whole, reasonable and are supportive of nonlinear relations in several cases. Indeed, of the seven place attributes that had significant linear terms (DI is not considered in this group), five of the quadratic terms were also significant and another was marginally so. Also, the coefficients of the linear and quadratic terms of most attributes are such that the attribute's marginal utility is positive. Indeed, all attributes for which both coefficients are significant have positive marginal effects on expected utility.

With regard to the linear terms of the amenity attributes, the effects of eight variables are of the anticipated sign, and of these only two, UR and WFW, are not significant. On the other hand, five have unexpected effects, but only one of these, HC, is significant. The results suggest that potential migrants are attracted to densely populated areas, where the housing is owner-occupied but not of the most recent vintage and where rental units are available. The migration to areas where the housing stock is growing, typically suburban areas, is apparently not of the type examined here. Such migrants may be intraregional migrants who stay at the same job rather than interregional migrants who change jobs. Other amenity factors attracting migrants are the social environments associated with the presence of educated residents and, for nonwhites, the presence of other nonwhites. It is interesting that NFN is significant while WFW is not. This suggests that nonwhites have a stronger preference for their own than do whites, or that housing markets operate more restrictively for nonwhites than whites.

The coefficient of VA, the measure of the common variance regarding a place's attributes, is negative as expected, but is insignificant. On the other hand, the origin-specific constant DO has a positive and highly significant effect. This result is certainly a tribute to the role of inertia in migration decisions whether it is due to separation costs of migration not captured by the personal attributes or to the first-hand information one has of the origin. Empirically, DO and VA may vary similarly. In particular, for the origin DO equals 1 and VA is close to 0, and for the destinations DO equals 0 and VA is close to 1. The two variables might be expected to be collinear, and our diagnostic examination of the data supports this possibility. As columns (2) of Table 5.2 show, estimation of a model in which DO was omitted resulted in a fivefold increase in the absolute value of the coefficient of VA and a 50% decrease in the coefficient's standard error.

This observation, that VA has a highly significant negative effect, is supportive of risk-averse behavior on the part of potential migrants, when considered along with the results for the quadratic terms. Of the six place attributes with positive significant effects for their linear terms, all of the squared terms had negative effects, as would be expected if risk aversion characterized the behavior (see Eqs. [3.9]). Moreover, the effects of four of these quadratic terms were significant and one other's was marginally so; only one of the six was clearly insignificant.

The coefficient estimate for LP, the logarithm of population, is positive, as expected. Also, the estimate is significantly different from both 0 and 1, which is consistent with nested dependence among the grouped alternatives within the counties.[16]

One other specification using the total sample was considered in which the linear and quadratic terms UR and UR2 were deleted and a relative urbanization variable, RUR, was included. RUR is the percentage of the urbanized population urban at an alternative minus the percentage urban at the origin:

RUR = (% urban at an alternative − % urban at the origin) · 10.

This specification was used to examine a specific form of the notion that utility derived from destination attributes depends on conditions at the origin as well as at the destination, suggesting a dependence between the origin and destination alternatives.[17] Potential migrants might view the amenities associated with urbanization at a destination relative to those at the origin. And other things equal, increases in relative urbanization might well lead to increases in the potential migrant's expected utility. As inspection of columns (3) of Table 5.2 indicates, the estimated coefficient of RUR is positive, as expected, but insignificant.

---

[16] If the true alternatives within a county have certain identical attributes such as a common tax rate there may be dependence among the nested or grouped alternatives comprising the observational alternatives or counties. A coefficient of LP that is significantly different from zero and one is consistent with nested dependence. See McFadden (1977, pp. 25–30).

[17] The hypothesis examined here is similar to a diagnostic test of the validity of the IIA assumption. The difference between the approach here and the diagnostic test is that in this specification the variables UR and UR2 are omitted. In the diagnostic test, the variables would be included and a χ^2 variable would be used to test whether RUR was a factor in a manner similar to that of an F test on a group of coefficients in a regression context. The reason the diagnostic approach was not used here is the potentially high collinearity between RUR and UR. In this model approximately 75% of the cases would have RUR equal to UR. For a detailed discussion of diagnostic tests, see McFadden, Tye, and Train (1976).

RESULTS FOR SAMPLE STRATIFICATIONS

If groups of potential migrants with heterogeneous behavior are used in the analysis of the total sample, the aggregate results may obscure underlying behavioral differences. Our work with stratifications by race, sex, and income indicates that the migratory behavior of certain subgroups, especially nonwhites, females, and high-income potential migrants, differs from that of the total sample. The results for each stratification are described below.

Race. The basic model was separately estimated for each race with the appropriate omission of the variables NW, NFN, and WFW. The results are presented in Table 5.3. Since about 90% of the 1996 potential migrants considered in our empirical analysis are white, the results for whites are expected to be similar to those of the total sample reported above, and indeed they are (see columns [1]). Only a few differences are noteworthy. The effects of two variables, owner-occupied housing, OH, and the college educated, CG, are noticeably greater for whites than for the full sample. Moreover, the coefficients for the linear and quadratic terms for both variables are significant.

For nonwhites, the estimation results in columns (2) are substantially different from those for the total sample. In the labor market, job tenure is an exceptionally important factor in impeding migration for nonwhites. The estimated effect of JT on nonwhite migration is over 20 times that for whites. This may be because nonwhites have a more difficult time establishing tenure than whites, given the practice of restricting nonwhites to entry-level positions. Also, nonwhites may have fewer specific (in particular, industry-specific) job skills than whites, since DI, the measure of employment in one's industry type, is not a significant factor for nonwhites.

The housing market may operate differently for nonwhites as well. The effects of four housing attributes—HC, VO, UH, and OH—have opposite signs for nonwhites and whites. Nonwhites apparently prefer, or are guided to by market practices, highly urbanized areas, where rental housing is available and of an early vintage and where local residents are predominantly nonwhite and not highly educated. (These observed effects may also be partly due to low income; 66% of nonwhites in the sample had incomes of no more than $5000 in 1969. This figure for whites was about 40%.)

Also, noteworthy is that VA is significant for nonwhites. Apparently, information regarding an alternative is more valuable to nonwhites than to whites or whites have supplemental information regarding alternatives not reflected in the measure VA. The influence of DO is also significant

TABLE 5.3
Estimates for the Migratory Choice Model: Whites and Nonwhites

Variable	Whites $1^{a,b}$	Whites 1^{c}	Nonwhites $2^{a,b}$	Nonwhites 2^{c}
TRN	-.67E-02	-5.61	-.25E-03	-.08
JT	.50E-01	1.13	.12E 01	2.82
NW				
YNG	-.18E-00	-1.02	-.30E 00	-.51
OLD	.46E-00	1.74	.10E 01	1.04
LR	.69E 00	12.82	.69E 00	3.77
FM	.25E-01	.16	.29E 00	.55
WAG	-.26E-05	-1.05	-.25E-05	- .63
ER	-.16E 00	- .76	.34E 00*	.30
DI	.27E 00	2.30	.39E 00	1.19
UR	.43E-03	.54	.11E-01*	2.91
DN	.67E-04*	2.31	.11E-03*	1.24
HC	-.17E-02*	-2.18	.59E-03*	.25
P50	.47E-02*	2.28	.18E-01*	2.57
VO	-.88E-02*	- .65	.15E-01*	.28
VR	.97E-02*	1.72	.57E-01*	2.11
UH	-.52E-02*	- .21	.29E 00	1.20
OH	.97E-02*	2.42	-.69E-02*	- .91
GS	-.11E-02*	- .37	-.54E-02*	- .45
NFN			.90E-02*	2.03
WFW	.15E-02*	.45		
CG	.14E-01*	3.17	-.36E-01*	-2.91
AP	-.18E-02*	- .21	-.38E-01*	-1.30
WAG2	-.13E-10	- .29	.13E-09	1.00
ER2	.89E-04	.78	-.17E-03	- .29
UR2	-.48E-06	-.68	-.65E-05	-2.31
DN2	-.30E-09	-.85	-.19E-08	-1.93
HC2	.87E-06	1.94	.86E-06	.85
P502	-.33E-05	-1.82	-.16E-04	-2.47
VO2	.97E-04	.84	.43E-03	.48
VR2	-.30E-04	-1.14	-.31E-03	-2.10
UH2	.27E-05	.19	-.16E-03	-1.18
OH2	-.69E-05	-2.12	.38E-05	.55
GS2	.16E-05	.34	.65E-05	.32
NFN2			-.11E-04	-1.87
WFW2	-.97E-06	- .43		
CG2	-.28E-04	-2.05	.11E-03	3.46
AP2	.25E-06	.04	.26E-04	1.35
VA	-.73E-06	-.68	-.13E-04	-1.69
DO	.30E 01	5.41	-.51E 01	-1.24
LP	.17E 00	2.92	.51E-01	.29

K		38		38
χ^2_K		7,520		933
ρ^2		.66		.68
N		1,789		207
C		48,236		5,881

[a] Coefficient estimates.

[b] Asterisk denotes place attributes for which the estimates of the coefficients of the linear and quadratic terms are such that the marginal utility of the attribute is positive, (3.9.a) holds, when evaluated at the national-average value of the attribute.

[c] Asymptotic t statistics.

but, unlike the case for whites, is negative, suggesting that nonwhites have fewer ties to the origin than whites.

Sex. The estimation results for males and females are portrayed in Table 5.4.[18] As inspection of columns (1) indicates, the results for males are fairly similar to those for the total sample. This is not unexpected, since 60% of the sample are males. Nonetheless, there are a few important differences.

The effect of job tenure is negative, contrary to its expected effect, albeit insignificantly. (In the following, we see that job tenure has a significant negative effect for those with high incomes. Since over 40% of males have incomes in excess of $8000 [the figure is only 5% for females], the observed effect of job tenure for males reflects two opposite effects, a positive effect for low-income males and a negative one for those with high incomes.) The effect of DI, the presence of employment in one's industry, is almost twice that for the total sample. The effects of residential density DN, pre-1950 housing P50, and the college educated CG, on the other hand, are no longer significant. Other differences are the effects of the common variance VA and the origin-specific constant DO. The coefficient of VA is five times that for the total sample and is significant. On the other hand, the effect of DO is insignificant and is a mere .3% of its value for the total sample. The sensitivity of the coefficients of DO and VA are likely the result of their suspected collinearity.

The estimates for females, columns (2), provide some surprises that may point out possible weaknesses in our migration data. The observed effects of JT and DI for females are similar to those described above in the case of nonwhites, and they differ from the results for males in much the same way as they did between the races. The results suggest that females place a high value on job tenure, perhaps because of a difficulty in acquiring tenure, and lack specific, industry-specific, job skills.

The most surprising findings indicate substantial differences in the importance of amenity attributes between males and females. Three attributes—DN, P50, and CG—which are insignificant for males are significant positive factors for females. And of the amenity factors significant for males—HVC, VR, and NFN—none are significant for females. This is surprising, since each group's observed choices were expected to coincide

---

[18] It should be noted that the estimation process for the sex groups required adjustments in the step-size of the Newton–Raphson algorithm. In the case of females, 50% step-sizes were used for several iterations; full step-sizes were then used until convergent values for the estimated coefficients were obtained. Step-sizes of 25% were initially required in the case of males. In both cases, the starting values for the coefficients were the convergent values resulting from the use of all the data.

TABLE 5.4
Estimates for the Migratory Choice Model: Males and Females

Variable	Males 1[a,b]	Males 1[c]	Females 2[a,b]	Females 2[c]
TRN	-.53E-02	-4.26	-.72E-02	-3.26
JT	-.12E-01	- .23	.33E 00	3.02
NW	-.17E 00	- .58	.93E-01	.24
YNG	-.11E 00	- .48	-.17E 00	- .68
OLD	.82E 00	2.56	-.64E-01	- .15
LR	.81E 00	11.10	.55E 00	7.65
FM				
WAG	-.28E-05	-1.07	-.89E-06	- .27
ER	-.96E-01	- .35	-.20E 00*	- .62
DI	.46E 00	3.26	.58E-01	.32
UR	.14E-02	1.43	.34E-03*	.27
DN	.35E-04*	1.02	.13E-03*	3.02
HC	-.19E-02*	-2.16	-.59E-02*	- .48
P50	.34E-02*	1.43	.10E-01*	3.06
VO	-.16E-01*	- .69	-.58E-04	- .01
VR	.14E-01*	2.16	.65E-02*	.77
UH	-.74E-02	- .21	-.12E-01*	- .37
OH	.64E-02*	1.39	.69E-02*	1.25
GS	-.39E-03*	- .09	-.41E-03*	- .09
NFN	.11E-01*	2.77	.62E-02*	1.31
WFW	-.12E-02*	- .30	.58E-02*	1.06
CG	-.15E-02	- .31	.28E-01*	3.70
AP	.25E-02*	.21	-.87E-03*	-.07
WAG2	.38E-11	.07	.11E-10	.15
ER2	.56E-04	.39	.10E-03	.62
UR2	-.13E-05	-1.46	.85E-07	.08
DN2	.57E-10	.14	-.15E-08	-2.92
HC2	.11E-05	2.44	.59E-06	.76
P502	-.22E-05	-1.06	-.87E-05	-2.91
VO2	.33E-04	.07	.22E-03	.96
VR2	-.51E-04	-1.65	-.17E-04	- .45
UH2	.52E-05	.26	.50E-05	.27
OH2	-.48E-05	-1.27	-.46E-05	-1.02
GS2	.24E-07	.01	.43E-06	.06
NFN2	-.16E-04	-2.17	-.10E-04	-1.55
WFW2	.28E-06	.10	-.26E-05	- .71
CG2	.16E-04	1.18	-.65E-04	-2.73
AP2	-.96E-06	- .12	-.22E-05	- .28
VA	-.54E-05	-9.70	-.88E-06	- .54
DO	.89E-02	.16	.32E 01	3.85
LP	.21E 00	3.05	.51E-01	.56
K		40		40
χ_K^2		4,967		3,546
ρ^2		.64		.70
N		1,187		809
C		33,032		21,429

[a]Coefficient estimates.

[b] Asterisk denotes place attributes for which the estimates of the coefficients of the linear and quadratic terms are such that the marginal utility of the attribute is positive, (3.9.a) holds, when evaluated at the national-average value of the attribute.

[c]Asymptotic t statistics.

with household choices more frequently than not. However, these disparate findings are also consistent with a potential weakness in the migration data. If the location of work places and residencies are not within the same county for males or females, disparities in the effects of amenity attributes on locational choices could arise. The findings with respect to the effect of NFN indicate the disparity is due to the nature of the data. The estimated coefficient of NFN is insignificant for females, whereas it is strongly significant for males. Given the segregation in residencies, the insignificance of NFN in the migration of females is probably due to disparities between work places and residencies. Apparently, females, at least nonwhite females, tend to work in counties other than where they live.

Income. The sample was stratified into three income groups. The high-income group includes 532 potential migrants who earned income in excess of $8000 in 1969. Those with incomes of no more than $5000 in 1969 comprise the low-income group, and 969 potential migrants fall in this category. The middle-income group, those who earned between $5000 and $8000 in 1969, was not studied. The results for the low- and high-income groups are summarized in Table 5.5.

The results for the low-income group, columns (1), are, as expected, similar to those reported for the total sample, since this group constitutes about one-half of the sample. Some differences are marked, however. In particular, the effect of job tenure is relatively large for the low-income group. Apparently, as tenure increases, nontransport costs of migration increase more strongly for low-income potential migrants than for others. Also, UR and WFW, the percentage urban and the percentage white for whites, exert significant positive influences on utility; neither is significant for the total sample. Another notable difference is the effect of GS, per capita government expenditures. While its negative sign is contrary to our expectations, its influence is relatively strong and its statistical significance is considerably greater than that for the total sample.

The estimates for those with high income, columns (2), are strikingly different from the estimates for the entire sample. Among the personal attributes, the most notable difference is the effect of JT. Here, job tenure exerts a negative significant influence, even though the effect of length of residency is positive and significant. In the high-paying jobs, it may be that either better opportunities lie with firms other than one's own as experience accumulates or the tendency of job transfer is greater as one's tenure with a firm increases. These findings, once again, are consistent with those of Bartel. In the case of job transfers, Bartel found that increased job tenure increased the probability of migration, even though increased length of residency decreased the probability.

TABLE 5.5

Estimates for the Migratory Choice Model: Low Incomes and High Incomes

Variable	Low incomes $1^{a,b}$	1^c	High incomes $2^{a,b}$	2^b
TRN	-.76E-02	-5.19	-.43E-02	-1.68
JT	.12E 00	1.69	-.18E 00	-2.28
NW	-.87E-01	- .34	.37E 00	.41
YNG	-.31E 00	-1.49	-.86E-01	- .16
OLD	.21E 00	.66	.55E 00	.96
LR	.59E 00	9.26	.12E 01	7.65
FM	.61E-01	.32	-.29E 00	- .43
WAG	-.17E-05	- .68	-.18E-05	- .41
ER	-.34E 00	-1.33	-.15E 00	- .35
DI	.18E 00	1.27	.55E 00	2.30
UR	.18E-02*	1.85	.33E-02	1.64
DN	.74E-04*	2.22	.92E-04*	1.52
HC	-.14E-02*	-1.51	-.42E-02*	-2.61
P50	.60E-02*	2.39	.16E-02	.37
VO	.37E-02*	.23	-.30E-01*	- .50
VR	.79E-02*	1.00	.21E-01*	1.41
UH	-.23E-01*	- .89	.93E-02*	.13
OH	.62E-02*	1.45	.83E-02*	.94
GS	-.43E-02*	-1.55	.15E-01*	1.63
NFN	.73E-02*	2.39	.27E-01*	1.87
WFW	.87E-02*	1.77	-.13E-01*	-2.12
CG	.81E-02*	1.51	-.23E-02	- .28
AP	.40E-02*	.39	-.75E-02*	- .37
WAG2	.33E-10	.60	-.68E-10	- .77
ER2	.18E-03	1.35	.86E-04	.38
UR2	-.68E-06	- .79	-.38E-05	-2.22
DN2	-.79E-09	-1.94	-.50E-09	- .65
HC2	.81E-06	1.43	.18E-05	2.56
P502	-.40E-05	-1.79	-.40E-05	-1.07
VO2	.77E-04	.60	-.27E-03	- .16
VR2	-.35E-04	- .86	-.63E-04	- .81
UH2	.12E-04	.80	-.22E-05	- .05
OH2	-.40E-05	-1.13	-.65E-05	- .92
GS2	.51E-05	1.20	-.21E-04	-1.37
NFN2	-.12E-04	-2.42	-.62E-04	-1.79
WFW2	-.49E-05	-1.53	.68E-05	1.63
CG2	-.62E-05	- .38	.18E-04	.81
AP2	-.48E-05	- .71	.69E-05	.54
VA	-.99E-06	- .79	-.46E-06	- .10
DO	.32E 01	5.06	.21E 01	.83
LP	.13E 00	1.92	.15E 00	1.23
K	41		41	
χ^2_K	3,738		2,626	
ρ^2	.59		.74	
N	969		532	
C	27,102		15,228	

[a] Coefficient estimates.

[b] Asterisk denotes place attributes for which the estimates of the coefficients of the linear and quadratic terms are such that the marginal utility of the attribute is positive, (3.9.a) holds, when evaluated at the national-average value of the attribute.

[c] Asymptotic t statistics.

Other findings of interest are the effects of UR, CG, and WFW. Those of high income are surprisingly not attracted to areas where residents are highly educated, but are attracted to urbanized areas and, for whites, to areas where residents are not predominately white. If the migration data were of residencies instead of work places, these findings would be difficult to interpret. To the extent that potential migrants reside in counties other than where they work, the estimates of the effects of place attributes need to be interpreted solely in the context of the location of work places. That high-income workers tend to reside at greater distances from a central work place than low-income workers, because of a greater demand for housing, is a well-known aspect of residential location theory. We invoke it here to aid in understanding the surprising effects of UR, CG, and WFW.

Nonetheless, for those with high income, the effect of per capita government expenditures is positive and statistically strong. In the case of low-income migrants, GS has a significant negative effect. This supports the notion that public services are an attractive force but are abundant only in areas where entrance into the housing market requires high income. Thus, public services exert a positive influence on the choices of those with high incomes because they can afford the high entrance costs to areas where services are high. A negative influence is observed in the case for those with low incomes, not because of a preference for low levels of public services but because of an inaccessibility to highly priced housing in areas where services are high.[19]

Also, the estimated coefficients of VA and DO suggest that potential migrants of high income are less tied to the origin than others. Such potential migrants may have information supplemental to that measured in VA and either a greater ability to afford any pecuniary costs of migration, or lower nonpecuniary separation costs (captured by DO), than others.

SUMMARY

This chapter first discussed how the data, described in Chapter 4, were used to specify empirically the migratory choice model of Chapter 3. It then presented the results of estimating the model for a sample of 1996 potential migrants and for stratifications of the sample by race, sex, and income.

---

[19] There is likely to be an interrelationship between levels of income and public services. Those with high incomes are likely to locate in areas with high levels of services, and they are also likely to tax themselves such that high levels of public services are provided.

The results were, for most of the factors considered, consistent with prior expectations. The personal attributes of job tenure, job turnover, and length of residency were consistently significant factors. Other, personal attributes were typically of the expected sign but not statistically significant. Of the individual-specific economic attributes, one, the presence of employment in the potential migrant's industry, was statistically important. The other, lifetime earnings, was not. Our earnings data are for industries rather than occupations, and this measurement problem in all likelihood afflicts the performance of the income variable. Several amenity attributes relating to neighborhood characteristics were found to be important. Among those positively related to expected utility are residential density, vacant rental housing, pre-1950 housing, owner-occupied housing, the presence of the college educated, and, for nonwhites, the presence of nonwhites. The only important negative factor is the rate of change in the housing stock.

The results also provide some support for risk-averse behavior on the part of potential migrants. The variance or lack of information potential migrants have regarding alternatives is significant in certain specifications. Since there was some evidence of a possible collinearity between the variance term and the origin-specific constant, we explore this completely in the next chapter.

The stratified analysis uncovered some heterogeneity in migratory behavior. For example, per capita government expenditures on public services is a negative factor for low-income potential migrants and a positive factor for those with high incomes. Reflecting these opposite effects, the variable exerts an insignificant influence in the case of the total sample.

6

A Diagnosis of Collinearity

In this chapter we adapt an approach to diagnosing collinearity developed by Belsley, Kuh, and Welsch (1980) in regression analysis to the maximum-likelihood estimation of our MNL model of interregional migration. This application is of interest for two principal reasons. First, the estimated migration model reported in Chapter 5 uses quadratic terms, which have always been suspected of causing collinearity. To aid in understanding the estimates we observed, it is of interest to see if any such collinearity is borne out by the diagnostic. Indeed, some collinear relations between linear and quadratic terms are found. Second, this application extends the diagnostic beyond regression analysis. The adaptation of the Belsley *et al*. approach is developed first. Then the empirical results of applying the diagnosis are portrayed and interpreted.

THE DIAGNOSTIC IN MULTINOMIAL LOGIT ANALYSIS

In this section, we initially consider the estimation problem in the MNL model in order to understand the variance–covariance matrix of the maximum-likelihood estimators. This adaptation is based upon an eigenvalue decomposition of the information matrix for the likelihood function.

The MNL model necessitates this formulation instead of the singular value decomposition of the matrix of explanatory variates used by Belsley *et al.*[1] We then employ a sensitivity theorem developed by Belsley *et al.*, the BKW Theorem, to aid in detecting the presence of collinearity. The BKW Theorem shows that the sensitivity of the estimator variances for the MNL model to changes in elements of the information matrix for the MNL likelihood function has a measurable upper bound. Next, we decompose the estimator variance–covariance matrix to compute the upper bound and the so-called variance–component proportions needed for identifying variates involved in collinearity. The upper bound and the matrix of variance–component proportions are used in the next section to analyze collinearity in our MNL migration model.

The estimation problem in MNL analysis is to evaluate the maximum-likelihood estimators of the parameters of the multinomial likelihood function (3.20). The estimator variance–covariance matrix $\text{Var}(\hat{\boldsymbol{\theta}}) = \mathbf{R}^{-1}$. (Note the use of $\hat{\boldsymbol{\theta}}$ here is as the vector of estimators of all the parameters of (3.20) and not merely the coefficient estimator of σ^{*2}.) The information matrix $\mathbf{R}$ is the negative of a weighted moment matrix of the explanatory variates.[2] This is quite unlike the case of regression, in which the estimator variance–covariance matrix is the inverse of simply the moment matrix of the explanatory variates scaled by the error variance. Since $\mathbf{R}$ is a weighted moment matrix, the econometrician in MNL analysis cannot use simple correlations and auxiliary regressions as aids.

Nonetheless, since $\mathbf{R}$ is real symmetric, we can use the BKW Theorem to assist in determining whether collinearity is potentially degrading. The BKW Theorem shows that the telltale characteristic of degrading collinearity, a high sensitivity of estimator variances to small changes in the data, can be ascertained from the data. In the context of maximum-likelihood estimation, the BKW Theorem implies that the elasticity of the diagonal elements of $\text{Var}(\hat{\boldsymbol{\theta}})$ to elements of $\mathbf{R}$ is less than or equal to the upper bound $2\eta_{\max}$, twice the condition number of $\mathbf{R}$.[3] The condition number $\eta_{\max}$ is the square root of the ratio of $\mathbf{R}$'s maximal eigenvalue, $\sigma_{\max}$, to its minimal eigenvalue, $\sigma_{\min}$. (Note the use of σ here is as the

---

[1] Since the singular values of the matrix of explanatory variates are the positive square roots of the eigenvalues of the moment matrix for the variates, the two approaches are theoretically the same. However, the singular value decomposition is preferred in practice, since, when collinearity is present, calculations based upon it are more stable than those based upon the eigenvalues.

[2] See McFadden (1974, p. 115).

[3] What we have called the BKW Theorem is Theorem 2 of Belsley *et al.* (1980).

vector of eigenvalues rather than the standard deviations of the distribution of place attributes.)

$$\eta_{max} = \sqrt{\sigma_{max}} / \sqrt{\sigma_{min}}. \tag{6.1}$$

This is only one, the maximal, of K so-called condition indexes

$$\eta(k) = \sqrt{\sigma_{max}} / \sqrt{\sigma_k}, \qquad k = 1, \ldots, K, \tag{6.2}$$

where K is the number of explanatory variates in the model. Since the condition number of $\mathbf{R}$ indicates the difficulty of computing $\text{Var}(\hat{\boldsymbol{\theta}})$ from $\mathbf{R}$, it is a useful guide to detecting collinearity.[4] In previous experimental work, condition indexes in excess of the range 15 to 30 have been found to be indicative of degrading collinearity.

In addition to detecting collinearity, one can also identify the involved variates upon knowing the matrix of variance–component proportions. The elements of this matrix are the proportions of each estimator's variance associated with each of the variates in the model. In general, if there are two or more variates with high variance–component proportions associated with the same variate that also has a high condition index, then those variates are involved in the collinearity indicated by the condition index.

To see that each estimator variance is a sum of K terms yielding the proportions, we diagonalize $\mathbf{R}$ with an orthogonal similarity transform,[5]

$$\mathbf{R} = \mathbf{V}\boldsymbol{\Sigma}\mathbf{V}'. \tag{6.3}$$

In (6.3), $\boldsymbol{\Sigma}$ is a diagonal matrix of the K eigenvalues for $\mathbf{R}$, and $\mathbf{V} \equiv (v_{ij})$ has as its columns an orthonormal set of eigenvectors for $\mathbf{R}$. In the same manner, $\text{Var}(\hat{\boldsymbol{\theta}})$ is diagonalized, $\text{Var}(\hat{\boldsymbol{\theta}}) = \mathbf{V}\boldsymbol{\Sigma}^{-1}\mathbf{V}'$,[6] and the estimator variances are

$$\text{var}(\hat{\theta}_k) = \sum_{j=1}^{K} \frac{v_{kj}^2}{\sigma_j}, \qquad k = 1, \ldots, K. \tag{6.4}$$

[4] The extent to which the inverse of a matrix is unstable—the elements of the inverse of a matrix being highly sensitive to small changes in the elements of the matrix—is measured by the ratio of the spectral norm of the inverse matrix to that of the matrix itself. When the ratio is large, the inverse matrix is unstable. The spectral norm of $\mathbf{R}$ is its maximal singular value, the square root of its maximal eigenvalue $\sqrt{\sigma_{max}}$. And since the eigenvalues of the inverse of a matrix are simply the inverses of a matrix's eigenvalues, the spectral norm of $\mathbf{R}^{-1}$ is $1/\sqrt{\sigma_{min}}$, where $\sqrt{\sigma_{min}}$ is the minimal singular value of $\mathbf{R}$. Thus, the ratio of spectral norms is the condition number.

[5] For the condition indexes to be comparable in magnitude to those of other work, $\mathbf{R}$ was normalized by both columns and rows before the diagonalization.

[6] This follows directly from $\mathbf{V}' = \mathbf{V}^{-1}$, since $\mathbf{V}$ is orthogonal.

By using (6.4), the variance–component proportions π_{jk} ($j, k = 1, \ldots,$ K) are then the proportion of the kth variate's variance associated with the jth variate:

$$\pi_{jk} = \frac{v_{kj}^2 / \sigma_j}{\sum_{j=1}^{K} v_{kj}^2 / \sigma_j}, \qquad j, k = 1, \ldots, K. \qquad (6.5)$$

In (6.5), it is clear that π_{jk} varies indirectly with σ_j for constant v_{kj}. Thus, if the ith variate is that associated with a high condition number, $\sigma_i = \sigma_{\min}$ (with $\sigma_{\min}$ small relative to at least one $\sigma_j, j \neq i, j = 1, \ldots, K$), then π_{ik} would tend to be large for constant $v_{ki}, k = 1, \ldots, K$. Similarly, a collinearity indicated by a high condition index for the ith variate would give rise to large $\pi_{ik}, k = 1, \ldots, K$. In practice, π_{ik} in excess of 50% have been taken to be large.

However, in general not all the $\pi_{ik}, k = 1, \ldots, K$, will be large. For those variates nearly orthogonal to those involved in the collinearity, the v_{ki} are small; indeed, orthogonal variates have v_{ki} equal to zero. For the uninvolved variates, the small v_{ki} then offset the small σ_i, and the π_{ik} are small relative to those for the involved variates. Thus, the variates involved in a collinearity are identified by having high variance–component proportions associated with a variate which has a high condition index.[7]

In practice, the following three rules guide the usage of the condition indexes and the variance–component proportions:[8]

1. If there is a single condition index greater than a predetermined threshold level η^* and two or more variates have variance–component proportions associated with this index greater than a predetermined threshold level π^*, these variates are involved in a single collinear relation.

2. If there are two or more condition indexes of similar magnitude greater than η^* and two or more variates have aggregate variance–component proportions, when totaled over the associated competing condition indexes, greater than π^*, these variates are involved in competing collinear relations. The number of such relations corresponds to the number of condition indexes of similar magnitude.

3. If there is a condition index of an order of magnitude greater than one or more other high condition indexes, the variates in the dominant collinear relations cannot be ruled out from being simulta-

---

[7] Since "it takes two to tangle," there must be at least two high proportions associated with a high condition index for it to be indicative of collinearity.

[8] A detailed, illustrative discussion of these rules is provided by Belsley *et al.* (1980).

neously involved in lower-order collinear relations just because their variance–component proportions associated with the lower-order condition indexes do not exceed π^*. The dominant relation can obscure the simultaneous involvement of variates in lower-order relations.

The criterion for diagnosing collinearity is then essentially that there be two or more variance–component proportions in excess of π^* associated with a condition index in excess of η^*, given the appropriate qualifications for competing or dominant collinearities. An empirical assessment of collinearity using the rule above is undertaken in the following.

DIAGNOSTIC RESULTS

In this section, the results of the diagnoses of collinearity for the MNL migration model described in Table 5.1, and for subsequent restricted models, are interpreted. The diagnostic results, the matrix of variance–component proportions (in percentage), and the condition indexes, for the model of Table 5.1, are provided in Table 6.1. The estimation results for this model are presented in columns (1) of Table 5.2 and of Table A.1 in the Appendix.

When threshold values of $\eta^* = 20$ and $\pi^* = 50$ are used, eight collinear relations become apparent, as seen in Table 6.1. Inspection of the row associated with the dominant $\eta(15) = 247$ indicates that the two variates 10 and 24, the employment rate ER and its square, have π's in excess of 50%. While these may be involved in lower-order relations as well, they are clearly collinear. Also evident is another relation associated with $\eta(21) = 69$ involving variates 20 and 34, the percentage of uncrowded housing UH and its square.

The next highest condition index, $\eta(9) = 46$, competes with $\eta(23) = 39$, and four variates, 11, 21, 25, and 35—the percentages of families above the low-income level, AP, and of housing owner occupied OH, and their squares—appear to be involved in these two collinear relations. Each variate has aggregate π's in excess of 50% when totaled over the variates associated with the two condition indexes.

The next four largest condition indexes, $\eta(25) = 28$, $\eta(41) = 26$, $\eta(10) = 25$, and $\eta(5) = 23$, are so similar in magnitude that they compete. Eight variates are involved in these four collinear relations. The relation between variates 12 and 26 (the percentage of population white for whites, WFW, and its square, WFW2), appears to be strongly responsible for the condition index $\eta(25) = 28$. Two other variates, 17 and 31 (the percentage

TABLE 6.1
Condition Indexes and Variance-Component Percentages, Unrestricted Model

		VARIABLE NUMBER																																								
CI (A)	(B)	1	2	3	4	5	6	7	8	9	10	11	12	13	14	15	16	17	18	19	20	21	22	23	24	25	26	27	28	29	30	31	32	33	34	35	36	37	38	39	40	41
1	2	0	1	0	0	0	0	0	0	0	0	0	0	0	0	0	0	0	0	0	0	0	0	0	0	0	0	0	0	0	0	0	0	0	0	0	0	0	0	0	0	0
1	12	0	0	0	0	0	0	0	0	0	0	0	0	0	0	0	0	0	0	0	0	0	0	0	0	0	0	0	0	0	0	0	0	0	0	0	0	0	0	0	0	0
1	11	0	0	0	0	0	0	0	0	0	0	0	0	0	0	0	0	0	0	0	0	0	0	0	0	0	0	0	0	0	0	0	0	0	0	0	0	0	0	0	0	0
1	27	0	0	0	0	0	0	0	0	0	0	0	0	0	0	0	0	0	0	0	0	0	0	0	0	0	0	2	0	0	0	0	0	0	0	0	0	0	0	0	0	0
1	20	0	0	0	0	0	0	0	0	0	0	0	0	0	0	0	0	0	0	0	0	0	0	0	0	0	0	0	0	0	0	0	0	0	0	0	0	0	0	0	0	0
1	19	0	0	0	0	0	0	0	0	0	0	0	0	0	0	0	0	0	0	0	0	0	0	0	0	0	0	0	0	0	0	0	1	0	0	0	0	0	0	0	0	0
1	18	0	0	0	0	0	0	0	0	0	0	0	0	0	0	0	0	0	1	0	0	0	0	0	0	0	0	0	0	0	0	0	1	0	0	0	0	0	0	0	0	0
1	13	0	0	0	0	0	0	0	0	0	0	0	0	2	0	0	0	0	0	0	0	0	0	0	0	0	0	0	0	0	0	0	0	1	0	0	0	0	0	0	0	0
2	14	0	2	23	5	36	0	15	0	0	0	0	0	0	0	0	0	0	0	0	0	0	0	0	0	0	0	0	0	0	1	0	1	0	0	0	0	0	0	0	0	0
2	7	0	0	0	0	0	0	0	1	0	0	0	0	0	0	0	0	0	0	0	0	0	0	0	0	0	0	0	0	0	0	0	0	0	0	0	0	0	0	0	0	0
2	40	0	0	0	0	0	0	1	0	0	0	0	0	0	0	0	0	0	0	0	0	0	0	0	0	0	0	0	0	0	1	0	0	0	0	0	0	0	0	0	1	0
2	38	0	0	2	9	21	0	4	0	0	0	0	0	0	0	0	0	0	1	0	0	0	0	0	0	0	0	0	0	0	0	0	0	0	0	0	0	0	1	15	85	0
2	33	0	0	0	5	9	0	3	0	0	0	0	0	0	0	0	0	0	0	0	0	0	0	0	0	0	0	0	0	0	0	0	5	0	0	0	0	0	28	19	3	0
2	32	0	0	0	2	14	2	7	0	0	0	0	0	0	0	0	0	0	1	0	0	0	0	0	0	0	0	0	0	0	0	0	4	0	0	0	0	0	0	0	0	0
2	30	0	1	58	2	14	0	0	0	0	0	0	0	0	0	0	0	0	0	0	0	0	0	0	0	0	0	0	0	0	0	0	0	0	0	0	0	0	5	1	0	0
2	29	0	0	0	0	0	0	0	0	0	0	0	0	0	0	0	0	0	0	0	0	0	0	0	0	0	0	0	0	0	1	0	0	5	0	0	0	0	2	5	2	0
3	36	0	0	73	4	2	0	1	0	0	0	0	0	0	0	0	0	0	0	0	0	0	1	0	0	0	0	0	0	0	3	0	0	0	0	0	0	0	2	0	6	0
3	39	0	0	0	2	0	0	0	0	0	0	0	0	0	0	0	0	0	0	0	0	0	0	0	0	0	0	0	0	0	1	0	0	0	0	0	0	0	5	0	0	0
3	1	0	0	0	0	0	0	0	0	0	0	0	0	0	0	0	0	0	0	0	0	0	0	0	0	0	0	0	0	0	1	0	0	0	0	0	0	0	44	46	0	0

A CI DENOTES CONDITION INDEX.

B V DENOTES VARIABLE NUMBER (SEE TABLE 5.1).

of housing built before 1950, P50, and its square, P502), have their variances concentrated in the variables associated with $\eta(25) = 28$ and $\eta(41) = 26$. The variates 1 and 41 (the origin-specific dummy, DO, and the common variance, VA) have the majority of their variances distributed over the variables associated with $\eta(41) = 26$, $\eta(10) = 25$, and $\eta(5) = 23$.[9] The variates 14 and 28 (residential density, DN, and its square, DN2) have their variances concentrated in the two variance components associated with $\eta(10) = 25$ and $\eta(5) = 23$.

The degradation of estimates caused by collinearity can, of course, only be rectified by introducing new information, whether it be additional data or a Bayesian prior, to bear upon estimation. In regression analysis, the econometrician can do this using mixed estimation or ridge regression. However, no such flexible method is available to the analyst, in MNL analysis, which limits his or her ability to deal with collinearity, even when valuable information outside the data series is on hand.

The analyst can nonetheless introduce strong priors in the MNL case; that is, estimators might be constrained to constants. We have imposed just such strong restrictions in subsequent specifications of the model by selectively omitting variables. This procedure is not based upon economic justification (indeed such a procedure could lead to specification bias), but rather it is used only to observe how the structure of the collinear relations is affected. In most cases, this amounted to restricting the coefficient of a quadratic term to zero. This, of course, required estimating the restricted models and computing the condition indexes and variance–component proportions. The results for these models are summarized below; the tables of the Appendix detail the estimation results (Table A.1) and the diagnoses of collinearity (Tables A.2 to A.9).

Upon omitting ER2, variate 24, the dominant collinear relation is eliminated, and ER is seen not be be involved in any other collinear relation (Table A.2). The coefficient of ER and its standard error change substantially, and the estimate turns positive, its anticipated sign (Table A.1, columns 1 and 2).[10] The structure of the other collinear relations is unchanged.

[9] On a priori grounds, DO and VA might be suspected of being collinear. The origin dummy DO is "on" for the origin and "off" for other alternatives. The common variance VA is lowest for the origin, since the potential migrant's information is then most abundant, and is high for all other alternatives. The variates DO and VA would seemingly be strongly negatively correlated. For other evidence on this, see the discussion pertaining to Table 5.2 in the section beginning on page 133.

[10] The coefficients of the variates not involved in the collinear relation at hand are, as expected, stable. In the restricted models, aside from the variates in the collinear relation at hand, the only estimates that are unstable to any degree are those that have been involved in a more dominant collinear relation of a less restricted model.

In dealing with the next dominant condition index, $\eta(21) = 69$, UH2 variate 34 was deleted (Table A.3). Once again, the dominant relation is eliminated and the coefficient of UH and its standard error change notably (Table A.1, columns 2 and 3). When the structure of the collinear relations is examined, the two relations associated with the two competing indexes $\eta(5) = 47$ and $\eta(21) = 39$ interestingly appear to be separately identifiable. In particular, AP and AP2, variates 11 and 25, are those involved in the collinear relation indicated by $\eta(5) = 47$. The other relation involves OH and OH2, variates 21 and 35. The lower-order relations are unaffected by the omission of UH2.

Once AP2 (Table A.4) is deleted, the coefficient of AP and its standard error characteristically change greatly (Table A.1, columns 3 and 4). The three lowest-order relations associated with the strongly competing indexes $\eta(41) = 24$, $\eta(10) = 23$, and $\eta(14) = 21$ have now become separately identifiable; that associated with $\eta(21) = 28$, involving WFW and WFW2, variates 12 and 26, was initially so. The relation indicated by $\eta(41) = 24$ seems to involve primarily P50 and P502, variates 17 and 31. Similarly, the relation between DN and DN2, variates 14 and 28, appears to be chiefly responsible for the condition index $\eta(10) = 23$. This is unchanged by the deletion of OH2 (Table A.5) and the subsequent deletion of WFW2 (Table A.6).

After P502 (Table A.7) is omitted, the final two relations, indicated by the competing indexes $\eta(41) = 23$ and $\eta(1) = 22$, become distinct. By deleting DN2, it is seen that DN is not involved in the relation between DO and VA, variates 1 and 41 (Table A.8). This final collinear relation was eliminated by deleting DO, the origin-specific dummy (Table A.9), since the data series VA has greater behavioral content than its dummy counterpart.

SUMMARY

The restricted models discussed in this section are not a solution to the collinearity problem in our migration model. This would be so only if the analyst had some prior knowledge that the seven variates—ER, UH, AP, OH, WFW, P50, and DN—were not related to the potential migrant's utility in a nonlinear fashion.[11] To the contrary, however, the uncertainty

---

[11] In the case of DO and VA, constraining DO's coefficient to zero is more appropriate than the other restrictions, since DO may be largely redundant to VA. In the absence of data on VA, one might plausibly use a dummy like DO as a proxy measure of the extent of the potential migrant's knowledge of a place.

in the potential migrant's decision environment leads the analyst to consider important nonlinear relations, hence the quadratic specification.

Instead, the preceding restricted models show quite clearly that quadratic specifications can, and indeed do, lead to degrading collinear relations. Each of the seven relations indicated by the seven highest condition indexes involved a variable's linear and quadratic terms. This became obvious as successive restrictions were imposed and previously competing and separately unidentifiable relations emerged as fairly distinct. That these relations correctly emerged was readily apparent in that no linear term of any variable whose quadratic term was omitted was involved in any other relation.

Even though the relations were observed to be bivariate, correlations would not necessarily have provided any indication of collinearity, since the estimator variance–covariance matrix in the MNL model is more complex than that in regression. For the same reason, auxiliary regressions would not have been particularly useful. More to the point, one cannot know whether the relations are bivariate without a complete diagnosis of collinearity.

The diagnostic information does not solve the problem of collinearity; only information in addition to the data at hand can do this. It does, nonetheless, greatly improve the econometrician's ability to use the estimates by indicating which, if any, estimates suffer from degradation. In particular, the diagnostics show that, of the eight linear terms that were statistically insignificant, four—ER, UH, WFW, and AP—are involved in collinear relations with their respective quadratic terms. Thus, their statistical importance, or lack thereof, has not been credibly established. On the other hand, the four insignificant linear terms not involved in collinear relations—WAG, UR, VO, and GS—are clearly seen to have insignificant effects in the decisions of this sample of potential migrants. Recall, however, that the insignificance of GS is the result of aggregating two significant but opposite effects observed when the sample was stratified by income. Similarly, the diagnosis indicates that the effect of the common variance VA is not unambiguously insignificant. Indeed, in a very reasonable specification of the model, where the origin-specific constant DO is omitted (see Table 5.2), VA is clearly seen to have a significant effect, supporting risk aversion on the part of potential migrants. The diagnostic results also show that the variables of job tenure, JT, and length of residency, LR, variates 7 and 8, are not involved in a collinearity, as is typically suspected.

7

Summary, Recommendations, and Conclusions

SUMMARY

This study examines interregional migration in the United States in a disaggregate behavioral context. The value of such an approach to an understanding of the migratory process is twofold. First, it allows analysis of micro data on individual potential migrants, which are usually richer than aggregate migration data in personal attributes such as work histories and family characteristics. The importance of personal attributes in the migration decision is widely recognized. Second, the disaggregate approach allows the investigation of personally relevant measures of economic opportunity. Individuals with diverse jobs do not have the same economic opportunities at alternative locations, and studies of the importance of economic opportunity should analyze personally relevant measures. While this study was limited by data considerations to examining personal attributes mainly related to the potential migrant's work history and to industry-specific rather than occupation-specific personally relevant measures of economic opportunity, the methodological framework for interpreting and using these and other factors in studying migration was developed in Chapter 3.

The migratory choice model (Chapter 3) viewed the potential migrant as

157

a consumer who, for each alternative location open to him, had an indirect utility defined over the lifetime income he would earn and the amenity factors available to him at the place. The migratory decision problem was then seen to be that of choosing the alternative with the highest value of expected utility. The advantages of the model are several. First, the model does not require the potential migrant to select the alternative with the highest expected real lifetime income, even net of migration costs. Instead, the migrant is free to substitute amenity factors for income in selecting a desired location; indeed, estimation results detailed in Chapter 5 could be used to calculate the marginal rates of substitution between income and amenity factors. Second, explicit economic roles in the decision process are afforded certain popular aspects of migration such as the notions of the well-beaten path and social distance. The decision environment of the model is one of uncertainty with regard to place attributes. The variance associated with the attributes is then a factor in the decision. The information passed along by recent previous migrants, who have beaten the paths before and keep social distances low, is considered by the model as negatively affecting the variance associated with an alternative. Upon estimation, one could assess the dollar value of additional information or the marginal rate of substitution between income and variance. Third, the so-called mobility characteristics of potential migrants are given a behavioral economic meaning. In the model personal attributes are considered as factors related to unobservable migration costs, which have implicit monetary value to the potential migrant. Fourth, the possible importance of unobservable characteristics of both individuals and places is not overlooked. Unobservable attributes are important in the decision process in that their distribution over observationally identical potential migrants is considered to generate a distribution of choices. Thus, the model does not require all potential migrants with identical observable personal and place attributes to select the same alternative.

The behavior of a sample of potential migrants was viewed as a multinomial experiment with a finite number of trials, in which the possible outcomes on each trial are the alternative counties open to each of the potential migrants. Estimates of the parameters of the potential migrant's utility function were obtained by maximizing the multinomial likelihood function. The analysis was of the locational choices of a cross section of individuals in 1969. The data were assembled from four sources. The principal data covering personal attributes and locational choices were from the Social Security Administration's Longitudinal Employer–Employee Data (LEED) file. The aggregate characteristics of the sample from the LEED file, and the use of the other data sets, were described in Chapter 4. While other micro data sets are available that are rich in personal characteristics (such as the household information detailed in the National Longitudinal Survey), none are as suitable as the LEED file to the kind of analysis conducted in this study. The disaggregate study of place-to-place migration requires detailed geographic information, which is not typically provided by other micro data sets.[1]

The migratory choice model was estimated and the results were described in Chapter 5 for the full sample and for stratifications of the sample by race, income, and sex. The findings support the importance of both risk aversion and personal attributes in the migration decision. Additionally, interregional migrants select places that have employment opportunities specific to them. And they locate in established parts of urbanized areas, where population is dense and rental housing is available. Unfortunately, the results for the income measure were not significant, which did not then allow reasonable assessments of the dollar value of additional information and of amenity factors. The results for the stratified subgroups of the sample were also interesting in that they unveiled heterogeneous behavior in the case of several factors. For example, the apparent lack of influence of per capita government expenditures on the potential migrant's expected utility, observed when the full sample is used, was revealed to be the aggregate of two opposite relationships. For high-income potential migrants the relation was positive; it was negative for those with low incomes.

Since the empirical specification of the model used linear and quadratic terms of several variables, a diagnostic analysis of collinearity was undertaken in Chapter 6. An analytical diagnostic developed for regression analysis was first adapted to the maximum-likelihood estimation of the MNL model. Applying the diagnostic to the data indicated that some collinearities involving linear and quadratic terms existed. This understanding aided in clarifying the statistical importance, or lack thereof, of the estimates we observed.

RECOMMENDATIONS FOR FURTHER RESEARCH

In reviewing the research, several areas for further research become apparent. Some pertain to further work with the LEED data and these are discussed below:

1. One way to isolate the effect of common variance VA is to estimate the conditional choice model of destination given migration. The

[1] At the present time, the industry–county specific information used in this study is no longer made available by the Social Security Administration because of possible confidentiality disclosures.

origin-specific constant DO is not a factor in this model. In pursuing this experiment one should be cautious, however. The selection of alternatives, recall, was based on the relative frequency of recent migration, which is also the basis of the common variance term. Consequently, one might want to estimate the conditional model twice. The first estimation would use the alternative sets determined through systematic selection on the basis of relative frequency of migration, and the second would employ alternative sets determined through random selection. The estimated effects for the common variance term should be the same. If they are not, then the systematically selected alternative sets are not truly exogenous to the model.

2. One of the requirements for the reasonable use of the MNL model is that the group behavior of the sample be homogeneous. The results for the sample stratifications indicated important differences in group behavior for subgroups of the sample. The model might be estimated for additional stratifications by other salient characteristics. One possibly important stratification is by age. The effect of the income measure, in particular, is likely to vary according to age. The young are more footloose over occupations and industries than are older potential migrants. Thus, it may be that the industry-specific income measure is the appropriate variable in the case of older potential migrants, while an average income measure is appropriate for young potential migrants. Another useful stratification might be according to the type of labor market in which the potential migrant is employed. As discussed in Chapter 3, the apparent tastes for income are likely to vary according to the kind of labor market in which one is employed.

3. A caveat in the use of the MNL model is the reasonableness of the IIA assumption. Only a limited diagnostic examination of the IIA assumption was undertaken in this study. An extensive diagnosis of potential breakdowns of the IIA assumption seems to be in order if empirical work is to proceed using the model. It is necessary that practitioners have a working understanding of the robustness of estimates obtained using the IIA assumption.

4. Given the concern for the apparent immobility of those in depressed areas on the part of those debating regional policy, it may be useful to estimate the choice model for depressed-area and non-depressed-area potential migrants. It is quite possible that those outside the mainstream of economic activity do indeed behave differently with regard to the migration decision. Also, one might study the mobility characteristics—job tenure, length of residency, and so forth—of depressed-area and non-depressed-area potential mi-

grants to see if the lack of mobility of depressed-area residents is due to a disproportionate share of potential migrants with low-mobility characteristics.

5. The longitudinal nature of the LEED file provides an excellent data source for investigation into two areas of migration that have not received extensive study: the chain hypothesis and return migration. The chain hypothesis essentially considers migratory behavior as a chain of short-distance moves that eventuates a major movement from less industrialized to more industrialized areas. While the chain hypothesis may be of more importance in understanding previous migrations than in explaining current behavior, the behavior of the footloose could be intensively examined using the LEED file. Return migration is typically more heavy in depressed areas than elsewhere and is thought to be differently motivated than nonreturn migration. Since little empirical work has been done on return migration, any improvement in our understanding of the determinants of such behavior is likely to aid regional policy makers in formulating long-term development strategies. Again, the LEED file could be useful in investigating return migration.

Other recommendations for further research require other data sets:

1. This study is exclusively of labor force participants with jobs. Thus, certain segments of the population have been excluded from analysis and certain behavioral questions have not been addressed by this study. For example, the question regarding the responsiveness of migration to welfare payments is important for understanding the burdens and benefits associated with migration. Since welfare is not likely to be a factor in the migration of those earning job income, its effect was not examined. However, other studies of the migratory behavior of the total population could address such questions.

2. The LEED file, while rich in information on work histories, is limited with regard to information on other personal attributes. As seen in Chapter 2, geographic mobility studies have shown that other characteristics are certainly important in the migration decision. With 1980 Census data on counties, the Michigan Panel Study of Income Dynamics might be used to analyze intercounty migration. The Parnes data file or the National Longitudinal Survey only permits interregional analysis at the highly aggregate level of census divisions.

3. Improvements in the model's specification are also called for, even though data availability limits the implementation of improvements. First, the relevant income measure may be an occupation–

geographic specific measure instead of an industry–geographic specific variable, as used here. Second, the host of amenity factors considered might be improved by measures of household agglomeration economies more refined than residential density and degree of urbanization. However, the problem of a successful empirical measure of agglomeration economies is itself an area of research. Climatic variables and recreational amenities might also be included in a more extensive study of amenities.

4. The results of this study provide some evidence for a two-stage process of inter- and intraarea location decisions. In the interarea migration stage, destinations are established, highly urbanized, and dense areas. In the second stage, intraarea migration, destinations are apparently fringe areas, where housing is new and rapidly growing. (Recall that the rate of change in the housing stock HC was a negative and significant factor in our results for interregional migrants. Clearly, the newly built houses are being occupied by migrants, but apparently not the interregional migrants analyzed in our study.) Further investigation into the possibility of a two-stage process seems to be warranted from the results of this study. This, of course, would require data with capabilities beyond those of the LEED file.

CONCLUSIONS

The role of factor flows in regional growth and development is critical. The flow of labor is the result of individual decision making on the part of the labor force. This study is the first to examine the interregional decision-making behavior of potential migrants in the United States at the disaggregate level. It represents a step along the path to an improved understanding of the migration process, which, it is hoped, will enlighten our regional public policy efforts.

Migration policy in the United States could range from a comprehensive program of population dispersion to a limited policy of worker relocation. Although the former's goal would be to bring the private marginal net benefits of migrating into line with the social marginal net benefits, the goal of worker relocation is, more narrowly, to expedite the labor exchange process, largely through the provision of information.

Addressing the migrations that do not enhance the welfare of the migrants would seem to be a high priority of any migration policy. Since the migration of the unemployed tends to be of this sort, worker relocation assistance would be a fundamental aspect of migration policy.[2] The operational feasibility of worker relocation is shown by mobility demonstration projects like the Department of Labor's Job Search and Relocation Assistance Program (JSRA).[3] Even though worker relocation is limited in scope, it receives little attention from policy makers for essentially the same reason that shadows a more grand policy of population distribution. The consensus needed to raise congressional support for worker relocation runs counter to the territorial interests of the members of Congress.[4]

At present, the Department of Labor's United States Employment Service (USES) does, as mandated by the Wagner–Peyser Act, support an interarea job clearinghouse service. There are, however, major obstacles to the evolution of this service to interarea job placement and relocation assistance. In addition to the lack of political support for migration policy, the economics, especially the benefits, of worker relocation are not fully known. While the costs of worker relocation are indicated by JSRA, it is difficult to establish that the benefits associated with reducing structural unemployment through worker relocation exceed the costs. The private and social benefits associated with reduced spells of unemployment are not easy to quantify. This is especially so in the debatable context in which relocations are substitutes for local placements or for migrations which would have otherwise occurred.

Nonetheless, there apparently is a potential to improve migratory decision making, particularly of the unemployed. The results of this study point to the complexity of the migration decision. The separation costs of migration have a strong effect on mobility, and general information regarding an area and specific possibilities for employment are important in affecting the choice of location. Also, amenity factors such as housing conditions and neighborhood characteristics are factors. Since income appears to be less important, regional income disparities may not be sufficient to cause migration. Rather, migration to an area is encouraged by the availability of housing, job information and opportunities, and general information about the place.

In light of our findings, the current strategy of providing second-hand information to potential migrants, USES's newly automated interstate job

---

[2] Bartel (1979) found that migrants on layoff fared worse, in terms of wage growth, than nonmigrants on layoff; the opposite was true for those who had quit their jobs. Also, Mueller (1981) reports that unemployed migrants, more so than others, viewed their moves to be disappointing decisions.

[3] For a description of JSRA, see Mueller (1981).

[4] President's Carter's Commission for a National Agenda for the Eighties (1980, pp. 168), however, strongly urged that federal policies consist of people-to-jobs strategies that recognize the role of worker relocation: "Improved access to jobs involves helping people relocate to take advantage of economic opportunities in other places, as well as retraining them to take advantage of economic opportunity in their own communities."

clearance system, which addresses only the imperfect information on jobs, may be insufficient in reducing the uncertainties that unemployed potential migrants face. On the other hand, the first-hand information on jobs at other places that is provided by relocation assistance like that of JSRA is aimed at reducing social uncertainties as well as job uncertainties, both of which appear to be factors in the complex migration decision. While it is not clear that worker relocation is an economically justifiable structural employment program, it may well be that efforts to provide interarea information that are not multifaceted, unlike those of JSRA, fall short of being effective in improving migratory decisions.

Appendix

TABLE A.1
Estimates of the Migratory Choice Model and of Restricted Models

Variable	1[a]	1[b]	2[a]	2[b]	3[a]	3[b]	4[a]	4[b]	5[a]	5[b]	6[a]	6[b]	7[a]	7[b]	8[a]	8[b]	9[a]	9[b]
TRN	-.65E-02	-5.96	-.66E-02	-6.01	-.66E-02	-6.01	-.66E-02	-6.01	-.66E-02	-6.00	-.65E-02	-5.99	-.66E-02	-6.01	-.66E-02	-6.02	-.45E-02	-4.45
JT	.71E-01	1.60	.71E-01	1.60	.71E-01	1.59	.71E-01	1.59	.70E-01	1.59	.70E-01	1.58	.70E-01	1.58	.69E-01	1.55	.87E-01	1.87
NW	-.33E-01	-.15	-.33E-01	.15	-.34E-01	.15	-.33E-01	.15	-.35E-01	.16	-.37E-01	.16	-.34E-01	.15	-.31E-01	.14	.15E-01	.06
YNG	-.16E 00	-.98	-.17E 00	-1.00	-.17E 00	-1.00	-.17E 00	-1.00	-.16E 00	-.98	-.16E 00	-.96	-.16E 00	-.98	-.17E 00	-1.04	-.57E-01	-.34
OLD	.49E 00	1.90	.49E 00	1.91	.49E 00	1.90	.49E 00	1.90	.49E 00	1.90	.49E 00	1.92	.49E 00	1.91	.48E 00	1.88	.68E 00	2.59
LR	.69E 00	13.46	.69E 00	13.45	.69E 00	13.45	.69E 00	13.45	.69E 00	13.45	.69E 00	13.47	.69E 00	13.50	.69E 00	13.50	.77E 00	14.40
FM	.43E-01	.30	.38E-01	.26	.38E-01	.26	.38E-01	.26	.39E-01	.27	.39E-01	.27	.57E-01	.39	.56E-01	.38	.28E 00	1.88
WAG	-.20E-05	-.97	-.20E-05	.97	-.20E-05	.97	-.20E-05	.97	-.18E-05	.89	-.19E-05	.92	-.20E-05	.98	-.20E-05	.96	-.13E-05	.66
ER	-.21E 00	-1.04	.53E-02	1.42	.53E-02	1.42	.53E-02	1.41	.54E-02	1.43	.55E-02	1.47	.50E-02	1.34	.55E-02	1.48	-.57E-02	-1.74
DI	.25E 00	2.28	.25E 00	2.28	.25E 00	2.30	.25E 00	2.29	.26E 00	2.33	.26E 00	2.38	.24E 00	2.22	.24E 00	2.21	.26E 00	2.35
UR	.85E-03	1.11	.76E-03	1.01	.76E-03	1.01	.74E-03	.98	.83E-03	1.11	.82E-03	1.09	.96E-03	1.27	.91E-03	1.21	.72E-03	.97
DN	.69E-04	2.62	.68E-04	2.61	.69E-04	2.62	.69E-04	2.65	.54E-04	2.23	.56E-04	2.29	.37E-04	1.54	.61E-05	.93	.64E-05	1.03
HC	-.13E-02	-1.84	-.13E-02	-1.87	-.13E-02	-1.88	-.13E-02	-1.87	-.13E-02	-1.83	-.13E-02	-1.90	-.16E-02	-2.08	-.13E-02	-1.73	-.23E-02	-3.66
P50	.66E-02	3.40	.66E-02	3.39	.66E-02	3.38	.67E-02	3.44	.70E-02	3.65	.71E-02	3.70	.13E-02	1.81	.17E-02	2.57	.60E-03	.94
VO	-.54E-02	-.42	-.57E-02	.45	-.53E-02	.42	-.61E-02	.50	-.61E-02	.50	-.62E-02	.51	-.11E-01	.87	-.12E-01	1.02	-.34E-01	-2.89
VR	.11E-01	2.12	.11E-01	2.11	.11E-01	2.12	.11E-01	2.10	.11E-01	2.07	.11E-01	2.12	.98E-02	1.80	.95E-02	1.75	.86E-02	3.35
UH	-.56E-02	-.23	-.69E-02	.28	-.45E-02	.19	-.49E-03	.21	-.39E-03	.16	.58E-04	.03	-.27E-03	.12	-.31E-03	.13	.54E-03	.23
OH	.59E-02	1.69	.59E-02	1.69	.60E-02	1.71	.61E-02	1.76	.17E-02	1.66	.11E-02	1.54	.11E-02	1.52	.93E-03	1.35	.35E-03	.01
GS	-.14E-02	-.53	-.16E-02	.61	-.16E-02	.61	-.15E-02	.59	-.15E-02	.56	-.14E-02	.51	-.29E-02	1.02	-.31E-02	1.19	-.32E-02	-1.37
NFN	.90E-02	3.35	.90E-02	3.35	.89E-02	3.35	.89E-02	3.34	.95E-02	3.59	.92E-02	3.51	.97E-02	3.71	.98E-02	3.76	.99E-02	3.75
WFW	.16E-02	.50	.17E-02	.52	.16E-02	.50	.15E-02	.47	.26E-02	.85	.22E-03	.36	.83E-04	.14	.54E-04	.09	-.15E-03	.25
CG	.81E-02	1.97	.81E-02	1.97	.82E-02	2.00	.83E-02	2.02	.85E-02	2.07	.80E-02	1.98	.10E-01	2.55	.90E-02	2.29	.83E-02	2.18
AP	-.11E-02	-.13	-.20E-02	.24	-.28E-02	.36	-.10E-02	.82	-.11E-02	.92	-.13E-02	-1.03	-.82E-03	.68	-.80E-03	.66	-.14E-02	1.16
WAG2	.55E-11	.13	.53E-11	.13	.55E-11	.13	.58E-11	.14	.64E-11	.15	.70E-11	.17	.70E-11	.17	.77E-11	.18	.14E-10	.35

Each cell shows the coefficient estimate[a] and the asymptotic t statistic[b].

	41	40	39	38	37	36	35	34	33
ER2	.12E-03 / 1.06								
UR2	-.58E-06 / -.85	-.55E-06 / -.81	-.52E-06 / -.78	-.52E-06 / -.77	-.49E-06 / -.73	-.55E-06 / -1.09	-.55E-06 / -.84	-.55E-06 / -.84	
DN2	-.56E-09 / -1.78	-.56E-09 / -1.79	-.57E-09 / -1.80	-.60E-09 / -1.92	-.62E-09 / -1.96	-.62E-09 / -1.34	-.42E-09 / -1.34		
HC2	.85E-06 / 2.25	.84E-06 / 2.23	.84E-06 / 2.22	.85E-06 / 2.25	.86E-06 / 2.33	.88E-06 / 2.40	.62E-06 / 1.19	.47E-06 / .92	.98E-06 / 2.56
P502	-.49E-05 / -2.91	-.50E-05 / -2.93	-.49E-05 / -2.92	-.50E-05 / -2.98	-.52E-05 / -3.16	-.54E-05 / -3.29			
VO2	.92E-04 / .82	.92E-04 / .82	.89E-04 / .80	.93E-04 / .84	.94E-04 / .86	.94E-04 / .85	.12E-03 / 1.09	.13E-03 / 1.19	.19E-03 / 1.73
VR2	-.40E-04 / -1.59	-.39E-04 / -1.54	-.40E-04 / -1.55	-.39E-04 / -1.53	-.39E-04 / -1.53	-.40E-04 / -1.56	-.32E-04 / -1.22	-.30E-04 / -1.15	-.80E-05 / -1.16
UH2	.30E-05 / .21	.37E-05 / .26							
OH2	-.40E-05 / -1.40	-.41E-05 / -1.41	-.41E-05 / -1.43	-.42E-05 / -1.45					
GS2	.19E-05 / .47	.23E-05 / .56	.23E-05 / .55	.22E-05 / .54	.20E-05 / .48	.17E-05 / .39	.41E-05 / .88	.50E-05 / 1.19	.42E-05 / 1.14
NFN2	-.13E-04 / -3.09	-.13E-04 / -3.10	-.13E-04 / -3.10	-.13E-04 / -3.09	-.14E-04 / -3.36	-.13E-04 / -3.29	-.14E-04 / -3.43	-.14E-04 / -3.43	-.14E-04 / -3.29
WFW2	-.96E-06 / .44	-.10E-05 / .46	-.96E-05 / .44	-.87E-06 / .41	-.16E-05 / .80				
CG2	-.94E-05 / .77	-.93E-05 / .76	-.94E-05 / .77	-.93E-05 / .77	-.98E-05 / .81	-.91E-05 / .75	-.15E-04 / -1.19	-.12E-04 / -1.00	-.10E-04 / -.88
AP2	-.39E-07 / -.01	.66E-06 / .12	.12E-05 / .23						
VA	-.11E-05 / -1.07	-.71E-06 / -.77	-.71E-06 / -.77	-.72E-06 / -.78	-.62E-06 / -.68	-.66E-06 / -.72	-.79E-06 / -.86	-.75E-06 / -.81	-.49E-05 / -11.14
DO	.27E 01 / 5.42	.29E 01 / 6.33	.29E 01 / 6.34	.29E 01 / 6.33	.30E 01 / 6.47	.29E 01 / 6.39	.29E 01 / 6.18	.29E 01 / 6.23	.29E 01 / 6.23
LP	.17E 00 / 3.06	.16E 00 / 2.96	.16E 00 / 2.95	.16E 00 / 2.96	.16E 00 / 3.04	.17E 00 / 3.18	.19E 00 / 3.48	.19E 00 / 3.48	.11E 00 / 2.13
κ	41	40	39	38	37	36	35	34	33
χ^2_κ	8,454	8,453	8,453	8,453	8,451	8,450	8,439	8,439	8,351
ρ^2	.66	.66	.66	.66	.66	.66	.66	.66	.66

Notes: The summary measures of the table are: (1) κ is the number of parameters; (2) $\chi^2_\kappa = -2[L(0)' - L(\hat{\theta})]$ can be used to test the null hypothesis that all parameters are simultaneously zero, that is alternatives are equally likely, where $L(0)$ and $L(\hat{\theta})$ are evaluations of the log likelihood function at parameter values of zero and at the estimated values respectively; and (3) $\rho^2 = 1 - L(\hat{\theta})/L(0)$ is a ''goodness of fit'' measure.

[a] Coefficient estimates.

[b] Asymptotic t statistics.

TABLE A.2
Condition Indexes and Variance-Component Percentages, Restricted Model: ER2 Omitted

VARIABLE NUMBER

A	B	1	2	3	4	5	6	7	8	9	10	11	12	13	14	15	16	17	18	19	20	21	22	23	25	26	27	28	29	30	31	32	33	34	35	36	37	38	39	40	41
CI	V																																								
1	2	0	1	0	0	0	0	0	0	0	0	0	0	0	0	0	0	0	0	0	0	0	0	0	0	0	0	0	0	0	0	0	0	0	0	0	0	0	0	0	0
1	12	0	0	0	0	0	0	0	0	0	0	0	0	0	0	0	0	0	0	0	0	0	0	0	0	0	0	0	0	0	0	0	0	0	0	0	0	0	0	0	0
1	11	0	0	0	0	0	0	0	0	0	0	0	0	0	0	0	0	0	0	0	0	0	0	0	0	0	0	0	0	0	0	0	0	0	0	0	0	0	0	0	0
1	28	0	0	0	0	0	0	0	0	0	0	0	0	0	0	0	0	0	0	0	0	0	0	0	0	0	0	0	0	0	0	0	0	0	0	0	0	0	0	0	0
1	27	0	0	0	0	0	0	0	0	0	0	0	0	0	0	0	0	0	0	0	0	0	0	0	0	0	0	0	0	0	0	0	0	0	0	0	0	0	0	0	0
1	20	0	0	0	0	0	0	0	0	0	0	0	0	2	0	0	0	0	0	0	0	0	0	0	0	0	2	0	0	0	0	0	0	0	0	0	0	0	0	0	0
1	18	0	0	0	0	0	0	0	0	0	0	0	0	0	0	0	0	0	0	0	0	0	0	0	0	0	0	0	0	0	0	0	0	0	0	0	0	0	0	0	0
2	19	0	0	23	1	0	0	0	0	0	0	0	0	0	0	0	0	0	1	0	0	0	0	0	0	0	0	0	0	0	0	1	0	0	0	0	0	27	17	0	0
2	29	0	0	0	0	0	0	0	0	0	5	0	0	0	0	0	0	0	0	0	0	0	0	0	0	0	2	0	0	0	0	2	0	0	0	0	0	2	0	0	0
2	7	0	2	2	9	36	0	15	1	0	0	0	0	0	0	0	0	0	1	0	0	0	0	0	0	0	0	0	0	0	0	0	0	0	0	0	0	2	0	0	0
2	40	0	0	0	0	21	0	5	0	0	0	0	0	0	0	0	0	0	0	0	0	0	0	0	0	0	0	0	0	1	0	3	0	0	0	0	0	1	1	0	0
2	39	0	0	0	0	0	0	0	0	11	0	0	0	0	0	0	0	0	1	0	0	0	0	0	0	0	0	0	0	0	0	0	0	0	0	0	0	0	7	33	0
2	32	0	0	0	5	9	0	3	0	0	5	0	0	0	0	0	0	0	1	0	0	0	0	0	0	0	0	0	0	0	0	5	0	0	0	0	0	5	0	8	0
2	31	0	0	0	0	0	0	0	0	0	0	0	0	0	0	0	0	0	0	0	0	0	0	0	0	0	0	0	0	0	0	0	0	0	0	0	0	0	0	0	0
2	30	0	1	59	2	14	0	7	0	25	0	0	0	0	0	0	0	0	0	0	0	0	0	0	0	0	0	0	0	0	0	1	0	0	0	0	0	1	8	55	0
3	33	0	0	0	0	0	0	0	0	0	0	0	0	0	0	0	0	0	0	0	0	0	0	0	0	0	0	0	0	0	0	0	0	0	0	0	0	50	47	0	0
3	36	0	0	0	0	0	0	0	0	2	0	0	0	0	0	0	0	0	0	0	0	0	0	0	0	0	0	0	0	0	0	0	0	0	0	0	0	0	5	0	0
3	34	0	0	0	0	0	0	0	0	6	0	0	0	0	0	0	0	0	0	0	0	0	0	0	0	0	0	0	0	0	0	0	0	0	0	0	0	0	0	0	0
3	38	0	0	0	1	0	0	10	0	11	0	0	0	0	0	0	0	0	0	0	0	0	0	0	0	0	0	0	0	4	0	0	0	0	0	0	0	0	1	0	0
3	4	0	3	5	67	12	1	10	0	0	0	0	0	0	0	0	0	0	0	0	0	0	0	0	0	0	0	0	0	0	0	0	0	0	0	0	0	0	0	0	0

A CI DENOTES CONDITION INDEX.

B V DENOTES VARIABLE NUMBER (SEE TABLE 5.1).

TABLE A.3
Condition Indexes and Variance-Component Percentages, Restricted Model: ER2, UH2 Omitted

VARIABLE NUMBER

A	B	1	2	3	4	5	6	7	8	9	10	11	12	13	14	15	16	17	18	19	20	21	22	23	25	26	27	28	29	30	31	32	33	35	36	37	38	39	40	41
CI	V																																							
1	2	0	1	0	0	0	0	0	0	0	0	0	0	0	0	0	0	0	0	0	0	0	0	0	0	0	0	0	0	0	0	0	0	0	0	0	0	0	0	0
1	20	0	0	0	0	0	0	0	0	0	0	0	0	0	0	0	0	0	0	0	4	0	0	0	0	0	0	0	0	0	0	0	0	0	0	0	0	0	0	0
1	18	0	0	0	0	0	0	0	0	0	0	0	0	0	0	0	0	0	2	0	0	0	0	0	0	0	0	0	0	0	0	1	0	0	0	0	0	0	0	0
1	12	0	0	0	0	0	0	0	0	0	0	0	0	0	0	0	0	0	0	0	0	0	0	0	0	0	0	0	0	0	0	1	0	0	0	0	0	0	0	0
1	11	0	0	0	0	0	0	0	0	0	0	0	0	0	0	0	0	0	0	0	0	0	0	0	0	0	0	0	0	0	0	0	0	0	0	0	0	0	0	0
1	28	0	0	0	0	0	0	0	0	0	0	0	0	0	0	0	0	0	0	0	0	0	0	0	0	0	3	0	0	0	0	0	0	0	0	0	0	0	0	0
1	27	0	0	0	0	0	0	0	0	0	0	0	0	0	0	0	0	0	0	0	0	0	0	0	0	0	0	0	0	0	0	0	0	0	0	0	0	0	0	0
2	29	0	0	0	0	0	0	0	0	0	5	0	0	0	0	0	0	0	0	0	0	0	0	0	0	0	0	0	0	1	0	0	0	0	0	0	0	0	0	0
2	30	0	0	0	0	0	0	0	0	0	15	0	0	0	0	0	0	0	2	0	0	0	0	0	0	0	0	0	0	0	0	6	0	0	0	0	2	0	0	0
2	40	0	0	0	3	5	0	2	0	12	0	0	0	0	0	0	0	0	0	0	0	0	0	0	0	0	0	0	0	0	0	0	0	0	0	0	0	10	27	0
2	33	0	0	0	11	25	0	6	0	0	0	0	0	0	0	0	0	2	2	0	0	0	0	0	0	0	0	0	0	0	0	2	0	0	0	0	6	1	9	0
2	7	0	2	23	5	36	0	15	1	0	0	0	0	0	0	0	0	0	0	0	0	0	0	0	0	0	0	0	0	0	0	0	0	0	0	0	0	1	0	0
2	16	0	1	58	2	14	0	7	0	0	0	0	0	0	0	0	0	0	0	0	0	0	0	0	0	0	0	0	0	0	0	0	0	0	0	0	0	0	0	0
2	19	0	0	0	0	0	0	0	0	0	0	0	0	0	0	0	0	0	0	0	0	0	0	0	0	0	0	0	0	0	0	3	0	0	0	0	0	7	61	0
2	22	0	0	0	0	0	0	0	0	0	0	0	0	0	0	0	0	0	0	0	0	0	0	0	0	0	0	0	0	0	0	1	0	0	0	0	27	17	0	0
3	1	0	0	5	69	12	1	10	0	0	15	0	0	0	0	0	0	0	0	0	1	0	0	0	0	0	0	0	0	0	0	0	0	0	0	0	0	5	0	0
3	4	0	74	5	0	1	2	1	0	0	0	0	0	0	0	0	0	0	0	0	0	0	0	0	0	0	0	0	0	0	0	2	0	0	0	0	0	0	0	0
3	3	0	0	0	0	0	0	0	0	0	15	0	0	0	0	0	0	0	0	0	0	0	0	0	0	0	0	0	0	0	0	0	0	0	0	0	0	0	0	0
3	32	0	0	0	0	0	0	0	0	0	0	0	0	0	0	0	0	0	0	0	0	0	0	0	0	0	0	0	0	1	0	0	0	0	0	0	16	0	0	0
3	39	0	0	0	0	0	0	0	0	0	0	0	0	0	0	0	0	0	0	0	0	0	0	0	0	0	0	0	0	0	0	0	0	0	0	0	25	13	0	0
3	38	0	0	0	0	0	0	0	0	3	0	0	0	0	0	0	0	0	0	0	0	0	0	0	0	0	0	0	0	3	0	0	0	0	0	0	26	21	0	0

```
CI   V
4 25   0  0  0  0  0  0  0  0  0  0  0  0  0  0  0  0  0  0  0  0  0  0  0  0  0  0  0  0
4 17   0  0  0  0  0  1  1  0  2  0  0  0  0  0  0 18  0  1  0  0  0  0  0  0  0  2  0  0
5  8   0  0  0  0  0 39 81  0  0  0  0  5 10  0  0 38  0  3  0  0  0  0  0  0  0  9  2  0
5 26   0  0  0  0  0  0  0  0  0  0  0  0  0  0  2  1  0  0  0  0  0  0  0  0  0  0  0  0
6 31   0  0  0  0  0  0  0  0  6  0  0  0  0  0  0 11  0  0  0  0  0  0  0 14  0 37  0  0
9 13   6  0 83  5  0  1  0  0  0  0  0  0  7  0 49  0  0  0  0  0  0  0  0 49  0  0 24  4
9  6   8  6  6  0  0  0  0 82 82  0  0  0  0  0  0  0  0  0  0  0  0  6  0  0  1  3  0  0
10 37  0  0  0  0  1  0  0  0  0 59  0  0  0  0  0  0  0  0  0  0  0 82 66  0  3  1  0  0
12 35  0  0  0  0  0  0  0  0  0  0  0  0  0  0  0  0  0  0  0  0 86  0  0 15 83  0  0  0
15 36  0  0  0 26  0  0  0  0  0  0 42  0  0  0  3  0  0  0  0  1 24  0  0  0  0  0  0  0
16 10  0  0  0 35  0  0  0  0  0  0 27  0  0  0  0  0  0  0 20 32  0  0  2  0  0  0  1  0
17 23  0  0  0 25  0  2  0  0  0  0  6  0  0  0  0  0  0  0 64 24  0  0  5  0  1  0  5  0
22  9 20  1  0  0  2  0  0  2  0 17  9 18 26  0  0  0  2  0  7  0  0 28  0  2  7  5 16  1 22
24 15 34  1  0  0  4  0  3  4  0  0  5  6  0  1  0  0  4  3  0  2  0 52  0  3  3  6  1  0 35
25 41 35  0  0  0  8  0  1  0  0 10  0  4 43  1  1  0  8  0  7  0  0  7  0  7  0 41  0  0 34
28 14  0  0  0  0  0  1 62  1  0  0  0  0 18  6  2  6  0  2  0  3  0  3 63 26  0  3  1  0
39 21  0  0  0  0  0 16 15  7  4  0  1  0  0 16  0 67  0  0 67  0  0  7  0  3  0  3  0  0
47  5  0  0  0  0  3 82 82 13  1  1  2  8  2  0  5  0  0  1 25  0  2 13  0  0  1  1  0  0
```

TABLE A.4
Condition Indexes and Variance-Component Percentages, Restricted Model: ER2, UH2, AP2 Omitted

VARIABLE NUMBER

CI	V	1	2	3	4	5	6	7	8	9	10	11	12	13	14	15	16	17	18	19	20	21	22	23	26	27	28	29	30	31	32	33	35	36	37	38	39	40	41
1	2	0	0	0	0	0	0	0	0	0	0	0	0	0	0	0	0	0	0	0	0	0	0	0	0	0	0	0	0	0	0	0	0	0	0	0	0	0	0
1	18	0	0	0	0	0	0	0	0	0	0	0	0	0	0	0	0	0	0	0	0	0	0	0	0	0	0	0	0	0	0	0	0	0	0	0	0	0	0
1	12	0	0	0	0	0	0	0	0	0	0	0	0	0	0	0	0	0	0	0	0	0	0	0	0	0	0	0	0	0	0	0	0	0	0	0	0	0	0
1	11	0	0	0	0	0	0	0	0	0	0	0	0	0	0	0	0	0	0	0	0	0	0	0	0	0	0	0	0	0	0	0	0	0	0	0	0	0	0
1	28	0	0	0	0	0	0	0	0	0	0	0	0	0	0	0	0	0	0	0	0	0	0	0	0	0	0	0	0	0	0	0	0	0	0	0	0	0	0
1	27	0	0	0	0	0	0	0	0	0	0	0	0	3	0	0	0	0	0	0	0	0	0	0	0	0	0	0	0	0	0	0	0	0	0	0	0	0	0
2	29	0	0	0	0	0	0	6	0	0	0	0	0	3	0	0	0	0	0	0	0	0	0	0	0	0	0	0	0	0	0	0	0	0	0	3	0	0	0
2	33	0	0	2	11	25	0	0	0	0	0	0	0	0	0	0	0	0	0	0	0	0	0	0	0	0	0	0	0	0	2	0	0	0	0	0	1	0	0
2	40	0	0	0	0	0	0	0	0	4	0	0	0	0	0	0	0	0	0	0	0	0	0	0	0	0	0	0	0	0	1	0	0	0	0	2	9	62	0
2	39	0	0	0	3	4	0	2	0	0	0	0	0	0	0	0	0	0	0	0	0	0	0	0	0	0	0	0	0	0	7	0	0	0	0	4	0	9	0
2	38	0	0	0	0	0	0	0	0	17	0	1	0	0	0	0	0	0	2	0	1	0	0	0	0	0	0	0	0	0	1	1	0	0	0	2	6	19	0
2	20	0	0	0	0	0	0	0	0	0	0	0	0	0	0	0	0	0	0	0	5	0	0	0	0	0	0	0	1	0	1	0	0	0	0	0	0	0	0
2	1	0	1	58	2	15	0	1	0	0	0	0	0	0	0	0	0	0	0	0	8	0	0	0	0	0	0	0	0	0	2	0	0	0	0	0	0	0	0
2	4	0	2	23	5	36	0	6	0	0	0	2	0	0	0	0	0	0	0	0	3	0	0	0	0	0	0	0	0	0	0	0	0	0	0	25	18	7	0
2	7	0	0	0	0	0	0	15	1	0	0	0	0	0	0	0	0	0	0	0	0	0	0	0	0	0	0	0	0	0	0	0	0	0	0	0	0	0	0
3	19	0	0	0	1	0	0	0	0	0	0	0	0	0	0	0	0	0	0	0	0	0	0	0	0	0	0	0	3	0	0	0	0	0	0	1	0	0	0
3	37	0	0	0	0	0	0	0	0	8	0	0	0	0	0	0	0	0	0	0	0	0	0	0	0	0	0	0	1	0	0	0	0	0	0	0	5	0	0
3	36	0	0	0	0	1	0	0	0	3	0	0	0	0	0	0	0	0	0	0	0	0	0	0	0	0	0	0	0	0	0	0	0	0	0	0	22	0	0
3	32	0	0	0	0	0	0	0	0	14	0	0	0	0	0	0	0	0	0	0	0	0	0	0	0	0	0	0	0	0	0	0	0	0	0	27	13	0	0
3	31	0	76	0	0	0	0	0	0	17	0	0	0	0	0	0	0	0	0	0	0	0	0	0	0	0	0	0	0	0	0	0	0	0	0	0	16	0	0

CI	V																														
3	30	5	5	69	12	1	10	1	1	0	0	0	0	0	0	0	0	0	0	0	0	0	0	0	0	0	0	0	0	0	0
4	17	0	0	0	0	1	0	0	0	0	0	0	0	0	0	0	0	0	0	0	0	0	0	0	0	0	0	0	0	0	0
5	16	0	0	0	1	18	37	3	5	0	0	0	0	0	0	0	0	0	0	0	0	0	0	35	0	0	0	1	0	0	0
5	13	0	0	0	1	0	0	1	17	0	0	0	0	0	0	0	0	0	0	0	0	0	0	10	0	0	0	1	0	0	0
5	8	0	0	0	0	25	53	1	31	2	6	2	0	0	0	0	0	0	16	0	0	0	0	17	0	0	0	0	0	0	0
6	35	0	0	0	0	0	0	2	19	5	16	0	53	0	0	0	2	0	2	0	0	0	0	0	0	38	0	0	0	0	0
9	6	8	6	0	0	0	0	3	0	6	0	0	0	0	7	0	0	0	0	6	0	0	0	0	0	0	0	0	0	0	4
9	14	0	0	83	6	0	1	1	0	0	0	0	0	0	0	83	0	0	0	0	0	0	0	0	0	0	0	0	0	0	0
10	3	0	0	0	1	0	0	0	0	59	0	0	0	0	0	0	0	83	0	0	67	3	1	0	0	0	0	0	0	0	0
12	15	0	0	0	0	0	0	2	0	0	9	87	0	1	0	0	0	0	0	0	0	0	0	0	0	1	0	16	85	0	0
15	10	0	0	0	0	24	38	7	2	5	44	3	1	0	0	0	1	0	0	0	0	47	0	0	0	0	2	0	0	2	1
16	22	0	0	0	0	0	27	0	0	0	0	0	0	4	21	35	0	0	28	0	0	0	0	0	0	0	0	0	0	0	24
17	9	0	0	0	0	27	2	0	2	0	0	6	1	0	64	26	0	2	5	0	1	0	0	0	0	0	1	0	0	1	56
22	26	21	1	0	2	0	2	0	17	8	18	26	0	0	8	2	0	27	5	2	7	5	16	0	1	0	0	1	0	0	23
24	23	33	1	0	0	0	5	0	0	5	6	0	0	2	3	3	0	53	3	3	6	3	3	0	1	0	0	0	0	0	35
25	41	35	0	0	0	3	9	1	10	0	4	44	2	1	3	8	0	7	0	1	0	41	0	2	0	3	0	0	0	0	34
28	21	0	0	0	0	0	0	2	63	1	2	0	21	0	5	2	0	3	3	0	0	30	0	4	0	5	2	0	0	2	0
41	5	1	0	0	0	0	0	0	17	2	24	0	0	2	0	93	0	0	3	0	0	0	93	0	0	0	56	0	0	0	1

A

CI DENOTES CONDITION INDEX.

B

V DENOTES VARIABLE NUMBER (SEE TABLE 5.1).

TABLE A.5
Condition Indexes and Variance-Component Percentages, Restricted Model: ER2, UH2, AP2, OH2 Omitted

VARIABLE NUMBER

CI	V	1	2	3	4	5	6	7	8	9	10	11	12	13	14	15	16	17	18	19	20	21	22	23	26	27	28	29	30	31	32	33	36	37	38	39	40	41
1	2	0	0	0	0	0	0	0	0	0	0	0	0	0	0	0	0	0	0	0	0	0	0	0	0	0	0	0	0	0	0	0	0	0	0	0	0	0
1	12	0	0	0	0	0	0	0	0	0	0	0	0	0	0	0	0	0	0	0	0	0	0	0	0	0	0	0	0	0	0	0	0	0	0	0	0	0
1	11	0	0	0	0	0	0	0	0	0	0	0	0	0	0	0	0	0	0	0	0	0	0	0	0	0	0	0	0	0	0	0	0	0	0	0	0	0
1	28	0	0	0	0	0	0	0	0	0	0	0	0	0	0	0	0	0	0	0	0	0	0	0	0	0	0	0	0	0	0	0	0	1	0	0	0	0
1	27	0	0	0	0	0	0	0	0	0	0	0	0	3	0	0	0	0	0	0	0	0	0	0	0	3	0	0	0	0	0	0	0	0	0	0	0	0
1	20	0	0	0	0	0	0	0	0	0	0	0	0	0	0	0	0	0	0	0	5	0	0	0	0	0	0	0	0	1	0	0	0	0	0	0	0	0
1	18	0	0	0	0	0	0	0	0	0	0	1	0	0	0	0	0	0	2	0	0	0	0	0	0	0	0	0	0	0	2	0	0	0	0	0	0	0
2	16	0	1	58	2	15	0	7	0	0	0	0	0	0	0	0	0	0	0	0	0	0	0	0	0	0	0	0	0	0	2	0	0	3	0	0	0	0
2	29	0	0	0	0	0	0	0	0	0	6	0	0	0	0	0	0	0	0	0	0	0	0	0	0	0	0	0	0	0	0	0	0	0	0	0	0	0
2	7	0	2	24	5	36	0	0	1	0	0	0	0	0	0	0	0	0	0	0	0	0	0	0	0	0	0	0	0	0	2	0	0	0	1	0	6	0
2	1	0	0	0	2	0	0	1	0	0	0	0	0	0	0	0	0	0	0	0	0	0	0	0	0	0	0	0	1	0	0	0	0	0	0	0	0	0
2	40	0	0	2	12	25	0	6	0	0	3	0	0	0	0	0	0	0	0	0	0	0	0	0	0	0	0	0	0	0	2	0	0	0	2	8	65	0
2	39	0	0	0	0	0	0	0	0	0	0	0	0	0	0	0	0	0	0	0	1	0	0	0	0	0	0	0	0	0	0	0	0	0	1	19	6	0
2	38	0	0	0	0	0	0	0	0	0	17	0	0	0	0	0	0	0	0	2	0	0	0	0	0	0	0	0	0	0	0	0	0	0	1	7	17	0
2	33	0	0	0	3	4	0	2	0	0	0	0	0	0	0	0	0	0	0	0	0	0	0	0	0	0	0	0	0	0	7	0	0	0	5	0	8	0
2	32	0	0	0	0	1	0	0	0	0	10	0	0	0	0	0	0	0	0	0	0	0	0	0	0	0	0	0	0	0	0	0	0	0	39	21	0	0
2	31	0	0	0	0	0	0	0	0	0	19	0	0	0	0	0	0	0	0	0	0	0	0	0	0	0	0	0	0	0	0	0	0	16	0	0	0	0

[A] CI DENOTES CONDITION INDEX.

[B] V DENOTES VARIABLE NUMBER (SEE TABLE 5.1).

TABLE A.6
Condition Indexes and Variance-Component Percentages, Restricted Model: ER2, UH2, AP2, OH2, WFW2 Omitted

VARIABLE NUMBER

A	B	1	2	3	4	5	6	7	8	9	10	11	12	13	14	15	16	17	18	19	20	21	22	23	27	28	29	30	31	32	33	36	37	38	39	40	41
CI	v																																				
1	2	0	0	0	0	0	0	0	0	0	0	0	0	0	0	0	0	0	0	0	0	0	0	0	0	0	0	0	0	0	0	0	0	0	0	0	0
1	12	0	0	0	0	0	0	0	0	0	0	0	0	0	0	0	0	0	0	0	0	0	0	0	0	0	0	0	0	0	0	0	0	0	0	0	0
1	11	0	0	0	0	0	0	0	0	0	0	0	0	0	0	0	0	0	0	0	0	0	0	0	0	0	0	0	0	0	0	0	0	0	0	0	0
1	28	0	0	0	0	0	0	0	0	0	0	0	0	0	0	0	0	0	0	0	0	0	0	0	3	0	0	0	0	0	0	0	1	1	0	0	0
1	27	0	0	0	0	0	0	0	0	0	0	0	0	2	0	0	0	0	0	0	0	0	0	0	0	0	0	0	0	1	0	0	0	0	0	0	0
1	20	0	0	0	0	0	0	0	0	0	1	0	0	0	0	0	0	0	0	0	4	0	0	0	0	0	0	1	0	0	1	0	0	0	0	0	0
1	18	0	0	0	0	0	0	0	0	0	0	0	0	0	0	0	0	0	2	0	0	0	0	0	0	0	0	0	0	2	0	0	0	0	0	0	0
2	19	0	0	0	0	0	0	0	0	0	3	1	5	0	0	0	0	0	0	0	5	0	0	0	0	0	0	0	0	0	0	0	0	6	1	0	0
2	22	0	0	0	0	1	0	0	0	0	13	0	3	0	0	0	0	0	0	0	0	0	0	0	0	0	0	0	0	0	0	0	0	0	0	0	0
2	29	0	0	2	12	26	0	6	0	0	0	0	0	0	0	0	0	0	0	0	0	0	0	0	0	0	0	2	0	2	0	0	0	0	1	0	0
2	30	0	1	58	2	14	0	7	1	0	0	0	0	0	0	0	0	0	0	0	0	0	0	0	0	0	0	0	0	0	0	0	0	0	0	0	0
2	7	0	2	24	5	35	0	14	0	0	0	0	3	0	0	0	0	0	3	0	0	0	0	0	0	0	0	0	0	0	0	0	0	0	0	0	0
2	40	0	0	0	0	0	0	0	0	0	3	0	0	0	0	0	0	0	0	0	0	0	0	0	0	0	0	0	0	0	0	0	0	3	69	0	0
2	39	0	0	0	0	0	0	0	0	14	0	0	0	0	0	0	0	0	0	0	0	0	0	0	0	0	0	0	0	0	0	0	0	23	9	45	0
2	38	0	0	0	0	0	0	1	0	0	0	0	3	0	0	0	0	0	3	0	0	0	0	0	0	0	0	0	0	1	1	0	0	23	19	15	0
2	33	0	0	0	2	3	0	2	0	28	0	0	0	0	0	0	0	0	0	0	0	0	0	0	0	0	0	0	0	8	1	0	0	5	1	5	0
2	32	0	0	0	0	2	0	2	0	0	0	0	3	0	0	0	0	0	0	0	0	0	0	0	0	0	0	2	0	0	0	0	0	6	3	8	0
3	6	0	6	5	69	11	1	1	0	0	0	0	0	0	0	0	0	0	0	0	0	0	0	0	0	0	0	0	0	0	0	0	0	0	0	0	0

The rows of the following table are identified by the pairs (CI, V) listed at the left. The body of the table is a large numerical matrix.

CI	V																																		
3	4	0	73	5	0	1	2	0	2	2	0	0	0	0	0	0	0	0	0	0	0	1	0	0	0	0	0	0	0	0	0
3	31	0	0	0	1	0	0	4	4	0	8	0	0	1	1	0	0	0	0	4	0	0	0	0	0	0	0	0	0	0	0
4	16	0	0	0	0	0	0	0	2	0	2	36	0	2	0	0	11	0	15	0	1	0	1	12	1	0	0	19	10	0	0
4	10	0	0	0	0	0	0	2	0	0	50	5	0	0	0	20	4	0	1	0	4	0	0	2	0	0	0	0	0	0	0
5	8	0	0	0	0	0	43	1	21	0	1	16	1	0	9	0	0	0	1	0	0	0	0	4	0	0	0	0	0	0	0
5	13	0	0	0	0	0	47	1	23	0	0	16	4	0	9	0	0	0	0	32	0	26	0	0	0	0	0	0	0	0	0
5	17	0	0	0	0	0	0	4	47	0	7	11	0	0	11	0	0	10	0	0	0	2	0	0	0	0	0	2	0	0	0
6	21	0	0	0	0	0	0	0	0	1	0	0	0	0	12	0	0	71	0	0	2	0	4	0	0	11	0	0	0	0	0
8	15	6	0	0	84	0	0	0	0	0	1	1	0	0	0	0	0	0	0	0	0	0	0	0	0	3	0	0	0	0	4
8	1	0	8	0	0	0	1	0	6	0	87	0	0	5	0	0	0	0	60	0	0	0	68	0	3	0	16	0	0	0	0
9	37	0	0	0	0	0	0	0	0	0	6	0	0	5	89	0	9	0	0	0	85	16	0	3	0	0	0	0	0	0	0
11	5	0	0	0	0	0	0	0	0	2	0	2	0	2	0	3	1	0	0	0	0	0	0	0	0	0	0	0	0	0	0
14	9	0	0	0	0	1	27	0	0	0	0	7	0	0	1	0	45	60	47	0	0	0	0	0	25	0	34	0	0	0	0
15	36	0	0	0	0	0	55	7	0	0	0	1	1	2	0	0	32	5	34	51	0	0	0	51	79	4	1	0	0	0	0
16	3	0	0	0	0	8	8	0	0	0	0	1	0	1	1	0	2	0	1	0	1	2	0	0	7	0	1	0	0	0	0
21	23	31	1	0	0	0	2	2	0	0	0	1	0	0	0	0	0	19	10	27	0	2	0	4	20	0	0	0	0	0	0
22	41	42	1	0	0	0	0	3	0	0	0	1	0	0	0	0	0	5	10	1	3	51	21	6	73	1	0	0	0	0	43
24	14	17	0	0	0	0	0	0	0	0	0	2	1	2	0	2	0	0	4	65	0	17	0	71	2	0	9	0	0	16

A
CI DENOTES CONDITION INDEX.

B
V DENOTES VARIABLE NUMBER (SEE TABLE 5.1).

TABLE A.7
Condition Indexes and Variance-Component Percentages, Restricted Model: ER2, UH2, AP2, OH2, WFW2, P502 Omitted

VARIABLE NUMBER

CI	V	1	2	3	4	5	6	7	8	9	10	11	12	13	14	15	16	17	18	19	20	21	22	23	27	28	29	30	32	33	36	37	38	39	40	41
1	2	0	0	0	0	0	0	0	0	0	0	0	0	0	0	0	0	0	0	0	0	0	0	0	0	0	0	0	0	0	0	0	0	0	0	0
1	12	0	0	0	0	0	0	0	0	0	0	0	0	0	0	0	0	0	0	0	0	0	0	0	0	0	0	0	0	0	0	0	0	0	0	0
1	11	0	0	0	0	0	0	0	0	0	0	0	0	0	0	0	0	0	0	0	0	0	0	0	0	0	0	0	0	0	0	0	0	0	0	0
1	29	0	0	0	0	0	0	0	0	0	1	0	0	0	0	0	0	0	0	0	4	0	0	0	0	0	0	1	1	0	0	0	1	1	0	0
1	28	0	0	0	0	0	0	0	0	0	1	0	0	0	0	0	0	0	0	0	0	0	0	0	0	0	0	0	1	0	0	1	1	0	0	0
1	27	0	0	0	0	0	0	0	0	0	0	0	0	2	0	0	0	0	0	0	0	0	0	0	3	0	0	0	0	0	0	0	1	0	0	0
1	18	0	0	0	0	0	0	0	0	0	0	0	0	0	0	0	0	0	2	0	0	0	0	0	0	0	0	0	0	0	0	0	0	0	0	0
2	20	0	0	0	0	0	0	1	0	0	3	1	6	0	0	0	0	0	0	0	5	0	0	0	0	0	0	0	2	0	0	0	0	0	0	0
2	19	0	0	0	1	1	0	0	0	0	0	0	0	0	0	0	0	0	0	1	0	0	0	0	0	0	0	0	1	0	0	0	0	0	0	0
2	36	0	0	0	1	2	0	1	0	0	6	0	7	0	0	0	0	0	0	0	0	0	0	0	0	0	0	0	0	0	0	0	22	18	17	0
2	33	0	0	2	2	5	0	0	0	0	0	0	0	0	0	0	0	0	3	0	1	0	0	0	0	0	0	0	0	1	1	0	20	2	3	0
2	32	0	1	59	2	14	0	7	0	0	34	0	2	0	0	0	0	0	0	0	0	0	0	0	0	0	0	0	9	0	0	0	5	2	5	0
2	30	0	1	0	0	32	0	14	1	0	0	0	0	0	0	0	0	0	0	0	0	0	0	0	0	0	0	0	0	0	0	0	9	6	0	0
2	7	0	2	21	0	0	0	0	0	0	2	0	0	0	0	0	0	0	0	0	0	0	0	0	0	0	0	0	0	0	0	0	0	0	0	0
2	40	0	0	0	0	0	0	0	0	0	2	0	0	0	0	0	0	0	0	0	0	0	0	0	0	0	0	0	0	0	0	0	3	0	0	0
2	39	0	0	0	0	0	0	0	0	0	12	0	0	0	0	0	0	0	0	0	0	0	0	0	0	0	0	0	0	0	0	0	3	9	73	0
2	38	0	0	2	12	27	0	6	0	0	0	0	3	0	0	0	0	0	0	0	0	0	0	0	0	0	0	0	0	0	0	0	21	47	0	0

CI	V																														
3	14	0	73	5	0	4	2	0	0	0	0	0	0	1	0	16	0	1	0	0	0	0	4	0	0	0	0	0	0	0
3	13	0	0	0	0	0	5	0	0	0	0	0	6	0	1	0	3	1	2	19	4	0	0	4	0	1	0	2	0	6
3	6	0	7	0	0	0	0	0	0	0	0	0	0	0	0	0	0	0	0	0	0	0	0	0	0	0	0	3	0	0
4	3	0	0	0	11	0	0	29	0	0	0	21	19	2	0	19	3	1	0	1	0	0	1	0	0	2	0	0	1	0
4	16	0	0	0	0	0	0	22	37	0	0	4	1	2	1	1	3	2	2	0	0	0	1	2	0	2	0	1	0	0
5	17	0	0	0	0	46	1	10	0	0	0	0	0	1	0	6	0	0	0	0	0	0	0	27	0	0	0	0	0	0
5	21	0	0	0	0	0	0	9	12	0	0	41	2	0	0	7	0	0	0	0	0	0	34	1	0	0	0	0	0	0
5	8	0	0	0	0	0	2	9	0	0	0	0	0	0	0	9	0	0	0	0	0	0	0	0	36	0	0	1	0	0
6	4	0	0	0	0	0	21	0	0	0	0	0	0	0	0	5	1	0	0	0	0	0	7	0	13	0	0	0	0	0
8	9	0	0	0	0	0	0	0	0	0	0	0	1	55	0	19	0	87	0	0	0	0	0	0	0	0	0	0	0	0
8	22	6	0	5	0	85	0	0	0	1	0	0	0	0	6	0	7	0	0	0	0	0	0	0	0	0	0	0	0	4
11	15	0	0	0	0	0	0	0	0	0	0	0	0	0	0	2	1	0	1	57	50	0	0	0	0	0	0	2	0	0
11	37	0	0	0	0	0	0	3	0	0	0	68	7	0	0	4	1	18	1	0	0	0	0	0	0	1	12	66	0	0
14	23	0	0	0	0	0	26	6	0	0	26	1	1	0	0	7	1	0	2	50	32	0	1	0	0	0	0	1	0	0
15	5	0	0	0	0	0	0	1	0	0	60	0	1	0	0	0	0	0	0	1	0	0	0	0	0	34	0	0	0	0
17	10	0	0	0	0	3	0	0	0	0	0	0	0	0	1	1	0	2	0	2	5	0	0	8	0	0	0	0	0	0
22	1	6	1	1	0	0	0	0	1	1	3	0	1	0	1	0	1	0	5	0	5	35	0	4	0	73	0	0	0	53
23	41	0	40	0	0	0	2	0	1	0	19	0	0	0	0	0	8	0	8	14	5	52	1	0	14	0	6	0	0	40

^A CI DENOTES CONDITION INDEX.

^B V DENOTES VARIABLE NUMBER (SEE TABLE 5.1).

TABLE A.8
Condition Indexes and Variance-Component Percentages, Restricted Model: ER2, UH2, AP2, OH2, WFW2, P502, DN2 Omitted

VARIABLE NUMBER

CI	V	1	2	3	4	5	6	7	8	9	10	11	12	13	14	15	16	17	18	19	20	21	22	23	27	29	30	32	33	36	37	38	39	40	41
1	2	0	0	0	0	0	0	0	0	0	0	0	0	0	0	0	0	0	0	0	0	0	0	0	0	0	0	0	0	0	0	0	0	0	0
1	32	0	0	0	0	0	0	0	0	0	0	0	0	0	0	0	0	0	0	0	0	0	0	0	0	0	0	0	0	0	0	0	0	0	0
1	29	0	0	0	0	0	0	0	0	0	3	1	0	0	0	0	0	0	0	0	0	0	0	0	0	0	0	0	0	0	0	0	1	0	0
1	27	0	0	0	0	0	0	0	0	0	0	0	0	2	1	0	0	0	0	0	0	0	0	0	3	0	0	0	0	0	1	1	0	0	0
1	20	0	0	0	0	0	0	0	0	0	1	0	6	0	0	0	0	0	0	0	4	0	0	0	0	0	1	1	1	0	0	0	0	0	0
1	18	0	0	0	0	0	0	0	0	0	0	0	0	0	0	0	0	0	2	0	0	0	0	0	0	0	0	2	0	0	1	1	1	0	0
1	12	0	0	0	0	0	0	0	0	0	0	0	0	0	0	0	0	0	0	0	0	0	0	0	0	0	0	0	0	0	0	0	0	0	0
1	11	0	0	0	0	0	0	0	0	0	0	0	0	0	0	0	0	0	0	0	0	0	0	0	0	0	0	0	0	0	0	0	0	0	0
2	7	0	0	58	3	14	0	6	0	0	0	0	0	0	0	0	0	0	0	0	0	0	0	0	0	0	0	8	1	0	0	0	0	0	0
2	19	0	1	0	1	1	0	1	0	0	0	0	0	0	0	0	0	0	3	1	0	0	0	0	0	0	0	0	0	0	0	6	0	3	0
2	40	0	0	0	0	0	0	0	0	0	0	0	0	0	0	0	0	0	0	0	0	0	0	0	0	0	0	1	0	0	0	1	6	3	0
2	39	0	0	0	2	0	0	1	0	0	18	0	0	0	0	0	0	0	0	0	0	0	0	0	0	0	0	0	0	0	0	22	25	82	0
2	38	0	0	0	0	0	0	0	0	0	34	0	0	0	0	0	0	0	0	0	0	0	0	0	0	0	0	0	0	0	0	40	46	8	0
2	36	0	0	1	0	3	0	0	0	0	0	0	2	0	0	0	0	0	0	0	0	0	0	0	0	0	0	1	1	0	0	10	4	0	0
2	4	0	1	2	13	28	0	0	1	0	1	0	0	0	0	0	0	0	0	0	0	0	0	0	0	0	0	0	0	0	0	0	0	4	0
2	3	0	1	22	5	34	15	7	0	0	0	0	0	0	0	0	0	0	0	0	0	0	0	0	0	0	0	0	0	0	0	2	0	0	0
3	30	0	0	0	0	0	0	0	0	0	1	0	6	14	0	0	2	2	0	3	3	3	0	0	0	0	2	0	0	0	0	0	2	0	0

CI	V																											
3	13	0	74	5	1	1	2	2	0	0	0	0	0	0	0	0	0	0	0	0	0	0	0	0	0	0	0	0
3	6	0	6	5	69	12	10	0	0	0	0	0	13	0	0	0	0	0	2	2	0	2	4	0	7	32	27	12
3	9	0	0	0	0	0	0	6	0	0	0	0	0	0	0	0	0	0	0	0	0	0	0	0	0	0	0	0
4	10	0	0	0	0	0	6	0	1	2	3	6	0	0	1	35	12	44	0	9	0	0	2	4	0	0	0	0
4	8	0	0	0	0	1	24	49	38	0	0	0	8	0	0	7	0	0	0	0	0	0	0	32	0	0	0	0
4	22	0	0	0	0	0	19	38	0	1	0	6	6	21	3	14	0	0	0	0	0	5	29	6	0	0	4	27
4	37	0	0	0	0	0	0	0	2	20	0	0	0	0	0	0	0	0	0	0	5	29	2	26	1	0	4	0
5	15	0	0	0	0	0	7	0	0	0	0	0	0	0	36	15	3	0	0	14	33	0	14	10	0	0	0	0
6	14	0	0	0	0	0	0	0	0	0	0	6	0	0	21	0	0	0	0	13	5	11	76	0	0	0	12	0
8	17	0	0	0	0	0	0	0	0	0	0	0	0	0	0	1	1	86	0	0	0	0	0	0	0	0	0	0
8	1	6	8	84	6	1	0	0	0	0	0	0	0	0	0	0	0	86	8	0	0	0	0	0	0	0	0	4
10	33	0	0	0	0	0	0	0	0	0	0	0	0	3	0	0	0	0	2	0	0	37	7	31	0	0	0	0
11	21	0	0	0	0	0	0	0	0	0	0	0	0	0	0	0	0	0	0	0	30	10	59	0	0	0	0	0
13	5	0	0	0	0	0	0	31	0	6	0	0	0	0	0	0	0	0	0	50	0	0	0	4	0	0	0	0
14	23	0	0	0	0	0	0	52	0	1	0	2	2	48	0	0	1	0	0	45	0	0	0	1	5	0	0	0
16	16	0	0	0	0	0	0	9	0	0	89	13	0	1	0	0	0	0	3	0	10	0	0	88	0	3	5	0
21	41	91	2	1	0	1	3	0	0	0	0	1	1	0	1	2	0	0	1	0	0	0	2	0	1	0	1	94

A
CI DENOTES CONDITION INDEX.

B
V DENOTES VARIABLE NUMBER (SEE TABLE 5.11).

181

TABLE A.9

Condition Indexes and Variance-Component Percentages, Restricted Model: ER2, UH2, AP2, OH2, WFW2, P502, DN2, DO Omitted

VARIABLE NUMBER

A	B																																	
CI	V	2	3	4	5	6	7	8	9	10	11	12	13	14	15	16	17	18	19	20	21	22	23	27	29	30	32	33	36	37	38	39	40	41
1	5	1	0	1	0	0	0	1	0	0	0	0	0	0	0	0	0	0	0	0	0	0	0	0	0	0	0	0	0	0	0	0	0	0
1	3	0	0	0	0	0	0	0	0	0	0	0	0	0	0	0	0	0	0	0	0	0	0	0	0	0	0	0	0	0	0	0	0	0
1	13	0	0	0	0	0	0	0	0	0	0	0	0	0	0	0	0	0	0	0	0	0	0	3	0	0	0	0	0	0	0	0	0	0
1	10	0	0	0	0	0	0	0	0	0	0	0	3	0	0	0	0	3	1	0	0	0	0	0	0	0	2	1	0	0	0	0	0	0
1	9	0	0	0	0	0	0	0	0	0	0	0	0	0	0	0	0	0	0	0	0	0	0	0	0	0	0	0	0	0	0	0	0	0
1	18	0	0	0	0	0	0	0	5	0	0	3	0	0	0	0	0	1	1	2	0	0	0	0	0	0	3	0	0	1	2	0	0	0
1	16	0	0	0	0	0	0	0	1	0	0	0	0	0	0	0	0	0	1	5	0	0	0	0	0	1	0	2	0	0	0	0	0	0
1	14	0	0	0	0	0	3	0	0	0	0	0	0	1	0	0	0	0	0	1	0	0	0	0	0	0	0	4	0	0	2	0	0	0
2	19	0	0	3	5	0	0	0	0	0	0	2	0	0	0	0	0	2	2	0	0	0	0	0	0	0	7	0	0	0	25	31	5	0
2	20	0	0	0	0	0	1	0	1	0	0	0	0	0	0	0	0	0	0	0	0	0	0	0	0	0	0	0	0	0	11	4	4	0
2	22	0	2	1	1	0	0	0	36	0	0	2	0	0	0	0	0	0	0	0	0	0	0	0	0	0	1	0	0	0	1	2	0	0
2	12	1	1	15	26	0	7	1	0	0	0	0	0	0	0	0	0	0	0	0	0	0	0	0	0	0	0	0	0	0	1	0	0	0
2	4	4	25	7	34	0	12	0	0	0	0	0	0	0	0	0	0	0	0	0	0	0	0	0	0	0	0	0	0	0	2	4	0	0
2	40	0	0	0	0	0	0	0	0	0	0	0	0	0	0	0	0	0	0	0	0	0	0	0	0	0	0	0	0	0	0	0	88	0
2	39	0	53	2	16	0	8	0	0	0	0	0	0	0	0	0	0	0	0	0	0	0	0	0	0	0	0	0	0	0	40	42	0	0
2	38	0	0	0	1	0	0	0	18	0	0	0	0	0	0	0	0	0	0	0	0	0	0	0	0	0	0	1	0	0	0	0	0	0

Table of variance-decomposition proportions (condition indices and variable proportions).

CI[a]	V[b]																					
3	7	17	12	17	7	7	13	0	0	0	0	0	0	0	0	0	0	0	0	1		
3	6	0	50	3	1	0	0	59	0	9	11	0	9	9	3	0	2	0	0	0		
3	29	0	0	1	0	0	0	2	0	0	0	3	9	0	0	0	1	0	6	0		
3	27	0	0	0	0	0	4	0	0	9	0	0	0	0	0	2	5	0	2	0		
4	33	0	0	0	0	0	2	43	20	11	2	0	0	20	3	3	17	0	0	0		
4	30	0	0	0	0	1	6	0	2	9	9	0	0	0	2	0	0	0	0	3		
4	8	0	0	2	42	18	0	0	0	0	0	0	0	3	0	1	0	3	0	3		
4	2	5	0	0	1	0	0	0	0	0	0	0	0	0	0	0	2	0	3	1		
5	21	0	0	5	2	20	0	0	0	0	0	17	12	3	0	0	2	0	7	0		
5	37	0	0	8	13	15	0	0	17	0	0	13	50	32	8	0	10	7	45	0		
6	32	0	0	0	2	0	0	0	0	20	0	0	13	3	74	0	0	0	27	8		
8	23	0	0	1	0	1	2	94	1	20	1	0	0	0	0	0	0	0	5	0		
9	36	0	0	0	2	0	0	0	0	1	0	9	0	0	0	2	0	7	0	0	82	
10	11	0	0	0	0	0	0	0	0	0	0	81	0	0	5	0	0	58	0	0	0	11
13	15	24	0	0	0	0	5	0	0	1	49	50	1	4	0	0	11	0	0	48	1	13
14	17	13	0	0	0	0	0	0	0	1	41	1	2	0	3	0	43	26	40	0	0	47
14	41	55	0	3	0	1	0	1	0	0	6	1	0	0	0	0	40	58	0	6	4	36

[a] CI DENOTES CONDITION INDEX.

[b] V DENOTES VARIABLE NUMBER (SEE TABLE 5.1).

References

Adler, T. J. (1975). *A Joint Choice Disaggregate Model of Non-Work Urban Passenger Travel Demand*. M.S. thesis, Department of Civil Engineering, Massachusetts Institute of Technology.

Adler, T. J. (1976). *Modeling Non-Work Travel Patterns*. Ph.D. dissertation, Department of Civil Engineering, Massachusetts Institute of Technology.

Alexander, A. (1974). Income, experience, and the structure of internal labor markets. *Quarterly Journal of Economics* **88**, 63–85.

Alonso, W. (1972a). The policy implications of intermetropolitan migration flows. *Proceedings of the Regional Economic Development Research Conference,* U.S. Department of Commerce, Washington, D.C.

Alonso, W. (1972b). The system of intermetropolitan population flows, *in* U.S. Commission on Population Growth and the American Future, *Population, Distribution, and Policy,* Vol. V. Washington, D.C.

Alonso, W. (1973). *National Interregional Demographic Accounts: A Prototype*. Monograph No. 17, Institute of Urban and Regional Development, University of California, Berkeley.

Alonso, W. (1974). *Policy-Oriented Interregional Demographic Accounting and a Generalization of Population Flow Models*. Working Paper No. 247, Institute of Urban and Regional Development, University of California, Berkeley.

Alperovich, G., J. Bergsman, and C. Ehemann (1977). An econometric model of migration between U.S. metropolitan areas. *Urban Studies* **13**, 135–145.

Anderson, J. E. (1978). *A Theoretical Foundation for the Gravity Model of Factor Flows*. Working Paper No. 85, Department of Economics, Boston College.

Anderson, J. E. (1979). A theoretical foundation for the gravity equation. *American Economic Review* **69**, 106–111.

185

Archibald, G. C., and R. G. Lipsey (1976). *An Introduction to Mathematical Economics.* New York: Harper & Row.

Arora, S., and M. Brown (1971). *A Utility Maximization Approach to Multipolar Migration under Uncertainty.* Discussion Paper No. 209, Department of Economics, State University of New York at Buffalo.

Bartel, A. P. (1979). What role does job mobility play? *American Economic Review* **69,** 775–786.

Beale, C. (1969). *The Relation of Gross Outmigration Rates to Net Migration.* Mimeo; Economic Research Service, U.S. Department of Agriculture, Washington, D.C.

Beale, C. (1972). Rural and nonmetropolitan population trends of significance to national population growth and the American future, *in* U.S. Commission on Population Growth and the American Future, *Population, Distribution, and Policy,* Vol. V. Washington, D.C.

Beals, R. E., M. B. Levy, and L. M. Moses (1967). Rationality and migration in Ghana. *Review of Economics and Statistics* **49,** 480–486.

Belsley, D. A., E. Kuh, and R. Welsch (1980). *Diagnostics in the Linear Regression Model: Identifying Influential Data and Sources of Collinearity.* New York: John Wiley.

Ben-Akiva, M. (1973). *Structure of Passenger Travel Demand Models.* Ph.D. dissertation, Department of Civil Engineering, Massachusetts Institute of Technology.

Blanco, C. (1964). Prospective unemployment and interstate population movements. *Review of Economics and Statistics* **46,** 221–222.

Borts, G. H., and J. L. Stein (1964). *Economic Growth in a Free Market.* New York: Columbia University Press.

Böventer, E. von (1969). Migration into West German cities. *Papers of the Regional Science Association* **23,** 53–62.

Bowles, S. (1970). Migration as investment: Empirical tests of the human capital approach to geographic mobility. *Review of Economics and Statistics* **52,** 356–362.

Cebula, R. (1974). Interstate migration and the Tiebout hypothesis: An analysis according to race, sex, and age. *Journal of the American Statistical Association* **69,** 876–879.

Cebula, R. (1979). *The Determinants of Human Migration.* Lexington, Mass.: Lexington Books.

Cebula, R., and C. Curran (1974). Determinants of migration to central cities: A comment. *Journal of Regional Science* **14,** 249–253.

Cebula, R., R. Kohn, and R. Vedder (1973). Some determinants of black interstate migration, 1965–1970. *Western Economic Journal* **11,** 500–505.

Cebula, R., R. Kohn, and R. Vedder (1976). Interstate black migration: Reply to Ziegler. *Economic Inquiry* **14,** 454–456.

Conte, S. D., and C. de Boor (1965). *Elementary Numerical Analysis: An Algorithmic Approach.* New York: McGraw–Hill.

DaVanzo, J. (1972). *An Analytical Framework for Studying the Potential Effects of an Income Maintenance Program on U.S. Interregional Migration.* Report No. R-1081-EDA, The Rand Corporation, Santa Monica, Calif.

DaVanzo, J. (1977). *Why Families Move: A Model of the Geographic Mobility of Married Couples.* R & D Monograph, U.S. Department of Labor, Washington, D. C.

Doeringer, P., and M. Piore (1971). *Internal Labor Markets and Manpower Analysis.* Lexington, Mass.: D. C. Heath.

Domencich, T. A., and D. McFadden (1975). *Urban Travel Demand: A Behavioral Analysis.* Amsterdam: North-Holland Publishing.

Fields, G. S. (1979). Place-to-place migration: Some new evidence. *Review of Economics and Statistics* **61,** 21–32.

Gallaway, L. E., R. F. Gilbert, and P. E. Smith (1968). The economics of labor mobility: An empirical analysis. *Western Economic Journal* **5**, 211–223.

Glantz, F. (1973). *The Determinants of the Intermetropolitan Migration of the Economically Disadvantaged.* Research Report No. 52, Federal Reserve Bank of Boston.

Goldfeld, S. M., and R. E. Quandt (1972). *Nonlinear Methods in Econometrics.* Amsterdam: North-Holland Publishing.

Grant, E. K., and J. Vanderkamp (1976). *The Economic Causes and Effects of Migration: Canada, 1965–1971.* Minister of Supply and Services, Ottawa, Canada.

Graves, P. E., and P. D. Linneman (1979). Household migration: Theoretical and empirical results. *Journal of Urban Economics* **6**, 383–404.

Greenwood, M. J. (1969). An analysis of the determinants of geographic labor mobility in the United States. *Review of Economics and Statistics* **51**, 189–194.

Greenwood, M. J. (1973). Urban growth and migration: Their interaction. *Environment and Planning* **5**, 91–112.

Greenwood, M. J. (1975a). Research on internal migration in the United States. *Journal of Economic Literature* **13**, 397–433.

Greenwood, M. J. (1975b). A simultaneous-equations model of urban growth and migration. *Journal of the American Statistical Association* **70**, 797–810.

Greenwood, M. J. (1976). A simultaneous-equations model of white and nonwhite migration and urban change. *Economic Inquiry* **14**, 1–15.

Greenwood, M. J., and P. J. Gormely (1971). A comparison of the determinants of white and nonwhite interstate migration. *Demography* **8**, 141–155.

Greenwood, M. J., and D. Sweetland (1972). The determinants of migration between standard metropolitan statistical areas. *Demography* **9**, 665–681.

Hansen, N. (1970). *Rural Poverty and the Urban Crisis.* Bloomington, Ind.: Indiana University Press.

Hansen, N. (1972). The case of government assisted migration, *in* U.S. Commission on Population Growth and the American Future, *Population, Distribution, and Policy,* Vol. V. Washington, D.C.

Hansen, N. (1973). *The Future of Nonmetropolitan America.* Lexington, Mass.: D. C. Heath.

Herrick, B. (1973). *Urban Self-Employment and Changing Expectations as Influences on Urban Migration.* Discussion Paper No. 46, University of California, Los Angles.

Hicks, J. R. (1932). *The Theory of Wages.* London: Macmillan Press.

Hoover, E. (1972). Policy objectives for population distribution, *in* U.S. Commission on Population Growth and the American Future, *Population, Distribution, and Policy,* Vol. V. Washington, D.C.

Hoover, E. (1975). *An Introduction to Regional Economics.* New York: Alfred A. Knopf.

Hunter, L. C., and G. L. Reid (1968). *Urban Worker Mobility.* Paris: Organization for Economic Development.

Intrilligator, M. D. (1971). *Mathematical Optimization and Economic Theory.* Englewood Cliffs, N.J.: Prentice–Hall.

Isard, W. (1969). *Methods of Regional Analysis: An Introduction to Regional Science.* Cambridge, Mass.: M.I.T. Press.

Jenness, R. (1969). Manpower mobility programs, *in* G. G. Somers and W. D. Wood, eds. *Cost Benefit Analysis of Manpower Policy.* Industrial Relations Centre, Queen's University, Kingston, Ontario.

Kahne, H. (1975). Economic perspectives on the roles of women in the American economy. *Journal of Economic Literature* **13**, 1249–1292.

Kain, J. F., and J. J. Persky (1967). *The North's Stake in Southern Rural Poverty.* Discussion Paper No. 18, Program on Regional and Urban Economics, Harvard University.

Kaluzny, R. (1975). The determinants of household migration: A comparative study by race and poverty level. *Review of Economics and Statistics* **57,** 269–274.

Keeney, R. L. (1969). *Multidimensional Utility Functions: Theory, Assessment, and Applications.* Technical Report No. 43, Operations Research Center, Massachusetts Institute of Technology.

Kendall, M. G., and A. S. Stuart (1961). *The Advanced Theory of Statistics,* Vol. 2. New York: Hafner Publishing.

Lansing, J. B., and E. Mueller (1967). *The Geographic Mobility of Labor.* Survey Research Center, Institute for Social Research, University of Michigan.

Lerman, S. (1975). *A Disaggregate Behavioral Model of Urban Mobility Decisions.* Ph.D. dissertation, Department of Civil Engineering, Massachusetts Institute of Technology.

Levy, M. B., and W. J. Wadycki (1972). Lifetime vs. one-year migration in Venezuela. *Journal of Regional Science* **12,** 407–415.

Levy, M. B., and W. J. Wadycki (1974). What is the opportunity cost of moving? Reconsideration of the effects of distance on migration. *Economic Development and Cultural Change* **22,** 198–214.

Lowry, I. S. (1966). *Migration and Metropolitan Growth: Two Analytical Models.* San Francisco: Chandler Publishing.

Luce, R. D., and H. Raiffa (1967). *Games and Decisions.* New York: John Wiley.

Manski, C. F. (1973). *The Analysis of Qualitative Choice.* Ph.D. dissertation, Department of Economics, Massachusetts Institute of Technology.

Mazek, W. F. (1966). *The Efficacy of Labor Migration with Special Emphasis on Depressed Areas.* Working Paper No. CWR 2, Washington University.

Mazek, W. F., and J. Chang (1972). The chicken or egg fowl-up in migration. *The Southern Economic Journal* **39,** 133–139.

McFadden, D. (1974). Analysis of qualitative choice behavior, *in* P. Zarembka, ed., *Frontiers in Econometrics.* New York: Academic Press.

McFadden, D. (1975). *On Independence, Structure, and Simultaneity in Transportation Demand Analysis.* Working Paper No. 7511, Institute of Transportation and Traffic Engineering, University of California, Berkeley.

McFadden, D. (1976a). *Properties of the Multinomial Logit (MNL) Model.* Working Paper No. 7617, Institute of Transportation Studies, University of California, Berkeley.

McFadden, D. (1976b). Quantal choice analysis: A survey. *Annals of Economic and Social Measurement* **5,** 363–390.

McFadden, D. (1977). *Modelling the Choice of Residential Location.* Cowles Foundation Discussion Paper No. 477, Yale University.

McFadden, D., W. Tye, and K. Train (1976). *Diagnostic Tests for the Independence of Irrelevant Alternatives Property of the Multinomial Logit Model.* Working Paper No. 7616, Institute of Transportation Studies, University of California, Berkeley.

Michigan Survey Research Center (1966). *Migration into and out of Depressed Areas.* U.S. Department of Commerce, Area Redevelopment Administration. Washington, D.C.

Miller, A. (1967). The migration of employed persons to and from metropolitan areas of the United States. *Journal of the American Statistical Association* **62,** 1418–1432.

Miller, E. (1973a). Is out-migration affected by economic conditions? *Southern Economic Journal* **39,** 396–405.

Miller, E. (1973b). Return and non-return inmigration. *Growth and Change* **4,** 3–9.

Mills, E. S. (1972). *Urban Economics.* Glenview, Ill.: Scott Foresman.

Mood, A. M., and F. A. Graybill (1963). *Introduction to the Theory of Statistics.* New York: McGraw–Hill.

Morrison, P. A. (1972a). Population movements and the shape of urban growth: Implications for public policy, *in* U.S. Commission on Population Growth and the American Future, *Population, Distribution, and Policy*, Vol. V. Washington, D.C.

Morrison, P. A. (1972b). *Population Movements: Where the Public Interests Conflict*. Report No. R-987-CPG, The Rand Corporation, Santa Monica, Calif.

Morrison, P. A. (1973a). *Migration from Distressed Areas: Its Meaning for Regional Policy*. Report No. R-1103-EDA/FF/NIH, The Rand Corporation, Santa Monica, California.

Morrison, P. A. (1973b). Theoretical issues in the design of population mobility models. *Environment and Planning* **5**, 125–134.

Morrison, P. A., and D. A. Relles (1975). *Recent Research Insights into Local Migration Flows*. Paper P-5379, The Rand Corporation, Santa Monica, Calif.

Moss, W. G. (1979). A note on individual choice models of migration. *Regional Science and Urban Economics* **9**, 333–343.

Mueller, C. F. (1978). *Labor Force Migration: A Behavioral Approach*. Ph.D. dissertation, Department of Economics, Boston College.

Mueller, C. F. (1980). *Diagnosing Collinearity in Multinomial Logit Analysis: A Case Study of Interregional Migration*. Unpublished paper presented at the 1980 WEA Meeting, San Diego, Calif.

Mueller, C. F. (1981). Migration of the unemployed: A relocation assistance program. *Monthly Labor Review* **104**, 62–64.

Muth, R. F. (1968). Differential growth among large U.S. cities, *in* J. P. Quirk and A. M. Zarley, eds., *Papers in Quantitative Economics*. Lawrence, Ka.: The University Press of Kansas.

Muth, R. F. (1971). Migration: Chicken or egg? *Southern Economic Journal* **37**, 295–306.

Muth, R. F. (1972). The chicken or egg fowl-up in migration: Reply. *Southern Economic Journal* **39**, 139–142.

Nelson, K. P. (1975). *Evaluating Social Security Measures of Migration: Basic Considerations*. Research Paper No. ORNL-UR-119, Regional and Urban Studies Department, Oak Ridge National Laboratory.

Niedercorn, J. H., and B. V. Bechdolt (1969). An economic derivation of the "gravity law" of spatial interaction. *Journal of Regional Science*. **9**, 273–282.

Olvey, L. D. (1970). *Regional Growth and Inter-Regional Migration—Their Pattern of Interaction*. Ph.D. dissertation, Harvard University.

Pack, J. R. (1973). Determinants of migration to central cities. *Journal of Regional Science* **13**, 249–260.

Pack, J. R. (1974). Determinants of migration to central cities: A reply. *Journal of Regional Science* **14**, 291, 292.

Parnes, H. S. (1970). Labor force participation and labor mobility, *in* A Review of Industrial Relations Research, Vol. I. Madison, Wisc.: Industrial Relations Research Association.

Persky, J. J., and J. F. Kain (1970). Migration, employment and race in the deep South. *Southern Economic Journal* **36**, 268–276.

Polachek, S., and F. Horvath (1977). A life cycle approach to migration: Analysis of the perspicacious peregrinator, *in* R. Ehrenberg, ed., *Research in Labor Economics*, Vol. 1. Greenwich, Conn.: JAI Press.

Pratt, J. W. (1964). Risk aversion in the small and in the large. *Econometrica* **32**, 122–136.

Quigley, J. M. (1976). Housing demand in the short-run: An analysis of polychotomous choice. *Exploration in Economic Research, Occasional Papers of the NBER* **3**, 76–102.

Rabianski, J. (1971). Real earnings and human migration. *Journal of Human Resources* **6**, 185–192.

Raiffa, H. (1970). *Decision Analysis*. Reading, Mass.: Addison–Wesley.

Raimon, R. L. (1962). Interstate migration and wage theory. *Review of Economics and Statistics* **44**, 428–438.

Renshaw, V. (1970). *The Role of Migration in Labor Market Adjustment*. Ph.D. dissertation, Massachusetts Institute of Technology.

Richardson, H. W. (1973). *Regional Growth Theory*. New York: John Wiley.

Riew, J. (1973). Migration and public policy. *Journal of Regional Science* **13**, 65–76.

Rogers, A. (1967). A regression analysis of interregional migration in California. *Review of Economics and Statistics* **49**, 262–267.

Rothschild, M., and J. E. Stiglitz (1970). Increasing risk I. A definition. *Journal of Economic Theory* **2**, 225–243.

Rothschild, M., and J. E. Stiglitz (1971). Increasing risk. II. Its economic consequences. *Journal of Economic Theory* **3**, 66–84.

Samuelson, P. A. (1965). *Foundations of Economic Analysis*. New York: Atheneum.

Schultz, T. P. (1977). *A Conditional Logit Model of Internal Migration: Venezuelan Lifetime Migration within Educational Strata*. Discussion Paper No. 266, Economic Growth Center, Yale University.

Schwind, P. J. (1971). *Migration and Regional Development in the U.S., 1950–1960*. Chicago: University of Chicago Press.

Sjaastad, L. (1962). The costs and returns of human migration. *Journal of Political Economy, Supplement* **70**, 80–93.

Social Security Administration (1971). *The 1% Sample Longitudinal Employee Employer Data File*. Mimeo, Office of Research and Statistics.

Stigum, B. P. (1972). Finite state space and expected utility maximization. *Econometrica* **40**, 253–259.

Taeuber, C., and I. Taeuber (1971). *The People of the United States in the Twentieth Century*. Washington, D.C.: U.S. Government Printing Office.

Theil, H. (1958). *Economic Forecasts and Policy*. Amsterdam: North-Holland Publishing.

Theil, H. (1965). Linear decision rules of macro policy, *in* B. Hickman, ed., *Quantitative Planning of Economic Policy*. Washington, D.C.: The Brookings Institution.

Theil, H. (1967). *Economics and Information Theory*. Chicago: Rand McNally.

Tobin, J. (1958). Liquidity preference as behavior towards risk. *Review of Economic Studies* **25**, 65–86.

Todaro, M. (1969). A model of labor migration and urban development in less developed countries. *American Economic Review* **59**, 138–148.

Trott, C. (1971a). *An Analysis of Outmigration*. Mimeo, Office of Business Economics, U.S. Department of Commerce.

Trott, C. (1971b). *Differential Responses in the Decision to Migrate*. Unpublished paper presented at the RSA Meeting.

U.S. Congress, House (1972). *Rural Development Act of 1972*. Report No. 92-385, 92nd Congress, Second Session.

U.S. Department of Agriculture (1969). *U.S. Population Mobility and Distribution*. Economic Research Service, ERS-436, Washington, D.C.

U.S. Department of Commerce (1966). *County Business Patterns, 1965*. Washington, D.C.

U.S. Department of Commerce (1970). Use of Social Security's Continuous Work History Sample for population estimates. *Current Population Reports*, Series P-23, No. 31, Washington, D.C.

U.S. Department of Commerce (1971a). Components of population change by county. *Current Population Reports*, Series P-25, No. 461, Washington, D.C.

U.S. Department of Commerce (1971b). Preliminary intercensal estimates of States and components of change, 1960 to 1970. *Current Population Reports*, Series P-25, No. 460, Washington, D.C.

U.S. Department of Commerce (1972a). *1970 Census of Population, Migration Between State Economic Areas.* Subject Report PC(2)-2E, Washington, D.C.

U.S. Department of Commerce (1972b). *1970 Census of Population, Mobility for States and the Nation.* Subject Report PC(2)-28, Washington, D.C.

U.S. Department of Commerce (1973a). *County Business Patterns, 1972.* Washington, D.C.

U.S. Department of Commerce (1973b). *County and City Data Book, 1972.* Washington, D.C.

U.S. Department of Commerce (1973c). Farm population of the United States: 1972. *Current Population Reports,* Series P-27, No. 44, Washington, D.C.

U.S. Department of Commerce (1974a). Female family heads. *Current Population Reports,* Series P-23, No. 50, Washington, D.C.

U.S. Department of Commerce (1974b). Mobility of the population of the United States, March 1970 to March 1973. *Current Population Reports,* Series P-20, No. 262, Washington, D.C.

U.S. Department of Commerce (1976). A statistical portrait of women in the United States. *Current Population Reports,* Series P-25, No. 58, Washington, D.C.

U.S. National Advisory Commission on Rural Poverty (1968). *Rural Poverty in the United States.* Washington, D.C.

U.S. President's Commission for a National Agenda for the Eighties (1980). *A National Agenda for the Eighties,* Washington, D.C.

Wadycki, W. (1974a). A note on opportunity costs and migration analysis. *Annals of Regional Science* **8,** 109–117.

Wadycki, W. (1974b). Alternative opportunities and interstate migration: Some additional results. *Review of Economics and Statistics* **56,** 254–257.

Wilde, D. J. (1964). *Optimum Seeking Methods.* Englewood Cliffs, N.J.: Prentice–Hall.

Winnick, L. (1966). Place prosperity vs. people prosperity: Welfare considerations in the geographic redistribution of economic activity, *in Essays in Land Economics,* Real Estate Research Program, University of California, Los Angles.

Ziegler, J. A. (1976). Interstate black migration: Comment and further evidence. *Economic Inquiry* **14,** 449–453.

Index